THE AUTHORS Sheila Tames is a Blue B
tours of Bath, Salisbury and Stonehenge, us̩
Spanish. Her specialist guiding interests include gardens, interior decor, food,
shopping and the eighteenth century.

Richard Tames is also a Blue Badge guide and the author of *A Traveller's
History of Oxford*, *A Traveller's History of London* and *A Traveller's History of
Japan*. He teaches history for Syracuse University's London programme and
for the Blue Badge guide training course

SERIES EDITOR Professor Denis Judd is a graduate of Oxford, a Fellow
of the Royal Historical Society and Professor of History at the London
Metropolitan University. He has published over 20 books including the
biographies of Joseph Chamberlain, Prince Philip, George VI, historical and
military subjects, stories for children and two novels. He has reviewed and
written extensively in the national press and in journals and is an advisor to
the *BBC History Magazine*.

Other Titles in the Series
A Traveller's History of Athens
A Traveller's History of Australia
A Traveller's History of Canada
A Traveller's History of Cyprus
A Traveller's History of Egypt
A Traveller's History of England
A Traveller's History of France
A Traveller's History of Greece
A Traveller's History of India
A Traveller's History of Ireland
A Traveller's History of Italy
A Traveller's History of Japan
A Traveller's History of London
A Traveller's History of Mexico
A Traveller's History of New Zealand and the South Pacific Islands
A Traveller's History of Oxford
A Traveller's History of Paris
A Traveller's History of Poland
A Traveller's History of Portugal
A Traveller's History of Scotland
A Traveller's History of Spain
A Traveller's History of Turkey
A Traveller's History of The USA
A Traveller's History of Venice
A Traveller's History of York

THE TRAVELLER'S HISTORY SERIES

'Ideal before-you-go reading' *The Daily Telegraph*

'An excellent series of brief histories' *The New York Times*

'I want to compliment you. . . on the brilliantly concise contents of your books.' *Shirley Conran*

Reviews of Individual Titles

A Traveller's History of France

'Undoubtedly the best way to prepare for a trip to France is to bone up on some history. *A Traveller's History of France* by Robert Cole is concise and gives the essential facts in a very readable form.' *The Independent*

A Traveller's History of China

'The author manages to get 2 million years into 300 pages. An excellent addition to a series which is already invaluable, whether you're travelling or not.' *The Guardian*

A Traveller's History of India

'For anyone. . . planning a trip to India, the latest in the excellent Traveller's History series. . . provides a useful grounding for those whose curiosity exceeds the time available for research.' *The London Evening Standard*

A Traveller's History of Japan

'It succeeds admirably in its goal of making the present country comprehensible through a narrative of its past, with asides on everything from bonsai to zazen, in a brisk, highly readable style ... you could easily read it on the flight over, if you skip the movie.' *The Washington Post*

A Traveller's History of Ireland

'For independent, inquisitive travellers traversing the green roads of Ireland, there is no better guide than *A Traveller's History of Ireland.' **Small Press***

A Traveller's History of Bath

AQVAE · SVLIS

For Phyllis Tames, a West Country Girl

A Traveller's History of Bath

RICHARD AND SHEILA TAMES

Series Editor DENIS JUDD
Line Drawings PHIL GLEAVES

CHASTLETON TRAVEL
An Imprint of Arris Publishing Ltd
Gloucestershire

First published in Great Britain in 2009 by
CHASTLETON TRAVEL
An imprint of Arris Publishing Ltd
PO Box 75
Moreton-in-Marsh
Gloucestershire GL56 0AS
www.arrisbooks.com

The front cover shows *The Royal Crescent c.*1820 by David Cox (1783–1859)
Private Collection/The Bridgeman Art Library.

The map on page 72 is reproduced by permission of Bath Central Library
www.bathintime.co.uk

The illustration on page 83 is reproduced by permission of the Trustees of
the British Museum

ISBN 978 1905214 65 5

Printed and bound in Great Britain

Telephone Arris Books at 01608 659328
Visit our website at www.arrisbooks.com or email us at
info@arrisbooks.com

Table of Contents

Preface

Bath is one of the most admired, best known and most frequently visited of Britain's many tourist spots. It is easy to see why this should be the case, for the city is extraordinarily rich in almost every quality that attracts visitors and travellers: it is ancient, beautiful, accessible, packed with literary, religious and historical associations and, above all, just good to be in. Bath became a World Heritage Site in 1987 and has about four million day visitors each year.

The city, set among hills in the Avon Valley, and on the edge of the Cotswolds, owes its origins to the warm springs that bubble up through the limestone and which emerge at a temperature of between 64 degrees Celsius (147.2 degrees Fahrenheit) and 96 degrees C (204.8 degrees F). Although it was the Celts who first worshipped at the hot springs, dedicating them as a shrine to the goddess Sulis, it was the Romans who constructed a temple there between 60-70 AD and who founded the town they called Aquae Sulis. Over the next 300 years the Romans developed the bathing complex.

After the Roman withdrawal and the Anglo–Saxon invasion – the town was taken by the West Saxons in 577 - the baths fell into disrepair, but the new rulers named the settlement Badum or Badon (meaning 'at the baths') which may explain the legend that Bath was the site of the battle of Mount Badon where King Arthur is said to have repulsed the Saxon invaders.

The first monastic house was established there in 675, and King Offa of Mercia gained control of the town and the monastery in 781, rebuilding the church and dedicating it to St. Peter. Later, King Alfred laid out the town afresh, and in 973 Edgar was crowned King of England in Bath Abbey.

In the medieval era new baths were built, and a bishopric was founded, based on Bath and nearby Wells, but the city did not particularly prosper. The Dissolution of the Monasteries in the 1530s destroyed the Priory, and the Abbey Church was allowed to become derelict.

The town's fortunes were revived under Elizabeth I, when various ecclesiastical buildings were restored and the spa baths were renovated and began to attract well-heeled visitors to take the waters. In 1590 a Royal Charter granted Bath the status of a city. Bath received a further boost in 1676 when Thomas Guidott, a former Oxford expert in medicine and chemistry, moved there and published a book, *A Discourse of Bathe, and the Hot Waters There.*

From now onwards, the city became a magnet for visitors, especially those seeking to restore their health, and a substantial and ambitious development during the Stuart, and especially the Georgian, periods turned Bath into a beautiful city of classical limestone-built squares, streets and crescents. Among the notable new buildings were the Theatre Royal, the Pump Room and the Assembly Rooms. Beau Nash, as master of ceremonies, presided over the city's social and cultural life from 1705 – 1761.

By the census of 1801, Bath's population had reached over 40, 000, making it one of Britain's larger cities. It has continued to flourish, despite the German bombing of the city in April 1942, undertaken in reprisal for the RAF's raids on the historic cities of Lubeck and Rostock, and which left over 400 dead and some 19,000 building damaged or destroyed. Today development and regeneration work are part of maintaining Bath's enduring appeal.

Nobody could be better qualified to have written this detailed, insightful and completely absorbing book than Sheila and Richard Tames. Their knowledge of Bath itself, and its surroundings, not to speak of British history and British tourism, shines out from every page of this marvellous history. Future visitors to Bath will be fortunate indeed to have them as their literary and historical guides.

Denis Judd, London

CHAPTER ONE

Introduction: Pageant of the Past

A hundred years ago, in 1909, the city of Bath caught the prevailing pageant bug and staged a lavish re-enactment of its brilliant past. A century past its apogee, Bath still celebrated and exploited its heritage to a degree perhaps unrivalled by any other British city. London, of course, celebrated and exploited its past – but it was also a major port and financial powerhouse. Ancient Oxford drew tourists – but it did also have a university. York had its Minster but was also a centre for the manufacture of confectionery and the maintenance of railways. Bath, by contrast, has largely chosen to ignore or minimise its commercial and industrial aspects in favour of its cultural and architectural achievements, its archaeological legacy and its therapeutic tradition. The streets of eighteenth-century Bath might have been paced by politicians and poets, but the backstreets were packed with cutlers and coopers, clock-makers and coach-builders, makers of mirrors and mops, brushes and birdcages, scissors for the city's seamstresses, razors for its barbers and scalpels for its surgeons.

From the floods of tourists thronging the city's streets the visitor might guess that his or her own pilgrimage to Bath is what provides the lifeblood of the local economy. In fact, the biggest local sources of employment are the city's institutions of higher education and the Ministry of Defence and its role as a retail centre serving some a regional population of some 300,000.

A Genius for Reinvention

As Peter Borsay has argued at length in *The Image of Georgian Bath*, an outstanding academic study in the best senses of the word, the city of Bath has for three centuries, at least, exhibited a positive genius for reinventing itself. And very well, too. Just over twenty years ago UNESCO recognised Bath as a World Heritage Site, an accolade confirmed ever since by the annual arrival of some four million visitors. Bath Abbey's yearly visitor intake of 350,000 generates half its income. Almost two-thirds of the city centre is a conservation area, the largest in Britain. Some six thousand of Bath's buildings are 'listed' as structures of historical or architectural significance. One in six of the city's houses was built before 1850, almost half before the twentieth century. The city's attractions include not only the Roman baths and the majestic abbey, its

historic theatre, two major art galleries and half a dozen museums but also one of only four bridges in the world with shops on both sides and Britain's last remaining Georgian pleasure gardens.

Much of Bath's attraction, like that of Florence, lies in the fact that its historic core is largely of one piece and period. With the notable exception of the abbey, pre-Georgian Bath is long gone. The architectural glories of the eighteenth century were achieved by acts of destruction no less unflinching than the demolitions of the 1950s and 1960s, which brutally and thoughtlessly swept away much of the city's artisan quarters. As the poet Robert Southey observed two centuries ago 'If other cities are interesting as being old, Bath is not less so for being new. It has no aqueduct, no palaces, no gates, castle or city walls, yet it is the finest and most striking town that I have ever seen.'

As Jan Morris, like Southey another sometime resident, once put it with characteristic clarity and elegance –

> ... the city we now know is more or less a fluke. For twelve centuries after the departure of the Romans it was an ordinary country town ... and it was a sudden flare of fashion and fortuitous genius that made it ... a city *sui generis* ... the most fashionable resort in England, and almost everything unique about it was created then, for a particular local purpose, mostly by local men.

In its continuing concern to maintain its visitor appeal Bath has established tight controls over virtually every aspect of building and construction, from the colours of exterior paintwork to the placement of advertising, the design of street furniture and the style of shop frontages. Plagued with beggars in its Georgian Golden Age, the city has established its own Guild of Buskers to regulate the street performers of today. On the positive side Bath has promoted itself as a city of festivals – devoted variously to theatre, film and literature, Jane Austen and Mozart, cricket and the guitar, beer, banjos and balloons. With the opening of Sir Nicholas Grimshaw's striking new £40,000,000 Thermae Spa complex Bath entered the twenty-first century by reasserting its original identity as a uniquely therapeutic location.

Bath, for centuries renowned as a place to visit, from Jane Austen's time, at least, became a highly desirable place to live in. At a price – as

Jane herself knew all too well (see page 150). In 1982 a house in the Circus would have cost £125,000; twenty years later it would have cost £2,000,000. In 2007 a two-bedroom flat on the Royal Crescent changed hands for over a million pounds. Even so, at the time of writing five of the houses in the Royal Crescent remain in single occupation.

J.B. Priestley's odyssey of 1934, published as *English Journey*, included the following tribute to the city of Bath and its residents:

> Bath, like Edinburgh, has the rare trick of surprising you all over again. You know very well it is like that, yet somehow your memory must have diminished the wonder of it, for there it is, taking your breath away again. There is a further mystery about Bath – which Edinburgh does not share – for I have never been able to imagine who lives in those rows and rows of houses really intended for Sheridan and Jane Austen characters. They all seem to be occupied; life is busy behind those perfect facades; but who are the people, where do they come from, what do they do?

Writing over thirty years after he first saw Bath, the architectural historian Mark Girouard recalled his initial sight of Lansdown Crescent on a summer evening as a moment of epiphany:

> The long level road snaked along the hill and below it a field dropped steeply down to a curving line of trees. In the field a herd of cows were chewing peacefully … Far below … the lower half of Bath was spread out … Surveying the field, the cows, the trees and the view was a high curving line of exquisitely simple houses … I had a sudden realization of a way of living in towns as enticing as it was sophisticated.

(This Arcadian vision was confirmed by a contrasting encounter with Bristol on a blustery winter Sunday):

> The town was extraordinarily dramatic. A terrace of Georgian houses perched high above a harbour. Warehouses and breweries as massive and exotic as Egyptian temples … There was water everywhere; the town clung to hills as steep as those of Bath, but unlike Bath it exuded the flavour of ships, cargoes, merchants, manufacture and money.

RAIDS, FIRE, PLAGUE AND FLOOD

The journalist Katherine Whitehorn once wrote that you just knew that nothing could ever go wrong when you were standing in the linen department of the John Lewis department store. Bath exudes a similar sense of security. But appearances can be misleading. The city was raided by Vikings in 1012 and razed to the ground twenty years *after* the Norman Conquest. Much of its newly-rebuilt abbey was devastated by fire in 1137. A city renowned for restoring health, Bath was ravaged by plague in 1604 and 1635, by typhus in 1643 and by cholera in 1831 and 1848. In 1715 and again in 1780 the city's normally serene streets were disfigured by anti-Catholic riots. The Theatre Royal was destroyed by fire in 1862. In 1881 a landslip carried away 175 houses. In 1882 the entire city centre was flooded, as it was again in 1947 and 1960. In 1942 three horrendous Luftwaffe raids killed over four hundred of the city's inhabitants and damaged some twenty thousand of its buildings. So – a history not without incident.

Literally hundreds of plaques mark the former residences of historic personalities associated with Bath, another evidence of the city's skill in self-promotion. The Circus alone boasts the names of Robert Clive, Thomas Gainsborough, David Livingstone and Pitt the Elder. Great Pulteney Stret was home to Louis XVIII and Napoleon III, not to mention William Wilberforce. Tobias Smollett and Sir Walter Scott both lived on South Parade, Burke, Goldsmith, Garrick and Wordsworth on North Parade. But, as Jan Morris has mischievously reminded us regarding Bath's celebrity residents – 'they have seldom done much in Bath – they have simply been there … in rented lodgings, recuperating for another battle or correcting proofs.'

In paying fulsome tribute to its visitors Bath has, perhaps, been less than fair to itself. There is, perhaps surprisingly, no statue, indeed no memorial of any kind, to honour its local academic superstar, the medieval scholar Adelard of Bath, a figure of European reputation for centuries after his death (see page 43). More prosaic, but also more typical, is a figure like Thomas Guidott (1638?-1706), who tipped up in Bath just short of his thirtieth birthday and turned out a series of publications promoting himself and the city in equal measure, extolling the properties of the local waters, chronicling its history as a centre of healing and recording the lives of its eminent physicians. Unfortunately Guidott also harboured a compulsion to satirise his contemporaries so savagely that he was obliged to leave for London. Eventually he returned to pursue his antiquarian interests, notably recording the inscriptions in the Abbey, where he was himself to be laid to rest.

Few cities have been – and are - more fortunate in the quality of their local historians, whose works are listed in the Reading and Reference section. The writers' debt to them is obvious and gladly acknowledged. But whereas many of them have written for an informed and enthusiastic local readership, our task has been to address the visitor, rather than the resident. While taking a certain amount of familiarity with the major outlines of our past for granted we have also tried to link our narrative with the national story. To quote a recently-arrived resident of the city, Kenneth Hylson-Smith, author of *Bath Abbey: A History*: ' ... what went on at Bath can only be fully understood if it is seen as part of what was happening at the same time in the overall ... life of the rest of England. Indeed, for some periods such a background context entails reference to Europe-wide events and ... global transformations...'.

A Full Chronological Survey

Whereas most accounts of Bath's history focus on the Roman and Georgian periods, skipping over much of the rest, this *Traveller's History* offers a chronological survey of the entire span of Bath's existence, supplemented by concise accounts of several of its many delights – its food, its fashions, its theatrical and artistic heritage, its music and its memorials. Inevitably this has been at the expense of such aspects of Bath's history as its religious life, its philanthropic institutions and its educational provision. 'The Society for the Suppression of Common Vagrants and Imposters, the Relief of Occasional Distress and the Encouragement of the Industrious Poor', founded in 1805, was but one of more than a dozen charitable initiatives taken against the anxious background of the wars with revolutionary France but its activities, like those of the 'Bath Association for Preserving Liberty, Property and the Constitution of Great Britain against Republicans and Levellers', must remain unexplored in the following pages. Alongside the historic personalities of national significance and enduring fame associated with Bath we have, however, tried to pay special attention to those, like Catherine Macaulay, Hannah More or William Beckford, who have been largely forgotten, or those, like Sir William Holburne, Sir Jerom Murch, Ernest Cook and George Perry Smith, who made a special contribution to the city and even to those, like Sally Lunn, who may never have existed – or Prince Bladud, who certainly didn't. Our purpose has been to brush in the background of what is still remembered, what has been lost to memory, what can still be seen – and what cannot.

CHAPTER TWO

Roman Bath

43 – *c*.400

Origins : Of Pigs and Princes

Visitors who have never been to Bath before, seeing the breath-taking architecture of the Circus for the first time, might well be so swept away by the majestic, uninterrupted curvature of its honeyed facades that they fail to notice the giant stone acorns crowning their parapets. Unless they had been unusually conscientious in doing their homework they would be unlikely to know that the Circus is exactly 311 feet in diameter – which is also exactly the breadth of Queen Square, both being equal to the diameter of the immense stone circle at Stonehenge (see page 261). Unless they happen to be seeing Bath for the first time from a balloon – or care to look at a street map of the city with a highly selective squint – they are unlikely to notice that the Circus, Brock Street and the Royal Crescent, when viewed from above, assume the shape of a gigantic key. All of which is by way of emphasising that the architectural author of Georgian Bath, the archetype of the neo-classical city, Bath-born John Wood the Elder (1704-54) (see page 106), was a fully-paid up member of the Prince Bladud Fan Club - at the very time that the notion that Bladud as the authentic historical founder of Bath was finally being discarded as complete nonsense.

The legend of Bladud, of which Wood gives an extensive and detailed exposition in his *Essay Towards a Description of Bath* (1742-3), runs like this. Bladud was the son of Lud Hudibras, King of the Britons, founder of London and tenth in line from the first king, Brutus, great-grandson of Aeneas, who was in turn a descendant of the

Prince Bladud as imagined by Bath artist William Hoare

royal house of Troy, which had fled abroad following the fall of their
city to the Greeks. Bladud, to his shame and horror, became afflicted
with leprosy and was expelled from the royal court (or was imprisoned
and escaped). Wandering the realm, he eventually found employment
as a swineherd at Swainswick and infected his pigs with the contagion.
The pigs, after wallowing in the mud of some curiously hot springs,
came out completely cured – and doubtless raring for a celebratory
feast of acorns, hence the back-reference to them on the Circus. Yet
another version has the pigs plunging to their apparent doom like the

Gadarene swine and being lured out of the steaming morass by being tempted with acorns. The only element of this story with any historical veracity is the fact that acorns, pretty much useless to humans, were traditionally a staple fare for the medieval peasant's main source of meat, his much-prized pig. Acorns *also* represent an indirect reference to the Druids, for whom the oak was sacred, and Druids loomed large in Wood's understanding of history (see page 107).

Bladud, taking the porcine hint, likewise tried the mud-bath treatment and was similarly cleansed of his disfiguring affliction. Restored to health, Bladud went to study in Athens for eleven years and returned bringing much Greek learning to Britain, According to another version of the legend he contracted leprosy while he was abroad on this academic odyssey. Yet another spin has him bringing back four Greek philosophers to found a university at Stamford in Lincolnshire. (There was a breakaway faction from Oxford there briefly in the fourteenth century). Bladud, supposedly a contemporary of the prophet Elijah, succeeded to his father's throne in 863 BC and in recognition of the therapeutic properties of the magic mud, founded the city of Bath. Whether or not he got leprosy in Greece he does seem to have contracted a fatal case of hubris because his newly-acquired taste for science (or in another version necromancy) led him to try flying with a pair of home-made wings which let him down – literally – and thus prematurely curtailed an otherwise brilliant reign of twenty years. So the throne passed to his son – King Lear, who supposedly founded Leicester. But that is another story ....

The fabricator of the Bladud blarney was Geoffrey of Monmouth (died 1155), better known as the most successful promoter of the King Arthur legend. Geoffrey taught at Oxford and between 1135 and 1139 published his *Historia regum Britanniae (History of the Kings of Britain),* in which the Bladud story appears as part of the long build-up to King Arthur. Much of Geoffrey's source material was probably Welsh and Bladud in Welsh – Bleiddudd – when the double ds are pronounced like th sounds a lot more like Bath than it does in English. And there were at least three royal Bleiddudds mentioned in early Welsh genealogies. The bits about Bath were based on a third century Roman travel-guide. Geoffrey credited Bladud absolutely with founding Bath and the baths, with heating them with stones (?coal) and with flying but he made no mention of leprosy or pigs, which were details added subsequently. Geoffrey's book was a huge hit, inspiring many knock-off versions (known as Bruts, from Brutus) throughout Europe and remaining immensely influential down to the time of the Tudors. Certainly the people of Bath believed it and a visitor to medieval Bath entering the city by the North Gate would pass directly under a huge statue of the mystic monarch, which was still being repainted as late as 1637.

John Leland (1502?-52), the royal historiographer, who visited Bath at the time of the dissolution of its abbey (see page 54) studiously ignored the Bladud legend in his account of the city. The antiquarian William Camden (1551-1623), half a century later, was agnostic – 'The finding of these springs is by our own traditions referr'd to a British king call'd Bleyden Cloyth i.e. Bleyden the Soothsayer; with what show of truth I leave to others.' But the legend still had legs as far as Bath was concerned and when the Pump Room was opened in 1706 a new song in praise of Bladud was included in the proceedings.

Although one of Bath's most eminent physicians, Dr William Oliver (1659-1716), dismissed Bladud in 1707 as 'mere fable and romance', John Wood's *Description*, however, not only recounted the whole Bladud myth but additionally claimed that Bladud was the founder of the whole Druidic order and that Bath was the Druids' capital and as such not Roman, but British, in origin. As a capital it was adorned with Britain's first architecture, like 'the great court of justice of the ancient Britons', a massive mausoleum containing the remains of Bladud and his imposing palace, which stood where the Parades were to be built. North Parade, built by Wood in the 1740s, had a commanding view of Solsbury Hill, where Wood claimed there was once a temple of Apollo, onto which Bladud had crashed on his fatal flight. Wood's imagined Bath was, moreover, far larger than the city in which he had been born, stretching away in one direction as far away as Wookey and in another to Stanton Drew, where the ancient standing stones were all that remained of a famed Druidic university.

Bath's leading resident artist, William Hoare (see page 163), obliged Wood by coming up with a full-length portrait of Bladud. Shaggily bearded, sporting baggy pants, a close-fitting jacket, a wrap and slippered feet and carrying an unstrung bow, he looks like an Ottoman archer on his day off. Wood included the picture in his *Description*. The corporation was still, in 1755, sufficiently taken with the legend to name its first punt at property development Bladud's Buildings. When Thomas Baldwin, the city's official architect, rebuilt the Cross Bath in the 1780s a statue of Bladud was placed there in a niche as a sort of presiding deity. But by then the legend was under scholarly challenge. An anonymous verse panegyric of *Bath and Its Environs*, published in 1775, gave the myth its last literary outing. Philip Thicknesse, writing in 1778, dismissed Bladud as 'fabulous'. Collinson, a cleric and serious historian, went beyond dismissal to demolition in his *History and Antiquities of the County of Somerset* (1791). Richard Warner, another clergyman, concurred in his pioneering *History of Bath* (1801), condemning 'wild reveries of imagination in lieu of the sober details of authentic history'. From then on nobody seriously disputed Bath's Roman origins, although in 1886, when five stained-glass panels were installed in the Pump Room, depicting scenes from Bath' history, one was of Bladud and his pigs. The devisers of the great Bath Pageant of 1909 initially considered making Bladud the narrator but thought better of it and demoted him to a comic appendage of the Elizabethan section.

Roman Bath

In terms of scale, interest and state of preservation Bath's Roman remains are second only to Hadrian's Wall as a legacy of four centuries of Roman imperial administration. Bath also lies at the centre of the largest concentration of Roman villa sites in Britain, with more than thirty within a twenty kilometre radius of the city. This is all the more remarkable given that, at a mere twenty-four acres, the Roman city of Bath was only about a quarter the size of an average Romano-British cantonal capital like Winchester or Silchester. Although modest in extent, however, Roman Bath was cosmopolitan in atmosphere and famed throughout the western half of the empire as a therapeutic and cultic centre, attracting sufferers and votaries from as far away as Trier and Metz. Like a modern day holistic health farm Bath offered its patrons the opportunity to be cleansed spiritually as well as cured physically.

Julius Caesar's expeditions of 55 and 54 BC were essentially punitive raids in force, intended to intimidate British chieftains against aiding further resistance in newly-conquered Gaul. They were also a key element in Caesar's personal strategy of political self-advancement. They were not the preliminary phase of a permanent occupation. The invasion undertaken by the Emperor Claudius in AD 43 was. Before the year was out the legions had swept across from their supply base in Kent into the south-west, establishing a presence at Bath. This was initially significant as one element of an early frontier communications network, the point at which the route westwards out of London crossed the Fosse Way, which ran diagonally north and east from Exeter to Lincoln. Immediately to the north of Bath a Roman settlement developed at North Wraxall, where there was a shrine. To the south lay Comerton, which became an important centre of pewter production, and beyond that there were further settlements at Shepton Mallet and Ilchester.

A subsidiary route also linked Bath with the south coast harbour at Poole and another went west to the port of Sea Mills at the mouth of the Avon. Bath continued as a military base for perhaps a couple of decades. The cash paid to its garrison doubtless attracted traders eager to supply troops with the little luxuries and indulgences that made army life more bearable in an alien outpost. An informal *vicus* (unplanned village) seems to have emerged around Walcot, to the north of Bath's hot springs, around AD 50, where there were potter's kilns and blacksmith's forges. Ribbon development after AD 60 then served to link this area up with the more formal structures erected around the main spring. A cemetery was established at Bathwick, on the far side of the river, as Romans were well aware of the health hazards of burying the dead too close to sites of human habitation. There were also burials along the line of the road leading to Walcot, the most numerous being soldiers but also including a mason, a sculptor and a temple official who performed auguries. (This was normally done by examining the innards, especially the liver, of a slaughtered animal.) It is possible that there may also have been a fort at Bathwick, where early Samian pottery has been found. This was dinner party ware, imported from Gaul, perhaps the first inkling of Bath's future destiny as a place of gracious living.

Given their addiction to the pleasures of the bath, the Roman occupying forces can scarcely have failed to notice and make use of Bath's unique asset of natural hot springs. Every sizeable Roman settlement had its bath-house. Even forts on remote, windswept Hadrian's Wall had them. In cities Romans went to the baths not simply to bathe but to exercise and to relax, to network and to gossip, to nibble snacks and to gamble. The grandest bath complexes included temples and gymnasia and even art galleries and libraries. Most were haunted by fast-food sellers, touts, pimps and petty thieves. Bathing not only kept one clean, it almost certainly minimised the danger from infections so easily caused by minor cuts and abrasions. Presumably the earliest Romans to patronise Bath's springs were therefore off-duty soldiers, glad to soothe tired muscles and, on occasion, to lark about.

The Roman take-over received a severe set-back in AD 60-61 when high-handed maltreatment of a formerly collaborationist tribe provoked the Iceni of Norfolk, led by a formidable warrior queen, Boudicca, to go on the rampage, destroying major Roman settlements at Camulodunum (Colchester), Londinium (London) and Verulamium (St Albans). Her uprising, despite massive native support, proved too unwieldy to coordinate and was crushed by the accustomed discipline of the legions, despite their manifestly inferior numbers. But the Romans as well as the British had learned a lesson. While there were no more armed revolts, the Romans also adjusted their strategy to embrace a 'hearts and minds' component, promoting the benefits of the Roman way of life. The conversion of Bath from rudimentary military outpost to a sophisticated urban centre began, therefore, as a product of 'the decade of reconciliation', intended to demonstrate that the Roman presence in Britain was not only permanent but could be benevolent and beneficial.

Provided conquered peoples were prepared to show outward respect to the cult of the divine emperor, Roman authorities were fairly relaxed at whatever else they – or the legionaries who had conquered them – might care to believe. The pantheon of Roman gods was no exclusive club and its members were capable of sustaining multiple identities. Romans had little difficulty in equating the Bath region's local Celtic god, Sulis, with their own Minerva, goddess of wisdom and healing. Smartening up the spring-head associated with her became a welcome project to demonstrate Roman technological superiority.

Gorgon's Head

Legionary engineers first drove a circuit of wooden piles to surround and contain the major spring, then dug a foundation trench around that, piling its base to support a reservoir wall of massive stone blocks. In its first incarnation, then, the 'Roman bath' consisted of an open pool in the corner of a paved temple courtyard. The temple, raised on a podium, stood to its north-west, facing east; its pediment, featuring a compelling Gorgon's head, was borne by four Corinthian columns. Sacrifice was offered at outdoor altars in the walled courtyard in front of the temple, the interior of the temple being accessible only to members of the priestly caste. To the south of the pool was a bath complex with a pool lined with lead locally procured from the Mendip hills. This was certainly functioning by AD 75.

OFFERINGS TO SULIS AND MINERVA

The spring itself was used for the receipt of offerings. These might be in the form of coins, of which some twelve thousand have been recovered, or messages for the bi-polar deity Sulis-Minerva, These were scrawled on plaques of lead or pewter. Usually they were curses, many of them deeply vindictive. Over a hundred curses have been found. One victim of theft begged Sulis to afflict the perpetrator 'with maximum death and not allow him sleep or children, now and in the future, until he has brought my hooded cloak to the Temple of Divinity.' Other finds have included libation vessels of pewter, bronze and silver. It is clear that the bath complex and the temple were planned to be interlinked both visually and functionally. Their presence was a continuing source of local employment as their priestly cadre would have required a subsidiary staff of domestics, doormen, attendants, masseurs, janitors etc. One of the most impressive Roman funerary monuments, found at Sydney Gardens (see page 140), was erected by Trifosa, the widow and former slave of Gaius Calpurnicus Receptus, a priest of Sulis who attained the venerable age of seventy-five.

Apart from attracting patronage from the immediate locality Bath also became – another prefiguring of the eighteenth century – a retirement centre for veterans of the military. Most served for twenty or more years and so would have been in their forties, looking forward to marrying a local girl, often a slave they had bought and freed. Others may have retired younger, through injury. Doubtless many valued the opportunity to relieve the ache of old war wounds in the local soothing waters. Baths to the south-west of the main bath suite, drawing on the springs that would feed the later Hot Bath and Cross Bath, may have been under the tutelage of Aesclapius, god of healing. The local stone, having proved its worth, began to be exploited as an economic asset and has been found in Roman structures, not only in adjacent areas like Monmouth and Hereford, but as far away as London and Suffolk. Lead was another valued local resource, used for water-pipes and roofing and, combined with tin from Cornwall to make pewter, shaped to make bowls, spoons and other items of tableware. Meanwhile the fame of the locality spread so far throughout the empire that the geographer Ptolemy, writing in faraway Alexandria, could record its existence as Aquae Calidae – Hot Waters.

Early in the second century – perhaps in anticipation of a visit by the emperor – a new precinct was developed to the east of the main temple. Hadrian certainly came to Britain in AD 122 but there is, alas, no evidence that Bath was on his itinerary. Nevertheless it is not unreasonable to suppose that his imperial presence reverberated throughout Romanised Britain, spurring on new projects, much like a royal jubilee or the Millennium. The new precinct included a circular temple (*tholos*), ornamented with sculpture. Now inaccessible – under the abbey – this was very rare in western Europe and unique in Britain. Archaeologists also assume that somewhere there must have been a theatre, though its existence and whereabouts as yet remain an open question. Bath's walls, which were to constrain the city's development until the early eighteenth century, possibly originated during the succession crisis which threw Roman Britannia into turmoil in AD 192-196. Starting as a simple rampart and ditch, they acquired a masonry facing in the third century.

Another major reorganisation of the temple took place around AD 300 when a new retaining wall was built and two flanking chapels erected to complement the temple. The open spring was enclosed in a hall with a vaulted masonry roof and the baths themselves re-roofed in masonry. Two buildings were put up in the temple precinct, facing each other. The southern one featured on its façade Sol, god of the sun, the south and daytime, the northern one Luna, goddess of the moon, the north and night. The spring which later became the Cross Bath was enclosed by an oval wall. There was also a lead-lined plunge bath.

LOCAL AFFLUENCE

Apart from the economic stimulus provided by its bath and temple complex, Bath prospered through the production of wool, another prefiguring of a future industry. Pewter vessels were manufactured at Lansdown. Glass and footwear were also locally made. Evidence of the affluence of local residents is provided by the discovery of eight dwellings with mosaic floors, now covered by later structures like the Blue Coat School and the Crystal Palace pub on Abbey Green. With glazed widows, painted, plastered walls and hypocaust heating systems, these may have been the occasional residences of the owners of villas in the surrounding countryside.

Villas appear to have been established from *ca*. AD 270, possibly thanks to the in-migration of wealthy landowners from Gaul seeking either security from troubles over there or an obscurity in which they could discreetly practise the still forbidden cult of Christianity. Another possibility is the sale of imperial holdings to sustain a cash-strapped central administration. Not all of these villas were miles away in the countryside. Some were as near as Norfolk Crescent, Marlborough Lane and Wells Road, others across the river at Bathwick. For many of their builders the villa lifestyle may have seemed the beginning of a new chapter in the story of Roman Britain. In retrospect it looks more like the beginning of the end. (The standard work on Bath's Roman history is Professor Barry Cunliffe's *Roman Bath Discovered* (Sutton 2000)).

A TOUR OF THE BATHS

Today's visitor to the Roman baths (www.romanbaths.co.uk) enters via a domed Victorian reception hall, at right angles to the west door of Bath Abbey. From there one emerges onto a terrace, overlooking the Great Bath, and lined with late Victorian statues (1894). Three are of Roman generals. Ostorius Scapula defeated the leader of the British resistance, Caractacus. Suetonius Paulinus, crushed the revolt of Boudicca. Agricola was the father-in-law of the historian Tacitus, who wrote an account of the Roman conquest. Five of the statues are of emperors particularly associated with Britain – Julius Caesar, Claudius, Hadrian, Constantine the Great and Vespasian. Impressive as this view is, it represents only about a quarter of the site area of the whole bath complex. At the Sacred Spring hot water (46 C) rises at the rate of 1,170,000 litres (240,000 gallons) a day, as it has for thousands of years. The Roman baths at Bath were highly unusual in having so much hot water at their disposal that engineers actually had to devise a way of disposing of the surplus. Because artificially-heated water was expensive to produce most Roman bath complexes had far less available for bathers. They might be able to luxuriate in a hot tub or even a small pool but not swim around in a huge tank as they could at Bath. After crossing what was the courtyard of the temple of Sulis Minerva the visitor can see the overflow where surplus water was ducted via a drain to be carried off to the River Avon four hundred metres away.

THE GREAT BATH

The Great Bath constitutes the central feature of the entire baths complex. Aligned east-west, the chamber measures 34 metres (110 ft) by 21 metres (70 ft). The bath narrows slightly at one end but is approximately 19 metres (60 ft) by 9 metres (30 ft.) Lined with sheets of locally-mined lead, it was once covered by an immense barrel vault forty metres above the surface of the water. Steps on all sides led bathers down into the water, which was 1.5 metres (5 ft.) deep. The presiding statue of King Bladud dates from the seventeenth century, although it may be a composite from different medieval statues.   In the East Baths is a sequence of heated rooms and plunges, including a large tepid bath, the Lucas Bath of 26 x 10.5 metres (80 ft x 35 ft.). In the West Baths another sequence of pools and heated rooms, including a *laconicum* (dry sauna), also illustrates how the hypocaust heating system worked. Original arched windows show how Roman bathers could have looked out onto the Sacred Spring. It is possible that the existence of two suites of subsidiary facilities enabled the baths to be used by men and women simultaneously, but separated from one another in the interests of modesty. In many Roman baths it was more customary for bathers to come in shifts, with women coming in the morning, while men were attending to business, and male customers coming later in the day.

Among the highlights of the museum are the Gorgon's Head, which was probably carved by Gaulish craftsmen and was discovered when the foundations of the Grand Pump Room were dug in 1790, and the gilt bronze head of Sulis Minerva, found when Stall Street was being dug up in 1727. These are both rare items of exceptional workmanship. In 1965 a memorial stone was discovered in vaults beneath the Grand Pump Room. Set up by L. Marcius Memor, it records his status as a *haruspex* or soothsayer, a type of religious specialist of whom no other example is known in Roman Britain and therefore another indication of the unique standing of Bath as a cultic centre.

CHAPTER THREE

The Darkened Ages

410 – 1066

Roman Retreat

Britain's Romanisation had always been a patchy process, more or less skin deep the farther one went from the heart of the administration at Londinium. But Bath's peculiar character as a cultic and recreational centre for a large proportion of the Romanised elite made it more intensely an embodiment of 'Romanitas' than most other provincial centres, despite the absence of a large standing garrison. Any faltering in Roman self-confidence would be reflected in the character and quality of urban life in Bath. And Roman rule in Britain was already on the back foot by the fourth century. Some of the damage was self-inflicted as ambitious generals challenged imperial authority or sought to seize it for themselves. External pressures, by land and sea, from tribal peoples beyond the frontiers of empire escalated the costs of defence and therefore the consequent burden of taxation. The toleration of Christianity from 312 onwards and the later suppression of pagan worship introduced unpredictable new factors to complicate men's loyalties. Rome still valued the province of Britannia enough to despatch high-ranking generals to inspect its defences and to strengthen Londinium. But Roman occupation began to lose any air of inevitable permanence it might have had and became with growing clarity a holding operation.

Britain's Romanised elite came to resent the generally thankless and ever more burdensome tasks of urban administration and gravitated towards living in large and largely self-sufficient villas. This process was strongly marked in the south-west of England. From their villas

The Great Bath

the former city fathers administered agribusinesses which prefigured in scale the plantations, ranches and sheep-stations which their remote descendants would one day command at the economic outposts of another and even greater empire. Private affluence for the few was apparently only to be maintained at the expense of neglecting the public welfare of the many. Lifestyle took priority over duty.

In Bath itself there was unmistakable evidence of adaptive change to uncomfortable new circumstances long before the 'official' end of

Roman rule in AD 410. Daily life became less polished, reduced in circumstances and preoccupied with the satisfaction of material needs rather than indulgence in ritual, display, celebration or conspicuous consumption. By the mid-fourth century a large house on Walcot Street had become a tile factory. The bath suite of a villa at Lower Common had been cannibalised into a workshop, not for making, it should be noted, but for *recycling* coloured glass. In close vicinity to the baths a blacksmith and a pewterer had staked out their respective premises. The baths themselves must have suffered a major decline in visitor numbers because houses – admittedly imposing ones with mosaics and hypocausts – had been built over the outer courtyard. The floor of the inner precinct of the Temple became covered with a layer of mud, rubbish and refuse. Around 380-390 the main outdoor altar was thrown down, which would fairly correlate with the decrees of 391 and 392 of the emperor Thedosius, banning pagan worship henceforth. Over the subsequent half century pagan religious sculptures would be turned face down for use as paving.

Even more ominous was the reconstruction of the city walls, using copious quantities of demolished monuments, inscriptions and tombstones, clearly indicative of haste, limited resources of manpower and material and a willingness to discard heritage in the interests of security. Bath's walls may have been intended to deter raiders – or even rebels – but they would also have provided greater security for the increasingly onerous operations of the tax system. Whether contributions were exacted in cash or kind they would need to be stored safely. The walls would likewise have guaranteed a more secure setting for whatever level of trade and commerce still survived. Finally, in times of general disorder, a walled town offered a refuge for the population of the surrounding region, together with their livestock and movable possessions.

The less Bath functioned as a centre of pilgrimage and tourism the less distinctively Roman and, indeed, the less distinctly urban it became. As fewer visitors came to the city its economic base contracted, as did its physical extent. Quality houses outside the walls were abandoned for residential purposes, often to be taken over as makeshift workshops or storehouses. By 400, in Peter Davenport's terse summary 'the huge buildings still stood, the springs continued to flow but provincial officials, craftsmen, military officials, perhaps, staffed a secure storage depot and production centre, perhaps also a local market, rather than a tourist resort.'

Roman coins ceased to be imported to Britain around 402. Since military pay and spending had always been the largest single factor in driving the monetized sector of the economy this must have declined rapidly to be replaced by other mechanisms of exchange, barter and labour service. The legions, embroiled in yet another attempted usurpation, left in 407-8. In 410 the emperor Honorius confirmed that they would not be coming back. Pottery production on an industrial scale ceased in Britain around 420. The skill of making glass was entirely lost. Building in stone virtually ceased, apart from crude recycling. Around 450 there was a sufficiently large-scale migration from the West Country to Armorica (Brittany) for its Latin-based argot to be replaced by a Celtic tongue which would evolve into Breton.

Adventus Saxonum

What medieval chroniclers called the '*Adventus Saxonum*' – the coming of the Saxons - was a messy process with none of the strategic orches-tration and clear objectives of the Roman invasion. The Romans actually helped to start it themselves in the fourth century by recruiting Saxon mercenaries to bolster their over-stretched defences against other Saxon raiders. Inevitably some of the hirelings, after their period of active service, stayed on to settle and invited their relatives to join them. From the fifth century, possibly impelled by environmental deterioration in their own homeland – roughly the region where modern Germany meets the Netherlands and Denmark – they began to arrive in eastern England in ever greater numbers.

The ending of imperial Roman rule created a political vacuum which vestigial regional governors, petty British kinglets and bands of Saxon intruders, settlers or warriors jostled with one another to fill. The period between 410 and 577, when Bath fell under Saxon control, is the most obscure in the city's long history. The presence of what archaeologists, with disarming imprecision, call 'dark earth', covering at least three different sites around the baths – i.e. within the line of the city walls – is taken to imply the presence of continuing human activity. Consisting as it does of a silt flecked with traces of charcoal and fragments of mortar and bone refuse, dark earth suggests the possibility of activities involving cultivation, heating, cooking and building. A pattern of wear on paving along the north side of the Great Bath implies heavy human traffic in the post-Roman period, though not necessarily use of the bath itself. Early Christianity was vehemently hostile to bathing, with its undeniable associations with paganism, water deities, nudity, luxury, delight in the human body etc. But if Bath in the immediately post-Roman period was pretty much a wreck, compared with what it had been two centuries before, at least it was still an occupied one. It may well be that it was during this period that the former Roman resort of Aquae Sulis acquired a new hybrid cognomen, becoming known as Aquamania/Aquaemann – Place of Water (from the British mann = place), which was later Anglicised as Achamanni or Acemannesceastre (water-place-camp), from which the Saxons derived their name for the Roman road from Bath to St Albans – Akeman Street.

Between *ca.* 450-550 the native British managed to slow down the westward thrust of Anglo-Saxon (i.e. English) penetration, an achievement attributed by the monastic chroniclers Gildas (British, writing *ca.* 550) and Bede (English writing *ca.* 733) to Ambrosius Aurelianus – 'the last of the Romans'. The shadowy figure of Ambrosius was possibly a Romano-British cavalry commander and is a plausible inspiration for the legend of King Arthur, whose elaborated literary cult would appropriate Glastonbury, Cadbury and other West Country locations. The British strategic triumph led to the establishment of a 'stop line' running through the Hampshire-Wiltshire border up into western Oxfordshire and northwards to the Pennines.

This stop line began to disintegrate rapidly around 550, a development which may have been connected with a plague pandemic known to have devastated all Europe in the 540s and 550s. That this happened is undeniable but is not in itself immediately explanatory. As there is no *a priori* reason to believe the Britons suffered proportionately greater loss of population than the Saxons, why should their defences have collapsed after half a century of apparently successful resistance? Quite possibly they were always smaller in numbers (already weakened by out-migration to Armorica) and the plague undermined them to the point of losing the critical mass needed to provide adequate manning of their defensive perimeter – a consideration of which, as we shall see, Alfred the Great was acutely aware (see page 33). Another possibility is a crisis of faith. Gildas, writing around this very time, excoriates the British leaders as immoral petty tyrants and interprets the plague and Saxon successes as God's retribution. The explanation may even lie in the purely military sphere, the loss of a British cavalry arm which the Saxons might well have found difficult to deal with. Whatever the relationship between plague, powerlessness and panic, Bath would no longer be buffered by intervening territory from the ever-encroaching English.

In 552 the Britons were defeated at Old Sarum, near Salisbury, by Ceawlin, leader of the West Saxons. Another, this time indecisive, encounter was fought against him at Barbury, near Swindon in 556. In 577 Ceawlin finally prevailed at Dyrham (Deorham) eight miles north of Bath, killing three 'cyningas' (literally 'kings' but possibly leaders regarded as generals or governors) and consequently taking control of Cirencester, Gloucester and Bath. Henceforth Bath would be drawn into the as yet unstable realm of Anglo-Saxon political rivalries. The earthwork known as the Wansdyke may have been associated with this. It runs along the high ground, just south of the Avon valley, from Bath to Dundry Hill, near Bristol. The name 'Wansdyke' is Saxon in origin, from Woden's dyke, meaning an earthwork attributed to the most powerful of the Saxon gods, hence very impressive.

Bath's conquest by Ceawlin was not followed by immediate and permanent absorption into the West Saxon kingdom. Indeed, Ceawlin was still fighting British resistance in the area in 584. By 626 Bath had become a major component of the petty kingdom of the Hwicce, a people who acknowledged as overlord Penda, the powerful king of Mercia, the kingdom which controlled all of central England. Although peripheral to Mercia, Bath, under royal control, remained a significant frontier strongpoint as the junction of Roman roads and a river crossing, with an extensive royal estate to the immediate north of the city walls and a major palisaded rampart and ditch earthwork, the Wansdyke, to the south-west.

In 658 Cenwalh of Wessex crossed into Somerset, beat the British in a battle twenty miles south of Bath and then chased the survivors clear across the county, confining to Devon and Cornwall the last redoubt of British resistance to English rule in southern Britain. Henceforth Bath would be Anglo-Saxon – English - at least until the Normans came.

FAITHFUL FEMALES

For those of us whose knowledge of nuns is drawn from *The Sound of Music* and *The Nun's Story* life in a convent may seem of limited appeal – largely because it seems to be *so* limited, an endless cycle of work and worship, shaped and sustained by devotion and denial of the self. Seen from the perspective of the seventh century, however, a conventual life might have seemed as much liberating as confining. England really was a murderously unstable place in which the normal hazards of pre-modern existence – epidemic disease, harvest failure and casual interpersonal violence – were compounded by seemingly endless wars for territory or succession to a throne. Life in a nunnery, by contrast, offered a high degree of personal security and an ordered existence of comforting routine in surroundings which were, by the standards of the day, often beautiful and even impressive. Add to this freedom from worries about food or clothing, a lifestyle of relative cleanliness and comfort and access to probably the least ineffective medical care available. Nuns were, moreover, spared the punishing physical labour and endless childbirth which were the lot of the peasant women who made up the vast mass of England's female population. Taking these factors into account, life within closed walls may begin to look distinctly attractive – without even considering the enhanced hope of eternal salvation, which was actually supposed to be the primary consideration.

Not surprisingly many of the inhabitants of early nunneries were drawn from the upper ranks of society, including persons of royal blood. Some doubtless were consigned to a convent because they were deemed, on grounds of health, personality or looks, unsuitable for the marriage market or unworthy of a dowry, but many were women of ability who welcomed the opportunity of life in a sphere of relative female autonomy. Nunneries in the early medieval period were not what they were to become by Chaucer's time, when he could depict his prioress as a vain, pretentious, empty-headed, chattering, flirtatious fashion-victim. The women heading the female religious communities of early Saxon England were often forceful and charismatic, many of them recognised for their achievements by canonisation. It was St Hilda, founder and Abbess of Whitby, who hosted the landmark Synod of 664 which determined that the English church would accept the discipline of Rome rather than cling to Celtic traditions. London still has churches dedicated to Saxon saints Ethelburga and Etheldreda.

All of which is by way of introduction to the fact that Bath Abbey seems to have started out as a nunnery; not necessarily on the site occupied by the present abbey but almost certainly within the surviving circuit of the former city walls. According to a twelfth century copy of a charter held by the monks of Bath Abbey and used by them as evidence of both the abbey's antiquity and its origin as a royal foundation, on 6 November 675 Osric, king of the Hwicce, gave land at Bath (Hat Bathu – the Hot Baths) to a 'convent of holy virgins'. Although this institution may already have been in existence, it is usually assumed that the land grant was to enable one to be founded – in which case the adjective 'holy' becomes part of an implicit job description rather than the complimentary recognition of an established fact. Such a grant is certainly in character with what else is known of Osric, because he is also credited with founding both an abbey at Gloucester (in 681), which later became the cathedral and where he is buried, and the cathedral at Worcester. Bearing a Frankish name, Bath's first abbess, Berta, may have come from one of the missionising houses around Paris, which could imply either that she was invited in to set base-line standards in terms of current best practice or to upgrade those of an existing community which was deemed to have slipped behind, or failed to achieve, Continental standards. Telltale evidence of a 'French connection' is the fact that one of the signatories to Osric's charter was another Frank, Leuthere, bishop of Wessex. Top managerial talent, then as now, was liable to be head-hunted internationally, adding the possibility of foreign travel (admittedly an ambiguous benefit in uncertain times) to the attractions of a church career.

By 681 Berta had either returned to 'Frankia', her mission accomplished, or quite possibly had died, because a charter dated to that year refers to the abbess as Bernguida, a Latinised version of the English

Beornwyth, presumably an Anglo-Saxon aristocrat deemed worthy to fill Berta's sandals. Significantly, however, her second-in-command, the prioress, was one Folcburg, a Frank, possibly inserted, Davenport suggests, to keep things on course and even perhaps to report back to the Frankish mother-house that all continued well. The land granted by the charter of 681 was a hundred hides, almost certainly the former royal estate to the north of city, and therefore long a going concern and not a patch of wilderness yet to be brought under the plough.

Where the nunnery that this estate supported actually stood has yet to be confirmed by archaeology. It is entirely possible that it stood on the site occupied by the present abbey and consisted of a complex of refurbished Roman structures, other stone buildings made with recycled Roman materials and new timber buildings, perhaps to house the servants and workers whose labour made it possible for the nuns to devote so much of their time to their devotions. Much of the area within the circuit of the walls and around this complex may have been given over to farming or, at least, horticulture. Bede, writing *ca.* 733 in Northumbria, at the other end of the future England, recorded of Bath that 'warm springs … supply hot baths suitable for all ages and both sexes in separate places and adapted to the needs of each.' This terminology – 'suitable', 'separate', 'adapted' - sounds unambiguously like a resumption of *organised* bathing. As the 'baths', whatever state they were in, would have been under the control of the local religious community they may have become a source of income or perhaps a way of fulfilling the Christian duty of healing or even, Davenport suggests, a unique form of monastic hospitality to encourage visitors who might also make offerings at its church or buy any surplus produce from its estate.

'The Ruin'

Copied out in about 940, what was described as 'a great English book of divers things, written in verse', was donated by Leofric (died 1072), first bishop of Exeter, to his own cathedral, one of a bequest of sixty books, twenty-eight of them in English. Leofric, despite his English name, had been brought up in Lotharingia (roughly Alsace-Lorraine) but he seems to have valued the culture of his forefathers. What became known as the *Liber Exoniensis* (*The Exeter Book*) was rediscovered in the eighteenth century and recognised as one of the most important repositories of Anglo-Saxon verse to survive. Alongside a famous collection of the riddles so beloved around the Saxon fireside the book contained longer religious poems and a selection of highly admired 'elegies'. One of these, '*The Ruin*' is fragmentary but runs to some forty-five lines, containing two references to hot baths, the second of which is extensive, and is almost certainly a description of Bath as it looked in the early eighth century to an awe-struck onlooker aware of the city's past greatness:

> Wondrous is this masonry, shattered by the fates ... the buildings raised by giants are crumbling ... the owners and builders are perished and gone ... and so these courts lie desolate, and the framework of the dome with its red arch sheds its tiles. There stood courts of stone and a stream gushed forth in rippling floods of hot water. The wall enfolded within its bright bosom the whole place which contained the hot flood of the baths.

This is the oldest known description of Bath, quite possibly by a local resident.

FROM MERCIA TO WESSEX

A charter issued in 757 granted land south of the Avon to the 'brethren of the monastery of St Peter at Bath'. *Brethren* of the *monastery*? Berta's house of nuns had apparently metamorphosed into or been supplanted by a community of monks. It is entirely possible that it was for some time a double house, consisting of both nuns and monks. This was not unusual in the period. In such institutions the two communities lived strictly segregated from one another but often under an abbess, as had been the case with Osric's foundation at Gloucester, an arrangement which only ceased with the death of Abbess Eafe, coincidentally in 757. The female contingent may have been transferred en bloc to another institution or dispersed piecemeal or simply have failed to attract new recruits and died out. We do not know.

In 781 Offa the Great, king of Mercia, and as such the most powerful ruler in England, put forward a claim for some ninety hides of land at

Bath, which he alleged were wrongly held by Heathored, bishop of Worcester. A synod at Brentford decided, perhaps unsurprisingly, in favour of the monarch and threw in another thirty hides south of the Avon for good measure. Offa probably wanted to assert direct control of Bath because it was still a strategically significant pawn in his territorial chess-game with the rising power of Wessex but the synod scribe recording his victory in the dispute referred to St Peter's as *celeberrimus monasterium* ('a most celebrated monastery'), possibly just a touch of indirect flattery confirming the righteousness of the king's concern, possibly a simple statement that Bath had already begun to achieve a certain eminence. According to a later medieval tradition Offa may well have stayed at Bath himself in 793. His successor, Cenwulf, certainly did so in 796, the year of his succession, issuing a charter there. Offa, today, is chiefly remembered as the builder of Offa's Dyke, an immense border earthwork stretching over a hundred and twenty miles – much longer than Hadrian's Wall - intended to keep the Welsh penned in. It was a huge organisational and engineering achievement but it didn't work. Cenwulf spent much of his reign trying to hang on to his inheritance and the rest of it fighting the Welsh on and off, dying at Chester, in 821. His successor, Ceolwulf, lasted just two years. His successor Beornulf was beaten in battle by Egbert (Ecgbryht), who in 829 was recognised as Bretwalda ('overking') of England, making Wessex pre-eminent among the as yet to be united kingdoms of England. Bath was still part of Mercia but Mercia was now the junior partner of Wessex, rather than its superior neighbour or even credible rival.

Alfred's Bath

Wessex was to become the core around which a united England would be forged. That this was so was entirely due to the only king the English have ever called 'the Great' – Alfred. And for much of his reign (871-99) it was touch and go whether even Wessex would survive. The threat to its existence now came not from the long-established skirmishings with its neighbours and rivals but from the ferocious onslaught of foreigners, the Vikings.

The Vikings struck first in the south, in 793, when they murdered the reeve, the king's local representative at Portland Bay, as he tried to put them straight on the local trading regulations. For the southern half of

England this remained an isolated outrage until the Vikings launched a series of coastal raids in 835. In 838 Egbert in alliance with the Cornish beat them in battle. It had become a time for burying local differences.

In 853 Aethelwulf of Wessex joined forces with Burhred of Mercia to subdue the Welsh, who, acting on the principle that my enemy's enemy is my friend, saw the distractions and pressure brought about by Viking incursions as an opportunity to strike back against the Saxons. The Welsh got a thorough thrashing and Burhred got Aethelwulf's daughter as a bride. In 864 they held court together in Bath. Ten years later Burhred had been chased out of his kingdom by the Vikings to die in Rome and Wessex had passed in 871 into the hands of a fifth son, Alfred (849-99). Alfred would much rather have been a monk than a king and, to complete his lack of credentials for warrior status, was almost certainly periodically incapacitated by epileptic fits. Wessex was attacked by the Northmen in the year of Alfred's accession, again in 876 and again in 878, when Alfred's forces were crushed at Chippenham, just ten miles from Bath. 'All Wessex surrendered' – but not Alfred. Fleeing to the watery refuge of Athelney in the marshes of the Somerset levels, Alfred miraculously raised yet another army and decisively trounced the Northmen at Edington and forced them out of Wessex and all of the west.

As an institution Bath abbey, and the surrounding community which depended on it, was reliant on royal favour and power. The hammerblows endured by the dynastic houses of Mercia and Wessex in the ninth century almost certainly reverberated to affect the religious houses which had traditionally enjoyed their protection and support. There is no reason to believe that the estates from which Bath drew its sustenance were exempt from pillage and that therefore the abbey itself was reduced to a poor condition.

RECONSTRUCTION

Fortunately for Bath the restoration of monasteries, as centres of both sanctity and learning, was high on Alfred's list of priorities. What was truly terrifying about the Vikings was not just that they came to loot and then to conquer but that they delighted in extirpating Christian culture, targeting monasteries to plunder and trash and systematically massacring those who lived their lives for their faith. Alfred set an agenda of reconstruction for his successors and made it possible for them to pursue it by creating a credible navy, reorganizing the *fyrd* (militia) as a force capable of rapid mobilization and establishing a network of *burhs* (boroughs) as a system of defence in depth. Bath was one of some thirty such strongpoints, with Axbridge the next nearest to it to the south-west and Malmesbury to the north-west. *Burhs* combined to various degrees the functions of citadel, refuge, market, manufacturing centre and mint. Administrative details of the scheme are related in the *Burghal Hidage* which outlines the allocation of land designated to support the garrison of each *burh*, reckoning four men needed to defend each pole (=16.5 feet) of its circuit defences. The present known line of Bath's walls is 1250 yards (1143.3 metres) but the *Burghal Hidage* formula gives a length of 1375 yards (1257.6 metres), a discrepancy of 9 per cent. With a garrison of a thousand men this would yield a surplus of ninety-one – enough to serve as a useful mobile reserve to support a section of the defences under severe pressure. However, another explanation is also possible. Outside, but close to the walls, at the lip of the ditch that protected them from direct frontal assault, Alfred had a wooden palisade erected, possibly as a stop-gap first line of defence until the ditch itself could be thoroughly scoured and the old Roman walls fully restored. Being slightly longer than the circuit of the walls the palisade might well account for the *Burghal Hidage* discrepancy.

Within the walls the whole town of Bath was re-planned, as were the interiors of all the new *burhs*. The standard pattern was to include a circuit road running around the town immediately inside the defences to allow speedy access to them at times of emergency. Within that was a main street joining the main gates. Westgate Street and Cheap (i.e. market) Street survive as remnants of Bath's main east-west boulevard. (The city's main east gate was re-sited to the north of its original site after 1091). Either side of this a grid of streets divided the settlement into *insulae* - literally 'islands', but to us, blocks. Where the *burh* was new-built, as at Wallingford or Wareham, the grid could be strictly adhered to but in Bath it had to make allowance for existing structures, including the abbey, surviving Roman ruins, mounds of rubble and the three hot springs. The presence of the abbey thus made it impossible to establish a central crossroads, like Carfax at Oxford, because it stood athwart the line of a putative southern road. The market place was laid out just inside the north gate, a potentially useful open space to corral incoming livestock in times of flight from the countryside. The basic unit of measurement used in planning Bath's new layout seems to have been the pole of 16.5 feet. Streets were usually two poles wide, with blocks usually of six, eight or twelve poles. As part of the royal estate Bath was administered on the king's behalf by an appointed Reeve, exercising his master's delegated powers and safeguarding his interests. Bath's reeve, coincidentally named Alfred, was a sufficiently important personage for his death in 906 to be noted in the *Anglo-Saxon Chronicle*, the official record inaugurated by Alfred in the last decade of his reign and the first history written by any European people in their own language. In 909 a new see of Somerset was founded, with its episcopal seat at Wells, establishing an ecclesiastical connection with enduring consequences for both communities. To the north of Bath the royal estate was centred on Barton Farm, which served as the residence of a royal bailiff who supervised its running.

Bath is known to have had a mint by early in the reign of Alfred's son and successor, Edward the Elder (reigned 899-924). Essentially functioning as a sub-branch of the major mint at Winchester, Edward's capital, it used a Winchester design but with BAD on the reverse. In 928 Athelstan (reigned 924-39) decreed that all mints should be within a *burh*, probably in confirmation of existing practice.

Apart from seventh century nuns and Alfred the Reeve, Bath's Saxon moneyers are the earliest residents whose names are known. Herewis was the first recorded. The spelling of the name of Biorthulf suggests he may have been from Kent. Bath's sole mint (London had ten) lasted until the early twelfth century. Bath-struck coins have been found as far away as Scandinavia – but none in or near the city itself. Archaeological evidence suggests that cloth-making and iron-working were among the occupations practised in the late Saxon city.

A Crucial Coronation

Edgar 'the Peaceable' (reigned 959-75) might equally have been called 'the Fortunate'. The grandson of Alfred the Great of Wessex, Edgar was the beneficiary of the campaigns and victories of his predecessors and could, perhaps more plausibly than any of them, truly style himself king of all England. Inheriting a stable kingdom, free from immediate threat of foreign attacks, Edgar enthusiastically supported the efforts of his charismatic and energetic Archbishop of Canterbury, St Dunstan (924-88), to reform the Church and in particular to restore monastic life and the role of monasteries as centres of education. Edgar also went out of his way to win the co-operation of his Danish subjects in the north and east of England.

The *Anglo-Saxon Chronicle* eventually gave fulsome recognition of Edgar's tenure of the throne

> His reign was prosperous and God granted him
> To live his days in peace; he did his duty,
> And laboured zealously in its performance.
> Far and wide he exalted God's praise
> And delighted in his law, improving the security
> Of his people more than all the kings
> Who were before him in the memory of man.

Edgar's coronation was deferred for fourteen years. It is assumed that, soon after his accession, he was formally recognised as king at Kingston-Upon-Thames, the usual location for this procedure, which was more an administrative than a ceremonial occasion. What Dunstan orchestrated at Bath on Whit Sunday, 11 May 973, was a much grander pageant, modelled on the installation of a Holy Roman Emperor. In part the long delay in organising this event may reflect caution on Dunstan's part, a concern that Edgar should give sustained and unambiguous proof of his virtues as a monarch and his commitment to the revival of the English church. He was, after all, only a lad of fifteen or sixteen when he came to the throne. Another possible explanation for the delay in organising a coronation was the king's alleged extra-marital track-record, which may have led Dunstan to impose a lengthy penance on him, to be worked off over years by founding new monasteries or granting lands to existing ones. Whatever the reason the long interval between accession and coronation also meant that Edgar had attained his thirtieth year, then the lowest customary age at which a candidate might be received into the priesthood. This implicitly endorsed the sacral nature of monarchy as an institution divinely ordained and blessed, an emphasis redoubled by the choice of date for Edgar's coronation, Whit Sunday. To emphasise the unity of the country Dunstan shared the conduct of the ceremony with Oswald, Archbishop of York, a Northumbrian and a Dane by birth. Oswald, moreover, had but recently returned from Rome where he had met the Pope, quite possibly to gain his explicit approval of the proposed ceremony.

The king entered Bath's abbey church already wearing his crown and laid it aside as he knelt at the altar. Dunstan then led the singing of the '*Te Deum*', at the end of which all the assembled bishops of England raised the king from his knees. Edgar then swore an oath, repeating his pledges from the Archbishop's dictation – that the church and all Christian people should enjoy peace for ever, that all wrong and robbery should be forbidden and that all judgments should be made with justice and mercy. The oath was followed by prayers of conse-cration and the anointing of the king, an act symbolic of priestly status, by both archbishops. Next came the antiphon '*Zadok the Priest*' with the entire assemblage joining in the salutation 'Let the king live for ever!' Dunstan then invested the king with a ring and sword, placed the crown on his head and put the sceptre of power and rod of justice in his hands, after which both archbishops conducted the king to his throne. Edgar's queen, Elfrida, was also anointed and crowned. Following the coronation ceremony there was a huge banquet at which the king and queen presided over separate tables.

The *Anglo-Saxon Chronicle* laid less emphasis on the nature of the coronation as a ceremony than on the joyousness of the occasion and the brilliance of the company assembled to witness it :

> In this year, Edgar, ruler of the English
> Was consecrated King by a great assembly,
> In the ancient city of Acemanesceastre,
> Also called Bath by the inhabitants
> Of this island. On that blessed day,
> Called and named Whit Sunday by the children of Men,
> There was great rejoicing by all. As I have heard,
> There was a great congregation of priests and a goodly company of monks,
> And wise men gathered together.

What did this all amount to? The great Victorian medievalist, William Stubbs (1825-1901), himself a bishop, hedged his bets in every direction, suggesting variously that Edgar's coronation was:

> a solemn typical enunciation of the consummation of English unity, an inauguration of the king of all the nations of England, celebrated by the two archbishops, possibly with special instructions or recognition from Rome, possibly in imitation of the imperial consecration of Edgar's kinsmen, the first and second Otto, possibly as a declaration of the imperial character of the English crown itself.

Whatever the qualifications attached to the occasion by Stubbs, the order of the coronation service performed on that day was of the utmost significance, establishing its basic framework for future generations of English monarchs and inspiring imitative forms in France and other continental countries. The occasion was noted by all the contemporary chroniclers and inspired a national ballad. In the Abbey today the event is commemorated by a stained-glass Edgar Window. In terms of royal authority, however, Edgar's coronation marked a false dawn. The king died only two years later, just thirty-one. His eldest son and successor, a boy of twelve or thirteen, was crowned by Dunstan at Kingston-upon-Thames. Hacked to death four years later at the instigation of his stepmother, he is remembered as 'Edward the Martyr' (reigned 975-8). For reasons too complicated to discuss here his bones currently rest in a bank in Croydon. Edward's younger half-brother was likewise crowned at Kingston. A boy of just ten or eleven he would reign for nearly forty years, disastrously, as Ethelred II 'the Unready' (reigned 978–1016), a reference not to his personal standards of punctuality but to his lack of '*raed*' – wise counsel or advice.

CHAPTER FOUR

Medieval Bath

1066 – 1540

Regime Change

When William the Conqueror (reigned 1066-87) launched his invasion of England in 1066 he was entirely convinced of the validity of his claim to the throne but he also took the additional precaution of obtaining Papal approval for his project. The Bayeux Tapestry, which gives us such a vivid, propagandistic account of the Norman Conquest from the Norman point of view, clearly depicts a transport ship sailing under a Papal banner. In return for this endorsement William had promised to return the allegedly deviant Anglo-Saxon church to conformity with approved Continental practice – i.e. to put it more firmly under the Pope's authority. This, in effect, would give him carte blanche to make a clean sweep through the ecclesiastical hierarchy of his conquered realm, replacing English church leaders with Norman nominees. Within twenty years there were only two English bishops left in post. Within half a century virtually every Saxon cathedral would have been demolished or abandoned and replaced by a new Norman-built establishment. In 1075 William I and his bishops, meeting as the Council of London, confirmed that episcopal sees should all be located, or where necessary relocated, to substantial and defensible urban centres. As a prominent ecclesiastical centre Bath would inevitably be caught up in this programme of radical reform.

DOMESDAY BATH

The great survey of the newly-conquered kingdom ordered by William I in 1086 revealed Bath as the second largest town in Somerset after

Taunton and confirmed that its mint was still active. Of the town's 178 burgesses twenty-four paid rent to the king directly as their lord and sixty-four to the abbey but the largest number, ninety, were 'burgesses of the king' barons'. The lords of various Somerset manors had built houses in the town, for rent, as refuges in time of war and in the case of two named individuals, Ernulf de Hesdin and Edward of Salisbury, for their own use. Another named individual would have been a crucial intermediary in the post-Conquest decades – Hugh the Interpreter. He had a house in Bath and an estate out at Batheaston. Some of the larger residences may have had their own chapels, which may possibly explain the origins of such churches as St Michael Within, St Mary, Northgate and All Saints in Binnebury, none of which had church-yards. In Somerset 'The Lands of the Church of Bath' consisted of fourteen separate named estates, collectively valued at just over £70. Although most of the tied labour consisted of serfs of varying status some fifty were enumerated as actual slaves. Apart from two hides of arable (usually interepreted as 240 acres), the royal estate at Batheaston also included fifty acres of meadow, two watermills and 'scrubland two leagues (= six miles) in length and breadth'. Twerton was divided into two unequal holdings, but each with two watermills, both held by Normans; Geoffrey's of two and a half hides was valued at £3, Nigel's, three times as large, at £10.

Phoenix in the West

Bath became the focus of major change thanks to a coincidence of events in the years 1087-88. The death of Bath's abbot, Aelfsige, in 1087 created a vacancy. The death of the Conqueror that same year brought his son William II (reigned 1087-1100) to the throne – but not without opposition. The Conqueror's own brother, Odo, Bishop of Bayeux, backed by Roger Mowbray and other leading Norman barons, favoured another of the Conqueror's sons, Robert of Normandy, known as Curthose, and raised a revolt on his behalf. In 1088 a rebel force, based in Bristol, selected Bath as a royal possession and ravaged the city and the surrounding area, before being defeated. (This devastation, to look on the positive side, cleared the way for a major reconstruction project.) In the same year the bishop of Wells, one Giso, obligingly chose to die. This presented the new regime with a convenient opportunity to install a new administration. William II accordingly opted to install a court loyalist, John of Tours (died 1122), as his nominee. William, openly irreligious and a plunderer of church property, has not enjoyed a good press from the monastic chroniclers chiefly responsible for shaping his historic reputation. His ruddy complexion, foul temper and undisguised homosexuality gained him the nickname 'Rufus', with the implication of satanic associations. Whatever his motives in appointing John of Tours to Bath, a high-minded concern to further the on-going programme of church reform is unlikely to have figured much in the king's calculations. The *Anglo-Saxon Chronicle's* verdict on William was that he was 'loathsome to well nigh all his people and abominable to God'. His death while hunting may have been an accident or deliberate murder. What is certain is that he was buried without any religious ceremony whatsoever.

Bath's new master, John of Tours, was only recently consecrated - in July 1088 – but, as this had been done at the hands of the reformist Archbishop of Canterbury, Lanfranc, it can be assumed that his elevation had the full approval of the church as well as of the crown. John may well have been the 'Johannes medicus' who is recorded to have attended the Conqueror as he lay dying; he was certainly regarded as a skilled physician. Another potentially confusing aspect of his identity is the frequent reference to him as John de Villula. Villula is Latin for a country estate but in his instance may well be a distortion of his episcopal title in relation to the see of Wells. Whatever designation he is known by, John had it in for Wells, which, having been the seat of the bishopric since 909, was downgraded to a collegiate establishment. Its new conventual buildings were demolished and their inhabitants reduced from the privileged life of monastic seclusion and dispersed to live among the laity. John's brother, Hildebert, was installed as prior to ensure that Wells accepted its new, subordinate status as the location of the '*cathedra*' (bishop's throne) was henceforth transferred to Bath.

In 1091 John of Tours got William II to confirm the transfer of the abbey and city of Bath from royal to episcopal possession and soon after began a grandiose building programme to establish a huge, walled-in, religious precinct taking up over a quarter of the area within the circuit of the city's own walls. Dominated by a massive new church, three hundred and fifty feet long and ninety feet wide, this would also include a palatial new residence for the bishop and incorporate the demolition of the late Saxon abbey of St Peter, the demotion of the church of St James to become the bishop's private chapel and the refurbishment of the first century King's Bath to serve once more as a place of healing. So extensive was the consequent disruption to the pre-existing town plan that henceforth the city's main through route from west to east would be entirely truncated to swerve dramatically north into the High Street and an entirely new thoroughfare, Stall Street, would be created to define the western boundary of the cathedral close and coincidentally to afford the bishop a handy new income from street-front commercial lettings.

When Henry I visited Bath in 1106 Bishop John took the opportunity to renew royal confirmation of his possession – in return for £500 of silver, which then meant 500 lbs of silver. This consideration additionally secured him the right to hold an annual fair, another lucrative source of income. In 1117 building work suffered a severe setback as a result of a major fire, a disaster readily explained by the amount of timber that would have been on site in the form of masons' sheds, scaffolding, temporary roofings etc.

Formidable, arrogant John of Tours died in 1122, apparently at a great age. The chronicler William of Malmesbury conceded that he:

completed many things nobly in ornaments and books, and filled the abbey with monks eminent for literature and discharge of their duties.

(This was offset in William's view by manifest shortcomings)

According to report, his medical knowledge was founded more upon practice than science. He enjoyed literary society but indulged in sarcasm more than was fitted to his rank. He was a wealthy man and of liberal habits, but could not be induced, even on his death-bed, wholly to restore their lands to the monks.

John's great building project was completed by Robert of Lewes, who

Abbey Green

was appointed bishop in 1136, despite another major fire in 1137 and the background of the long-running anarchy which constituted the reign of King Stephen (reigned 1135-54). Robert's long tenure (1136-66) witnessed the completion not only of the cathedral church but also of a chapter house, cloisters, refectory and infirmary. In 1156 the Pope reiterated a confirmation that the seat of the bishopric had, indeed, been transferred from Wells to Bath. Of the Norman abbey built by John and Robert virtually nothing survives. The present Abbey takes up merely what had once been the nave of its mighty predecessor. Only the ghost of the monastic precinct remains, the Abbey Green being but a remnant of the former bishop's garden.

Scholar, Superstar

Adelard of Bath was a shining figure of international stature, much of whose life remains a matter of shadows and conjecture and whose outstanding achievements seem to have been largely forgotten. Neither the precise date of his birth nor of his death are known for certain. Writing in 1885 the Scottish philosopher Robert Adamson, author of the entry on Adelard in the first edition of the *Dictionary of*

National Biography, was scrupulously cautious to the point of vagueness, describing his subject as 'a writer on philosophy, of English birth, (who) flourished about the beginning of the twelfth century.' Adelard certainly was English, originally bearing the Anglo-Saxon name Aethelhard. His father, Fastrad, is known to have held land locally in the Bath area in 1087 as a tenant of the bishop of Wells. There is little reason to doubt that Adelard was born in Bath, probably around 1080, and was educated at the recently-founded priory academy. In Adelard's own writings he notes *en passant* that he was born in Bath and made the claim to be a citizen of Bath – not proof enough apparently for the sceptical Scottish professor. Adamson emphasised that one of the uncontested and documented facts of Adelard's life was a mention in the Pipe Rolls of the later reign of Henry I, dating from *ca.* 1130. Subsequent research has confirmed that Adelard's name appears as a witness to documents issued at the court of King Stephen between 1135 and 1139, making it unambiguously clear that he lived until at least the latter date and that his eminence was endorsed by royal recognition as a man of standing. From Bath Adelard as a young man had moved on to study at Tours, which it would be perverse not to assume was due to the patronage of John de Villula. It is known that Adelard accompanied the bishop to witness the coronation of Henry I's first wife, Matilda, in Westminster Abbey in 1100, surely a mark of signal favour for a man probably just out of his teens. As Adelard appears to have reached Tours around 1100 or shortly afterwards it is entirely plausible that bishop John invited him to accompany his entourage to Westminster so that he could ingratiate himself with the new royal regime by showing off his most promising protégé before despatching Adelard onwards to his studies overseas.

From Tours Adelard eventually progressed to Leon, capital of the Spanish kingdom of Leon, then on the frontier of Christian and Muslim Spain in more senses than the purely literal one. A strategic base for the Christian '*reconquista*' of Muslim-ruled territories, Leon was also a frontier of intellectual encounter, a crucial arena for the reception of the long-lost learning of ancient Greece, transmitted via translations into Arabic made by Muslim scholars and then rendered into Latin. The bearers of this new – or renewed – learning included many

Christian refugees from Toledo, which had been reconquered in 1085 and was already established as the foremost centre for Arabic-to-Latin translation. Western historians have hailed this process as the crucial component of a 'twelfth century renaissance' of classical learning in Christendom, pervading every realm of endeavour from architecture and astronomy to music, medicine and mathematics. Adelard was to be at the heart of this ferment of rediscovery.

Nowadays Leon is still dominated by two great architectural legacies of the Middle Ages, an immense Gothic cathedral, dating in its present form from the century after Adelard's residence, and the Colegiata de San Isidoro, a seat of learning dedicated in 1063 to honour the memory of Archbishop Isidore of Seville (?560-636), an intellectual giant, whose pioneering encyclopaedia preserved the framework of classical learning and set the model for all later medieval encyclopae-dists. Nowadays, if remembered at all, Isidore is credited with intro-ducing the notion that all human history should be divided by the crucial event in that history, the birth of Christ, into BC and AD.

Adelard seems to have advanced sufficiently in his studies to have joined the teaching faculty at Leon before moving on into the Muslim world itself. The extent of his subsequent travels implies fluency in Arabic as he moved through Muslim-ruled Spain and North Africa before diverting to Sicily, another arena of brilliant and fruitful cultural exchanges, brought under the control of Norman conquerors in 1059. Here Adelard is known to have visited both Syracuse and Palermo. From there he went on to Greece and what is now Turkey, where he would have had the opportunity to acquire or perfect a mastery of Greek, which he certainly also knew. Adelard additionally referred in another passage of his writings to experiencing an earthquake while on a bridge in Syria.

AN ODYSSEY OF LEARNING

Over what period of time these adventures occurred is unclear. Adelard was certainly in Bath in 1106 when he is known to have witnessed a document for John de Villula. Had he already undertaken his massive odyssey? It seems more likely that he had perhaps merely gone as far as he could, academically speaking, at Tours but that, having heard of the

marvellous opportunities in Spain, come home to request permission
(and funding?) from his patron to take an extended period of study-
leave thereafter. Adelard's academic achievements to that point would
almost certainly have brought him the privileged status of a cleric but
without subjecting him to the disciplines and restrictions that would
have bound a monk to his monastery. Given the enormous distances
he covered, the hazards he risked and the learning he amassed, it seems
much more probable that Adelard's excursion into the world of Islam
therefore took place after his return to Bath in 1106, rather than being
crammed into a frantic five years before that date.

We can speak with a little more certainty about Adelard's intellectual journey. Adamson's rather cavalier judgment was that 'on his
return from travel Adelard threw into systematic shape such of the
Arab teachings as he had acquired.' Writing as a professional philosopher and a gifted teacher of philosophy, Adamson's brief resumé of
Adelard's career devotes most interest to his epistemological treatise
De Eodem et Diverso (Concerning Sameness and Difference), in which
the author wrestles with the problem of reconciling the contrasting
views of Plato and Aristotle regarding the ultimate nature of reality
and how it may be known. Typically for a medieval scholastic he sets
his treatise in the form of an allegorical debate, with the soul of man
as its implicit prize. Philocosmia (Worldliness) is aided by the five false
values of fortune, power, dignity, fame and pleasure, while opposing
Philosophia (Lover of Wisdom) is supported by seven wise virgins,
representing the seven Liberal Arts which made up the basic course
of study at a medieval university – Grammar, Logic and Rhetoric, the
tools of disputation, and Arithmetic, Geometry, Astronomy and Music,
the means of investigating and ordering the created universe. The
problem was to square the circle between Platonic idealism – ultimate
reality consists of disembodied abstractions like the genus or species of
which living beings are but imperfect embodiments – and Aristotelian
pragmatism, which was insistent that the embodied individual was the
only true existent. Adelard appears to have cracked it – at least to his
own satisfaction. Such were, indeed, the major preoccupations of the
medieval mastermind and, indeed, of academic philosophers ever since.
As Davenport usefully reminds us, however, we should not 'make the

mistake of assuming Adelard was a modern thinker stranded in the Middle Ages.' On the one hand he was perfectly capable of accurately calculating the latitude of Bath. On the other he was perfectly happy to oblige the king by casting his horoscope.

That said, the modern reader might well be more impressed by the fact that Adelard made the first known translation of Euclid's *Elements* into Latin. Whether from a manuscript in the original Greek or from an Arabic version is not certain – he was capable of doing either – but as it remained the fundamental framework of mathematical thought for the next five centuries Adelard's achievement in this respect alone can hardly be underestimated. The work was also instrumental in the introduction of 'Arabic' numerals – actually Indian in origin – to northern Europe, although admittedly the government of Adelard's own native land continued to use Roman numerals for its accounting systems until Newton's lifetime.

Adelard's other major surviving works include an account of the abacus and a treatise on the use of the astrolabe in navigation and astronomy, which presumably benefited from practical experience gained in the course of his own wanderings. Undoubtedly a scholar of the first rank, Adelard was, however, neither a creature of the cloister nor a prisoner of the study but a multilingual polymath able to move easily among courtiers and kings. Having inevitably endured much hardship in the course of his travels he had no preference for monastic austerities but appreciated fine clothes and was expert at the royal pastime of falconry. He was also an accomplished musician and recorded in *De Eodem* that he had played the cithara, a sort of lyre plucked with a plectrum, for the amusement of Queen Matilda.

The enduring significance of Adelard's intellectual legacy is attested by the fact that more than three centuries after his death, when the invention of the printing-press at last made possible the dissemination of key works previously confined to precious manuscript copies, Adelard's other major philosophical treatise *Perdifficiles Quaestiones Naturales* (Very Difficult Questions about Nature) was published some time after 1472 and his version of *Euclid* was printed in Venice in 1482. Despite all this he has no memorial whatsoever in his native city of Bath. What price a statue? – a plaque? Street name?

Name Games

The painstaking research of Elizabeth Holland of the *Survey of Bath and District* has recovered the names of over two hundred holders of the office of mayor of Bath between the early thirteenth and the mid-sixteenth centuries. Surnames only began to become common in the twelfth century as a consequence of the general rise in and increased mobility of the population. Early surnames were often indicative of residence, personal appearance or place of origin. Hence among thirteenth century mayors of Bath John de Porta (of the Gate) and Roger of Dichegate, David Little, John de Dover and Stephen de Devizes. Many of the newly adopted surnames, indicative of occupation, illustrate the importance of textiles and provisioning to the local economy. In the thirteenth century Henry the Tailor held the office of mayor of Bath four times, John de Combe, a tailor from Combe Down, twice and Gilbert Cissor, another tailor once. Between 1332 and 1359 members of the Dyer family were mayors seven times. William Cook was mayor six times between 1283 and 1315 and another William Cook – surely a son or nephew? – in 1330. Whytesons, a family of millers, provided nine mayors between 1310 and 1345. Stephen de Devizes was also known as Stephen Baker. John Pistor, a baker, served around 1301. John the Baker served in 1316 and 1319. Other occupational surnames included Clerk, Taverner, Falconare (Falconer), Carpenter and Draper.

For decades at a time the mayoralty was dominated by particular families. Coles held the office seven, possibly eight times, between 1317 and 1343, Wasprays seven times between 1388 and 1411. Notably durable individuals included William Cubbel, who served in 1339,1344,1347 and 1348 and survived the Black Death to serve again in 1352; John Wittoksmede, mayor five times between 1355 and 1369; John Gregory eight times between 1362 and 1381; Roger Testwood four times between 1401 and 1407; Ralph Hunt, six times between 1408 and 1429 and William Phillips, seven, possibly eight, times between 1423 and 1444.

The names of the abbots, bishops and priors of Bath attest clearly to the Normanisation of England's ecclesiastical hierarchy. Anglo-Saxon abbot Aelfsige managed to hang on until 1087 but the twelfth to fifteenth century priors whose names are known all bear common foreign importations – John (8), Thomas (4), Walter (3), Robert (3) plus one each of Benedict, Peter, Hugh, Gilbert and William. The bishops of those centuries included five Johns, three Roberts, three Williams, three Walters, two each of Richards and Ralphs plus a single Godfrey, Reginald, Roger, Joscelin, Henry, Nicholas and Thomas. Their surnames indicate family origins in Lewes, Salisbury, Shrewsbury, Barnet and Stafford.

A Caring Community

The Hospital of St John the Baptist was established in 1180 – and still exists. The founder was Bishop Reginald Fitzjocelin (?1140-91), who was bishop from 1174 until his death. A member of the powerful Norman family of de Bohun, Reginald had been brought up in Italy and was a high-flyer whose career was as much diplomatic and political as clerical. At the coronation of Richard I, for example, he stood at the king's left hand, the bishop of Durham being to his right. Bishop Reginald was later involved in negotiating Richard's ransom after he had been kidnapped – and used his position to protect Bath's treasures from being pilfered for that particular pot. Despite the fact that Reginald was absent from Bath far more than he was ever there he ensured that he was buried in the abbey, clad in the robes of a monk – a custom often also followed by lay patrons of a religious house in the belief that it would secure a readier passage to paradise. Reginald's clout was posthumously attested by the fact that he secured the position of his successor for his cousin, Savaric.

Bishop Reginald's hospital stood by the Cross Bath and was intended to help the sick and poor of the city of Bath take advantage of the healing properties of the waters. It consisted of an infirmary, rather like a modern hospital ward, with an adjacent chapel, plus a kitchen and a house for the resident master. In its later existence it may have been mildly abused by being used as a retirement home for aged retainers from the abbey. Although the hospital received minor benefactions from the bishops of Shrewsbury and Lincoln, the canons of Wells and the inhabitants of Bath, it was never wealthy. In 1535 it was valued at £22.16s.9d. Perhaps because it was regarded as a primarily philanthropic, rather than religious, institution the Hospital of St John the Baptist escaped dissolution. By 1548 it was being used as an almshouse to accommodate 'six poor men'. After Elizabeth I confirmed that it should be controlled by the Mayor and city of Bath the institution was enlarged to provide lodgings for prosperous visitors whose fees helped to subsidise its philanthropic side. The appointment of a laundress implies a determination to set decent standards of cleanliness for both inmates and guests. The Hospital of St John the Baptist was subsequently merged with St Catherine's Hospital, which had been founded in 1444 by a Bath clothmaker, William Phillips; today it provides sheltered accommodation for the elderly.

The Hospital of St Mary Magdalen was established at Holloway, outside Bath, as the gift of Walter Hussey, a priory tenant. It was in existence by 1212 when it is known to have received a gift from the bishop of Lincoln. Situated on the far side of the river, well away from the city, it was intended for the care of lepers. As such it was as much a place of confinement as of care. Lepers were regarded as legally dead and their wills put into effect before they were admitted to the institution devoted to their care. With the gradual disappearance of leprosy in the later Middle Ages St Mary Magdalen fell into decay and in 1486 Prior John Cantlow amalgamated it with the abbey. It was later used as an asylum for the mentally handicapped.

Lantern of the West

At its peak in the early thirteenth century Bath abbey had a complement of some forty monks. A Lady Chapel was added to the fabric. In 1324 a major programme of repairs was undertaken. After the Black Death of 1348-49 the number of monks was halved and remained at around twenty for the rest of its existence. The church itself fell into serious disrepair. Its decline was matched by a marked falling off in spiritual standards. Neither manpower nor assets proved adequate for the upkeep of John of Tours' increasingly oppressive architectural legacy. When the monks' dormitory needed to be rebuilt in the mid-fifteenth century the bishop had to chip in with the necessary funds. Such was the impoverishment and ruinous condition of the monastic establishment that between 1485 and 1496 it was exempted from taxation

West Front of Bath Abbey

by the founder of England's new Tudor dynasty, the shrewd and steely Henry VII (reigned 1485-1509), a monarch noted for his ruthlessness in repairing the royal finances by every means available to him.

Bath Abbey was virtually re-founded barely a generation before it was to be extinguished for ever. Its would-be saviour was Oliver King (died 1503) another high-flyer much in favour with his king. Bishop King had held a succession of prestigious offices – royal secretary for French correspondence, registrar of the Order of the Garter and canon of Windsor – and had served on diplomatic missions overseas. In 1492 he was made bishop of Exeter, though it is doubtful that he ever went there. In 1495 he was advanced to the see of Bath and Wells, though he does not seem to have visited Wells until 1497. When he finally came to Bath in 1499 King found that the abbey church was 'ruined to the foundations' and placed the blame squarely on 'the laxity of many priors'. Laxity was also manifest in the behaviour of the residents – more inclined to feasting than fasting, desultory in the performance of their duties and habituated to the company of women at all hours.

During the course of his visitation Bishop King claimed to have had a visionary dream in which he beheld the Holy Trinity and beneath them a ladder with angels ascending and descending and at the foot of the ladder an olive tree bearing a crown. And - just in case the symbolism escaped him - a voice commanded 'Let an OLIVE establish the crown and a KING restore the church.' The modern sceptic may prefer to reflect on the fact that Henry VII had visited Bath in 1496 and 1497 and can scarcely have failed to notice the decay of its most prominent public building. Henry was, if not profoundly religious, certainly conventionally respectful of the church. He also had the knack of getting other people to pay for what he thought needed doing.

A HEAVENLY MISSION

Whether the hint had come from a heavenly or an earthly throne Bishop King had found his mission. Within a month the luckless Prior, John Cantlow, had died, to be replaced by William Bird, who proved to be just as much an enthusiast for rebuilding as his patron. King died only four years after initiating his project, Bird lived on for another twenty-two years, ensuring that King's death did nothing to divert or delay the allocation of resources to the venture in hand. King had calculated the monks' income at £480 a year and proposed to allocate £300 of that towards the building fund, topping it up as required from his own resources.

The rebuilding of Bath Abbey was placed in safe hands, those of the king's own masons, Robert Vertue (died 1506) and his brother William (?1465-1527). They promised King a vault in comparison with which there should be 'none so goodly neither in England nor in France'. This pledge, made in 1501, is the first recorded mention of the celebrated brothers. William, who would outlive his brother by more than twenty years, would become the foremost builder of his day, responsible for the Henry VII chapel at Westminster Abbey, St George's Chapel at Windsor, Corpus Christi College, Oxford and the chapel of St Peter ad Vincula in the Tower of London.

Foundations were being dug at Bath by 1502, which means that the demolition of the old nave had already been completed. New walls were rising as early as 1503. King wrote that the roof would be on by November – but himself died in August. Although he had prepared a handsome chantry chapel for himself at St George's Chapel, Windsor, in his will Oliver King asked to be buried in the choir of the new church rising at Bath.

Compared with the old Norman and early Gothic abbeys or cathedrals the King/Vertues' abbey was simple in conception and moderate in size, without the large transepts or retro-choir needed for the numerous side-chapels associated with the pilgrimage trade or a large community of monks. The resemblance to St George's Chapel at Windsor, which King knew well, is marked. Both feature elaborately adorned and symbolically sculptured west fronts with flanking, slightly projecting turrets. Both have pierced and panelled battlements. Both employ flying buttresses to contain the outward thrust of their daring vaulted roofs. The crucial difference is that St George's was finished the year after William Vertue's death. Bath wasn't. King's successor as bishop of Bath was an Italian cardinal, Adrian di Costello, who was sacked in 1518 for trying to poison the Pope. He never came near England, let alone Bath, but he does seem to have contributed to the work and his arms can be seen in the chancel vault which was, therefore, presumably completed before his disgrace.

Building continued as best it could on a limited budget but came to a complete halt in 1535.

Dissolution

Like dozens of other medieval cities, like Salisbury, Winchester, Ely and Bury St Edmunds, medieval Bath was dominated by its ecclesiastical establishment. In terms of their roles as landlord, employer and purchaser of goods and services such bodies most closely resembled a modern university campus, a place set apart yet influencing almost every aspect of the life of the local community. The sudden abolition of such a body and the confiscation of its assets would inevitably have the most profound impact on its locality. Which is exactly what happened to Bath when its ancient Benedictine abbey was suppressed on 27 January 1539.

The dissolution of the monastic houses of England and Wales was a by-product of Henry VIII's pursuit of a legitimate male heir. The king's first wife, Katherine of Aragon, gave him a daughter, Mary, but no son and once she had passed child-bearing age Henry sought to have the Pope overturn the original papal dispensation which had allowed him to marry his dead brother's widow in the first place. The Pope failing to oblige, Henry had broken the deadlock by rejecting papal authority to declare himself Supreme Head of the Church in – rather than *of* – England, thus enabling him to put away the luckless Katherine in favour of the fecund Anne Boleyn. This was endorsed by Parliament with the passage of an Act of Supremacy in 1534. Doctrinally the English church remained Catholic but Henry was readily persuaded by his favoured bureaucratic dogsbody Thomas Cromwell (1485?-1540) that its monastic arm was riddled with abuses. The religious houses were also possessors of immense wealth in the form of jewelled relics, great libraries and vast estates amounting to about a third of the entire country. An enquiry into church holdings, the *Valor Ecclesiasticus*, was set in train to itemise these assets in detail. Investigations of short-comings in monastic behaviour began the following year.

The *Valor Ecclesiasticus* recorded Bath Abbey as enjoying an annual income of £617. Translating the money values of Tudor times into a modern equivalent is notoriously difficult. Dr. J.H. Bettey, author of *The Suppression of the Monasteries in the West Country*, estimates Bath's £617 as worth about £1,000,000 in today's money. If this seems an amazing sum, consider that a sixteenth-century labourer could expect to earn about £5 a year; so the Abbey's annual income was worth roughly the earnings of 120 labourers. Compare that with the annual income of the same number on today's minimum wage of roughly £5 an hour (40 hours and 50 weeks) – say £10,000 a year - and a million pound estimate looks very plausible. In the case of Bath this went to support the lifestyle of just twenty monks. Admittedly there were dozens of servants to be fed and clothed out of this sum as well but even so the Abbey can plausibly be compared to an Oxbridge college with the monks in the role of well-cosseted dons. They, of course, might well have thought themselves hard done by compared to some of their plusher neighbours. Gloucester cathedral had an income of £1,846 and Glastonbury a whopping £3,500.

Bath was visited in August 1535 by one of Thomas Cromwell's most zealous enforcers, the pushy and none too scrupulous Richard Layton (?1500-44) who, in his confidential report to his master, dismissed Prior William Holleway as 'a man simple and not of the greatest wit'. What had become routine accusations of misconduct were alleged against the monks – 'worse than any I have found yet, both in buggery and adultery, some one of them having x (10) women, some viii and the rest fewer'. The fabric of the abbey was conceded to be 'well repaired' but at the expense of an outstanding debt of £400.

Holleway, by no means a simpleton, was a renowned physician with a passion for chemistry. Far from lacking in worldly wiles he presented Layton with a present of three Irish hawks as a gift for Cromwell. Layton also passed on a confiscated collection of relics of highly improbable provenance including the fetters which had bound St Peter in prison, combs belonging to Saints Margaret, Dorothy and Mary Magdalene and part of the stone manger in which the infant Jesus had been laid at Bethlehem. Layton also sent on 'a book of our Lady's miracles, well able to match the *Canterbury Tales*, such a book of dreams as you never saw, which I found in the library.'

Armed with this sort of ammunition, Cromwell proceeded to gain parliamentary approval for the suppression of the smaller religious houses, worth £200 a year or less, in 1536. At Bath meanwhile the monks lived in a condition of virtual house-arrest, forbidden to leave the abbey precinct. Prior Holleway used the breathing-space thus gained to try to muster local support for the abbey by granting out abbey lands on long leases in the hope that tenants would resist their curtailment. He also sent Cromwell another of the library's greatest treasures, a copy of the works of St Anselm, which had attracted the covetous attention of the royal librarian. In 1537 he even ordered that Cromwell be paid an annual pension of £5 out of Abbey funds. All proved in vain.

The royal commissioners sent to take possession of Bath Abbey on 27ᵗ January 1539 were John Tregonwell (died 1565) and William Petre (1505-72). Both were West Country men and trained lawyers. Both were destined for high office. Both would be knighted and die rich on their pickings from their service to the crown. Petre in the course of just the first three months of 1539 would accept the surrender of no less than thirteen religious houses. At Glastonbury Abbot Whiting refused to comply and was executed. One part of his quartered body was displayed in Bath as a warning of the price of non-compliance. At Bath there was no futile resistance to the authority of the king's commissioners. Depending on their age and seniority the monks were awarded pensions ranging from £4.13s.4d to £9. Prior Holleway was assigned a munificent £80, plus a house in Stall Street. Little good it did him. Devastated by the royal onslaught, he rapidly declined into dementia, his sufferings compounded by the onset of blindness. The crown disposed of the Abbey's lands. The abbey church was offered to the citizens of Bath for £333.6s.8d. When they failed to buy it, it was sold to one Humphrey Colles of Taunton. He stripped the lead off the roof and demolished the roof of the nave and in 1543 sold it to Matthew Colthurst, the MP for Bath.

The bishopric continued to be known by its joint title of Bath and Wells but with the dissolution of Bath's monastic foundation the cathedral at Wells became *de facto* as well as *de jure* the effective seat of episcopal authority.

Eyewitness

In 1533 Henry VIII's librarian John Leland (?1506-52) set out, with royal approval, to tour the kingdom with a warrant to search monastic and collegiate libraries for neglected ancient manuscripts so that they 'might be brought out of deadly darkness to lively light.' Leland's odyssey lasted a decade and brought him through Bath twice, before and after the dissolution of the abbey. He was very impressed by the fact that many residents had the benefit of a piped water supply, an unusual luxury for domestic houses, even in London – 'The City of Bath … is environed on every side with great Hills out of which come many springs of pure water that be conveyed by divers ways to serve the city. Insomuch that Lead being made there a hand many Houses in the Town have Pipes of Lead to convey Water from Place to Place.' At the Cross Bath he noted the less appetising consequence of Bath's hydraulic bounty – the presence of sufferers from 'Lepre, Pokkes, Scabbes and great Aches'

In Memoriam

'These walls adorned with monument and bust
Show how Bath waters serve to lay the dust.'

The funeral monuments and memorials of Bath Abbey are more remarkable for their sheer quantity than their outstanding quality. There are over 640 of them, more than in any other church outside Westminster Abbey. There were once even more but many were lost during the course of G.P. Manners' restoration work in the 1830s, when he cleared the nave pillars of monuments and transferred them to the walls. Abbey registers list 3,879 burials under the Abbey floor up to 1845.

The Oxford antiquarian and gossip Anthony Wood produced a short account of the memorials as long ago as 1676, John Britton a much more comprehensive survey in 1825. The vast majority date from the period 1740-1870, only about thirty having been added since then.

Monuments do not necessarily correlate with burials within the Abbey. Some commemorate people buried in other churchyards or in the Abbey cemetery outside the city at Widcombe. Not surprisingly many of the monuments were locally produced by Reeves and Sons or Thomas King but there are also examples of the work of distinguished London masters like Joseph Nollekens, John Bacon Senior, John Flaxman and Sir Francis Chantrey.

What follows is necessarily a small selection of the more interesting or unusual:

Choir, South side East end
Chantry chapel of **Prior Birde** – Birde's rebus – a bird – can be seen over the doorway and in the frieze.

'Outside' the chantry to the right of the altar is a brass of **Sir George Ivy** (d.1639) and his wife and an alabaster one for **Bartholomew Barnes** (d.1605) and his wife.

Opposite, left of the altar, a composition (by Bacon Sr.) to the literary hostess **Lady Miller** (1781) (see page 118).

South Chapel

S.wall **Mary Frampton** (d.1698) has an inscription by the Poet Laureate John Dryden

N. wall The Bath painter **William Hoare** (see page 163) died in 1792 but his monument, by Chantrey, was not made until 1828.

South Choir Aisle

Sir Philip Frowde (d.1674), a swaggering soldier; the lengthy inscription says less about his military career than about his three wives and nine children.

Admiral Sir Richard Hussey Bickerton (1759- 1832) (by Chantrey) who served as Nelson's deputy at the blockade of the French fleet at Toulon 1804-5.

Dr Sibthorp (by Flaxman), Professor of Botany at Oxford. Sibthorp (1758-96) compiled a definitive study of the plant life of Oxfordshire, identifying 1,200 different specimens. His second tour of Greece brought on his early death; the results of his studies there were published posthumously in ten volumes, illustrated by 966 plates, at the staggering cost of £30,000. Flaxman depicts him walking from the Styx, the river of death, towards a Greek temple, carrying an offering of flowers and wearing a Greek chlamys with a hat like the one worn by Hermes, messenger of the gods.

South Transept

Jacob Bosanquet (d.1767) has a relief of the Good Samaritan. A recumbent **Lady Waller** (d.1633) is shown with her husband, commander of the parliamentary forces at the battle of Lansdown (see page 80); the alabaster figures were defaced when Bath was occupied by royalist troops.

South Aisle

Beau Nash (d.1761) with an admirably concise epitaph – *Bathonie Elegantiae Arbiter* – Bath's Master of Manners.

Merchant **William Baker** (d.1770) is attended by Justice, Plenty and a Turk with a camel. The sarcophagus of eminent physician **Caleb Hillier Parry** (d.1822) is surmounted by books and a serpent, emblematic of healing. Parry was the most eminent Bath practitioner of his day, a Fellow of the Royal Society who made important discoveries in relation to angina and rabies. He was also a keen agriculturalist with a farm outside Bath where he promoted merino sheep.

Senator William Bingham (d.1804) is here commemorated (by Flaxman) and in New York state by the city of Binghamton. Against the S wall of the SW porch is a suitably theatrical tribute to **Rauzzini** (see page 137), a swagged curtain bearing a musical score.

Nave West wall

Herman Katencamp (d 1808), H.M. Consul General in the Two Sicilies and in Spain (by Bacon Jnr.) **Col. Champin** (d.1793) (by Nollekens).

Nave

The memorial to **Brevet Col. Jos.Matlock** (d.1860) tells a mini-saga of imperial sacrifice. Hardships endured in India killed him in South Africa en route for home. Leaving behind the body of an infant son, he lost a further two daughters, aged fifteen months and five, at sea. His widow got back to England only to have her surviving baby daughter die at four months.

North Aisle

The broken column on the memorial to **Lt.Col. Robt.Walsh** (d.1788) signifies that he was the last of his family line.

James Tamesz Grieve (d. 1787) was physician to Empress Elizabeth of Russia and his wife who predeceased him by thirty years is attended by Death and Father Time.

The monument to **Bishop Montague** (d. 1618) (see page 78) is the largest in the church.

North Choir Aisle

Physician and composer **Henry Harington** MD (d. 1816) was Mayor of Bath and founder of the Bath Harmonic Society, hence the organ and music on his memorial.

The Abbey's oldest monument shows **Richard Chapman** (d. 1572) and **William Chapman** (d.1627) flanked by skulls as memento mori. The memorial to **James Quin** (see page 131) is by local sculptor Thomas King with an inscription by David Garrick.

One of a Kind

'One of the best men and truest philosophers of any age or country.'

By far the most intellectually distinguished person memorialised (and buried) in Bath Abbey is the **Revd. T.R.Malthus** (1766-1834) who married Harriet Eckersall, a local girl from St Catherine's, and happened to die at her family home, Claverton House, one Christmas. Informally educated by a succession of unusually stimulating tutors, in his youth Malthus revelled in cricket, rowing, skating and 'fighting for its own sake' without the slightest malice. Malthus' brilliant academic career at Cambridge was followed by ordination and continued study which led in 1798 to the (initially anonymous) publication of the work that would make him famous – to many infamous – *An Essay on the Principle of Population as it affects the Future Improvement of Society*. The outbreak of revolution in France had inspired idealists like the radical philosopher William Godwin to proclaim the perfectibility of mankind. Malthus, who looked to facts rather than theories, would have none of it. Malthus argued that whereas population growth proceeded in geometrical progression, the means of subsistence would only increase in an arithmetic progression. Population would therefore inherently outrun subsistence and be cut back ruthlessly by famine, disease, war etc, unless otherwise checked by 'self-restraint' or 'vice', which for Malthus, included contraception. Poverty was therefore the inescapable lot of man. Hence the accusation that Malthus had made economics 'the gloomy science'. A second, much expanded, edition of the *Essay on Population* appeared in 1803, informed by Malthus' own extensive travels in Scandinavia, Russia, France and Switzerland and incorporating much factual material to back up his argument. Malthus continued to revise and expand the work until it reached a massive sixth edition in 1826. The effect of Malthus' teachings was to discourage traditional forms of charity and generous wages on the grounds that they only encouraged feckless fecundity. 'Malthusianism' was roundly attacked by radicals and conservatives alike, the critics including Godwin, Cobbett, Coleridge, Owen, Hazlitt and Southey.

Regardless of the furore caused by the *Essay* Malthus himself lived a retired life at the East India Company's college at Haileybury, Hertford as Britain's first professor of political economy. Indifferent alike to praise or abuse, Malthus, despite a serious speech defect, enjoyed many warm friendships and was renowned for his serenity and amiability. Elected a Fellow of the Royal Society, he was also a founder of the Political Economy Club and the Statistical Society of London, one of ten royal nominees to the Royal Society of Literature and an honorary member of the Academies of Paris and Berlin. A century after Malthus' death John Maynard Keynes rehabilitated Malthus' reputation in an essay hailing him as 'The First of the Cambridge Economists'. Malthus's monument is just beside the door in the west front by which one enters the Abbey.

A concise, inexpensive illustrated souvenir guide *Bath Abbey Monuments* by Bernard Stacel (Millstream Books/ Bath Abbey 1993) can be bought at the Abbey bookshop.

The Inner Man

Set in a thriving agricultural region, historic Bath was framed by market gardens, meadows and rich grazing land. The *Bath Guide* of 1800 boasted that 'Lansdown is one of the most conspicuous and happily situated hills in the west of England and famous for the number of sheep fattened by its herbage.' This claim was substantiated by the fact that the maverick, womanising politician John Wilkes (1725-97) had a self-confessed 'marked partiality for Bath mutton', which became something of a family joke. Wilkes may have been a conspicuously unsatisfactory husband but he was an affectionate father and delighted in sending his daughter Polly supplies from Bath. These included soles, gurnard, whiting and woodcock and also such simple things as local cheese and 'a country loaf of brown bread'which he judged to be 'exquisite'. Until the mid-eighteenth century, the city also had a six acre vineyard, although its output was anything but reliable; in 1720 it produced enough grapes to made sixty-six hogsheads of wine, in 1721 only enough for three.

Bath also had the immense advantage of being near Bristol. The nation's second greatest port ran an extensive trade with both the West Indies and the Mediterranean and was thus able to supply in quantity such tropical luxuries as sugar, chocolate and rice, as well as exotic items such as turtles ('will keep a good ten days') and pineapples, not to mention bulk supplies of port, sherry and rum.

If Bath wanted to put on a corporate bash it was fully capable, therefore, of matching anything London could come up with. When Frederick, Prince of Wales (1707-51), honoured the city with a visit in 1738 the banquet fare included salmon, crayfish, oysters and lobster, venison, veal, mutton, beef and tongue, plus partridge, duck, chicken, pheasant, capons, quail and guinea hens. This profusion of basic items was complemented by noodles, mangoes, asparagus, game ragout, calves' ears and 'Rhenish Wine Cream'.

Cooks employed at Bath's numerous inns could be hired to cater for particular occasions. When, in 1794, Lord Camden (1714-94) – 'an indolent dilettante and a temperate epicure' - decided to celebrate becoming Recorder of Bath by hosting a dinner for seventy at the Town Hall the arrangements were entrusted to the celebrated Mr Pickwick, proprietor of the White Hart Inn, who was given carte blanche in the matter of the budget. As a result 'the table was three times covered with every possible dainty of the season', to complement the main features of the feast – three turtles and three fat buck.

That indefatigable Bathonian booster John Wood boasted that, apart from its incomparable mutton, butter, 'herbage' and fish, the city also commanded superlative culinary talent – 'no City in the World can be furnished with better and cleaner Cook Maids … the extraordinary Abilities of those Maids have long rendered the Town a Nursery for supplying … such Kind of Servants.' Indeed, Wood claimed, every year visiting gentry, having hired a Bath cook, 'on their leaving the City' took them 'to their respective Places of Abode, even in London itself.'

Entertaining acquaintances to a meal was an essential element of Bath's social life but as many residents took rooms without cooking facilities there was a constant demand for prepared foodstuffs in the form of pies, pasties, tarts, pre-cooked poultry, cured meats, dishes preserved in aspic and such extravagances as chickens fattened on chopped almonds and raisins. These were supplied by the city's famed confectioners and cookshops, most notably Gill's of Wade's Passage and Molland's of Milsom Street. Dalmer the baker of Walcot, offered a delivery service to all parts of the city and had a portable oven to deliver items piping hot for the breakfast table. Perishable commodities, like greens, milk and fish were sold door-to-door by hawkers.

Food vied with fashion as a key component of Bath's retailing sector. The trade was sufficient to support specialist suppliers like an ice cream parlour at 13 Pulteney Bridge, which also sold jellies, cakes, biscuits and lemonade. So profitable was his business that Charles Gill, purveyor of pies, pastries, tarts and soups, became a virtual Bath institution, hymned at length in verses concluding triumphantly :

While he so well can broil and bake,
I'll promise and fulfil,
No other Physic e'er to take
Than what's prescribed by GILL

Gill was wealthy enough to keep a coach, something even Gains-borough never did in Bath. He could also afford to send his son, another Charles (see page 161), to train as a painter at the newly-established Royal Academy and in Reynolds's studio. Although Gill junior never achieved the first rank as a portraitist he was still able to live in the Circus in the 1780s, thanks to his father's accumulated wealth.

Tea-drinking became universal through all social classes in the course of the eighteenth century, though it was drunk at breakfast and in the evening rather than at what was to become 'tea-time' during the course of Victoria's reign. Guests in Bath's boarding houses were often expected to supply their own tea and sugar, the tea usually being kept in a locked caddy. Among ladies, especially, the ability to discriminate between the various types and grades of tea was as essential a social skill as an appreciation of a superior claret or burgundy was among men. The stock held by John Coles, proprietor of what he advertised as 'The Cheapest Tea Ware-House in Bath', ranged from the most basic 'Bohea', retailing at 1 shilling and 10 pence per pound, through 'Good Green Tea' at 3 shillings and 4 pence to 'the best superfine' at ten shillings. Coles claimed to purchase all his teas in person from the warehouses of the East India Company itself and even swore an oath before the mayor and an excise officer that he never bought smuggled tea and never adulterated it.

Which brings us to the subject of fraud and abuse in the food trade. A pamphlet of *ca.* 1737, entitled *The Art of Thriving at Bath*, accused the city's tradesmen of conducting a routine system of theft known as poundage. Realising that many fashionable visitors to Bath thought that examining their grocery bills in detail was beneath them, traders colluded with their servants to inflate their accounts by an agreed proportion of shillings in the pound and split this mark-up with them.

The corporation of Georgian Bath retained many of the regulatory powers of its medieval predecessor, such as the right to set the price of a standard loaf and to license publicans. It also appointed two bailiffs to supervise the market and to catch stallholders trying to sell stale or underweight items. These would be confiscated and given to the city's poor. It also proved necessary for the city to introduce a system of licensing for the porters and 'basketwomen' who carried shoppers' bulk purchases home for them. The chance to earn a living like this allegedly attracted vagrants to the city, competing with the city's own poor and often too ignorant of its layout – or too dishonest – to deliver goods to the correct address.

Apart from its numerous inns and taverns, Bath had many other venues for eating out. Cookshops like Gill's often had an eating area. There were many coffee-houses, some exclusively for female clientele. It was also possible to find refreshment in the city's pleasure gardens. After taking the waters early one could make breakfast a pleasant social occasion. In 1766 a Cornish visitor, John Penrose, considered himself a model of moderation in limiting himself to a single hot buttered roll and a single cake, sluiced down with a cup of chocolate, two cups of coffee and two cups of tea.

Pupils at Bath's many private academies had little choice in what they ate but some at least seem to have fared not too badly. The girls of Belvedere House were fortified with mutton, rice puddings, currant dumplings – known by them as 'chokedogs' – and, as a Saturday treat, stewed beef with pickled walnuts.

While Bath's well-heeled visitors were more than well served at table the provision of an adequate food supply for the poor was a worry for the city fathers. Indicators of anxiety were promptly reported in the columns of the *Bath Chronicle*. In 1782 the large number of sparrows being found dead was taken as evidence of an imminent harvest shortfall. In 1784 the newspaper published a recipe to enable the comfortably off to prepare a nourishing soup for the city's less fortunate residents. Starting with left-over bones and vegetables from the domestic table it suggested the addition of six pounds of oatmeal, water, the toppings from celery, onions and turnips, bolstered with 'one or two salt herrings, a bit of beef or bacon and a few potatoes', the whole to be boiled for 'three or four hours'. Fear of popular discontent was heightened by the outbreak of the French Revolution in 1789 and the onset of war with France in 1792. In that year the

Chronicle reassured its readers that the arrival of a bumper catch of large mackerel at Plymouth, to be sold a twopence and threepence a dozen, 'will allow the poor to eat well despite the high price of meat'. A particularly severe harvest crisis in 1795 brought readers of the *Chronicle* alarming reports of food riots in Norfolk, Hampshire, Sussex and Shropshire. The newspaper helpfully published a recipe for making loaves from barley and oatmeal. The government did its bit by banning the use of wheat flour for making starch or wig-powder – with immediate repercussions for Bath's highly fashion-conscious population. The *Bath Chronicle* announced portentously that 'The Duke of Northumberland has not only left off hair powder himself but given each of his servants two guineas a year additional wages on condition they go unpowdered.'

The Bath Oliver

Now readily available throughout Britain, the Bath Oliver biscuit was long a speciality of the city of its birth. Its invention is attributed to physician William Oliver FRS (1695-1764), who made it part of a regimen he prescribed for his patients. Oliver is said to have given the secret of its recipe to his coachman, Atkins, together with £100 and a supply of wheat flour. Atkins then set up in business at 13 Green Street and made a splendid living out of what he called 'Bath Olivers' in deference to his benefactor. The Bath Oliver was later produced by Fortt and Son of Bath. The blitzing of their premises in 1941 supposedly destroyed all the original documentation relating to the origin of the biscuit. Bath Olivers are nowadays manufactured by leading biscuit-makers such as Jacobs and Huntley and Palmer and are usually eaten with cheese.

The Bath Bun

'These Bath-buns are almost the same preparation as the Brioche cakes so much eaten and talked of in Paris.'
Mistress Margaret Dods *The Cook and Housewife's Manual* (1826)

Not to be confused with a Sally Lunn (see page 89), the original Bath Bun consisted of a rich egg and butter dough topped with crushed caraway seed comfits. It achieved national notice thanks to the Great Exhibition of 1851, when visitors consumed 943,691 of them. After Dr Edwin Lankester revealed that bakers (in London, not Bath !) were using sulfide of arsenic to colour Bath buns yellow Britain's Parliament hastened in 1860 to pass the world's first modern legislation against food adulteration. Frederick Hackwood writing in 1911 observed that the Bath Bun was 'sold everywhere throughout the kingdom' and described it as 'a sweet bun of a somewhat stodgy type ... popularly supposed to constitute, with a little milk, the average form of luncheon taken by mild curates.' In the 1920s Max Beerbohm characterised it as the standard fare of the railway refreshment room. The modern Bath Bun is made from a sweet yeast dough and sprinkled with crushed sugar, sometimes with a lump of sugar baked in the bottom as well. Variant forms can include raisins, sultanas, currants or candied fruit peel. Not surprisingly they feature on the menu in the Pump Room. References to Bath Buns date from 1763. Elizabeth Raffald's *The Experienced English Housekeeper* (1769) gave a recipe which omitted eggs but included both butter and cream. Bath Bun is also Cockney rhyming slang for son.

Bath Chap

The Bath chap (a variant spelling of chop) is the jawbone of the pig, with the attached cheek, which has been soaked in brine, cooked and pressed in a mould. In the past it was usually dried before cooking and, when treated with saltpetre, was expected to keep for several months. With its upper surface covered with breadcrumbs and its interior a streaky alternation of lean pink meat and white fat, the Bath chap looked like a cone cut in half vertically. The lower jawbone, which had the tongue as well as the cheek attached, sold for twice the price of the upper one. A great treat in the Victorian era, when it was often eaten cold (e.g. as a picnic dish), the Bath chap has proved rather too fatty for most modern palates.

Beauty of Bath

The Beauty of Bath is an early dessert apple, small, flattish, sharp and juicy, green but flushed with red, introduced into cultivation by a Mr Cooling of Bath in 1864. In 1887 it was awarded the Royal Horticultural Society's First Class Certificate. Ideally it should be eaten straight from the tree as it does not keep at all well and does not therefore appeal to the retail trade.

The Hole in the Wall

When George Perry-Smith (1922-2003) opened his Hole in the Wall restaurant in 1952 wartime rationing of food was still partially in force. Inspired by Elizabeth David's *French Country Cooking* (1951), Perry-Smith was the provincial pioneer of Mediterranean-style cuisine. And whereas the typical London establishment of that day would be offering two or at most three choices per course, Perry-Smith offered up to ten. He had a passion for fresh local produce and a capacity for taking infinite pains. His own signature dish was salmon with currants and ginger in a puff pastry wrap. Other offerings included home-made pâtés and quiches, mundane enough nowadays but incredibly exotic in the grim 1950s.

George Perry-Smith was educated at Kingswood, Bath's Methodist school, took a first in French at Cambridge and, as a Quaker and conscientious objector, drove an ambulance during World War Two. Rather than become a schoolmaster, he took to the restaurant trade and stuck with it in Bath till 1973. He is commemorated by the George Perry-Smith Memorial Prize which encourages local schoolchildren to devise their own menus, using Somerset produce. Strangely the Hole in the Wall's current website makes absolutely no mention of this remarkable man.

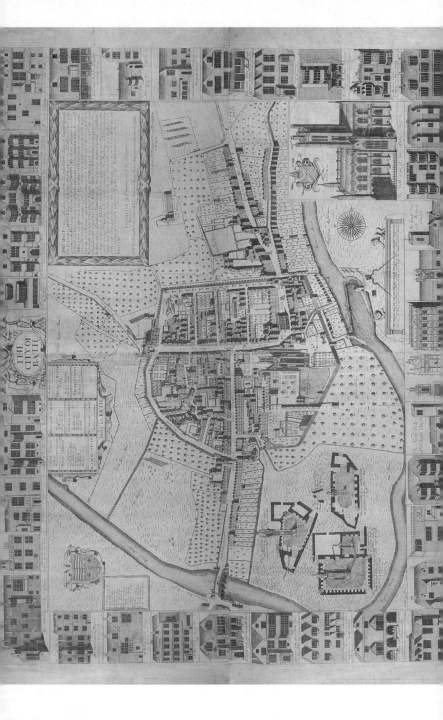

THE CITY OF BATH

CHAPTER FIVE

The Rise of the Spa

1540 – 1700

A Liquid Solution

The suppression of Bath Abbey deprived the city of its major economic driver. The decline of its cloth trade deprived it of another. Salvation was eventually found in the redevelopment of the resource which had made Bath a centre of resort and expenditure a millennium and a half before – the hot, healing waters which had never ceased to bubble out of the ground.

The first scientific endorsement of the medical value of Bath's mineral waters was made by William Turner (?1508-1568), 'the father of English botany' and sometime – or more accurately sometimes – Dean of Wells. A Cambridge don, Turner in his youth had an early and unwavering conversion to the cause of Protestantism, a commitment which was to cost him dear. His religious convictions blighted a promising academic career, forcing him into self-imposed exile. Turner spent over a decade abroad, studying botany in Italy, Switzerland, Germany and the Netherlands, while maintaining himself as a physician and Protestant chaplain. The accession of Edward VI, a keen reformer, in 1547 saw Turner come into royal favour, serve briefly as a Member of Parliament, and after several disappointments, gain the appointment of Dean of Wells. Scarcely had he been able to install himself, however, than the early death of Edward VI in 1553 and the consequent accession of his devoutly Catholic half-sister Mary forced him back abroad. Finally restored to his deanery in 1560, Turner managed to forfeit a comfortable old age by his uncompromising truculence in attacking the religious moderation of the new regime of Elizabeth I (reigned 1558-1603).

Opposite: Joseph Gilmore's detailed map of the City of Bath, 1694

RESTORATIVE WATERS

Turner's tribute to the medicinal value of Bath's waters – 'a book of the bath of Baeth' - was published in 1562 as an appendix to one of his pioneering 'Herbals'. In particular Turner praised the waters for the treatment of gout, palsey and sciatica and also claimed they could 'scoure away frekels'. Turner's groundbreaking contribution to English botany was the elementary but essential task of systematically recording the names of hundreds of plants and herbs, sometimes giving them names himself, such as goatsbeard and hawkweed. He also introduced new plants to England, most notably lucern, which he called horned clover. In 1548 Turner had published a pioneering comparative dictionary – *The names of herbes in Greek, Latin, English, Duch and French.* This was followed in 1551 by *A New Herball wherein are continued the names of Herbs.* The 1562 volume was a 'second part' of this work, long delayed by Turner's enforced exile. It was reprinted in 1580 and1589 and there were also later editions. Turner's contribution to botany was freely acknowledged by his successor John Ray (1627-1705), the founder of modern plant taxonomy. Perhaps equally important was Turner's contribution in making the *Herbal* a standard work of household reference. If a sixteenth century household possessed any printed book it was a Protestant Bible. After that, the most popular work was *Foxe's Book of Martyrs*, detailing the sufferings of English Protestants under Mary Tudor. Third would come a Herbal, an invaluable guide to the plants to be used for making up 'simples' (medicines), poultices, emetics, cosmetics and in cooking, preserving etc. The author of a successful Herbal like Turner's would, therefore, be as much a household name, at least among the literate, as one of today's celebrity chefs. Hence the importance of Turner's endorsement of Bath's baths.

Not that it could be called a ringing endorsement. Turner certainly praised the waters' healing virtues but lamented the baths' neglected condition, comparing them unfavourably to those he had seen on his travels in Germany and Italy, and even elsewhere in England. The baths at Bath had scarcely changed since medieval times, consisting of mere open pools with seats in niches around the sides. There were no changing rooms and no system for draining the baths periodically so that they could be cleaned. Turner noted acerbically that while the townsmen of Bath could always seem to find cash for cock-fights or tennis or travelling players 'I have not heard tell that any rich man hath spent upon these noble baths … one groat these twenty years.'Turner's suggestions for improving the baths included erecting a separate bath for women, another separate bath for sufferers with highly infectious diseases – and a third, separate bath, for horses. Turner's message was reinforced in 1572 with the publication of a volume by John Jones informatively entitled '*The bathes of Bathes Ayde: wonderfull and most excellent against very many Sicknesses, approved by authoritie, confirmed by reason and dayly tried by experience,with the antiquity, commodity, property, knowledge, use, aphorisms, diet, medicine, and other things to be considered and observed.*'

The city did gradually make the necessary investment in upgrading the bathing facilities. A new bath for women, known as the Queen's Bath, was created beside the King's Bath. Private donations enabled all the baths eventually to be equipped with changing-rooms, provided with sluices and embellished with decorative centre-pieces.

The reformation of the bathing facilities was complemented by an expansion in the facilities for worship. Edward Colthurst, son of the Bath MP who had bought the former priory church, was willing to turn it over to the city, which would enable it to be used by the city as a whole, as a single united parish. As the city fathers explained in a petition to the sovereign – 'There is in the spring time and at the fall of leaf yearly great repair to the … city of noble men, men of worship and others for relief at the baths there are no convenient church … for any company to resort together to hear the word of God preached.'

In 1572 the Queen graciously assented to set aside her patronage of the city's smaller churches – St Mary de Stalle, St Mary Within and St Michael's - to allow this to happen. In 1573 she issued a special warrant to allow collections toward the restoration of the Abbey church throughout England for seven years.This would eventually raise enough to roof in the chancel and repair the north transept. The full task of restoration would be spread out over forty-five years, longer than it had taken to build the church in the first place. In today's abbey a modern stained-glass window of great charm celebrates the achievement.

ROYAL ENDORSEMENT

In 1574 the Queen herself visited Bath to give her endorsement to the restoration project in person. Although restoration had scarcely begun, a preacher was lined up to give an inaugural sermon, choristers were borrowed from Wells and the half-ruined church cheered up with a plentiful garnish of fresh greenery. As royal visits were by definition high-profile occasions, the Queen travelled with a large entourage. As she was never off duty a meeting of the Privy Council was held in the course of her stay. All of which gave her courtiers ample opportunity to become familiar with the city and its facilities and, in due course, to spread the word to other potential visitors. The Queen's closest personal favourite, Robert Dudley, Earl of Leicester (1533-88) came four times. Sir Walter Raleigh (1554-1618) was another ardent patron. James I's consort, Anne of Denmark, visited Bath in 1613 and again in 1615. Her physician in Bath was Edward Jorden (died 1632) whose *Discourse of Natural Bathes and Mineral Waters* ran to five editions.

Royal courtiers especially favoured lodging in Abbey Church House whose builder, Dr Robert Baker (died 1596), had installed a private bath fed directly from the Hot Bath. Baker's widow married Dr Reuben Sherwood. During Sherwood's tenure the house was visited by the Queen's lady-in-waiting, the Marchioness of Northampton. A maid-of-honour to Princess Cecilia of Sweden, Helena Ulfsdotter Snakenborg, stayed no less than eight times. An up-market clientele was no infallible guarantee of impeccable behaviour as the courtier Sir John Harington (1561-1612) wittily observed :

> A common phrase long used here hath been,
> And by prescription now some credit hath;
> That divers Ladies coming to the Bathe,
> Come chiefly but to see and to be seene.
> But if I should declare my conscience briefly,
> I cannot think that is their Arrant chiefly.
> For as I hear that most of them have dealt,
> They chiefly come to feel and to be felt.

Harington had a good claim to local knowledge. He lived on an estate at Kelston, acquired by marriage, and was twice banished there by the Queen, his godmother – for writing scurrilous verses. This did not prevent him from serving as High Sheriff of Somerset or entertaining the Queen at Kelston when she visited Bath in 1592.

In 1590 Elizabeth conferred a final benefaction on Bath by granting it a charter which conveyed governmental powers to the mayor, aldermen and city councillors. This remains the basis for Bath's present system of administration. The charter also significantly extended the bounds of the city, adding the whole of the Barton Farm estate to the north-west and much of the parish of Walcot.

Surveying the Scene

Towards the end of the reign of Elizabeth I the schoolmaster and antiquarian William Camden set out to produce a county by county survey of the entire realm, the first such enterprise to be attempted. Of Bath's setting Camden wrote :

> Seated it is low in a plain, and the same not great, environed round about with hills almost all of one height, out of which certain rills of fresh river waters continually descend into the city, to the great commodity of the citizens.

Not surprisingly he devoted most of his account of the city to a description of its unique natural assets:

> Within the city itself there bubble and boil up three springs of hot water, of a bluish or sea colour, sending up from them thin vapours and a kind of strong scent withal, by reason that the water is drilled and strained through veins of Brimstone and a clammy kind of earth called Bitumen. Which springs are very medicinable and of great vertue to cure bodies over-charged and benumbed (as it were) with corrupt humours. For by their heat they procure sweat and subdue the rebellious stubbornness of the said humours.

Describing the baths in detail, Camden noted that the Cross Bath was flanked by twelve stone seats and was 'of a very mild and temperate warmth', the Hot Bath was 'much hotter' and the King's Bath was 'walled also round about and fitted with thirty-two seats of arched work, wherein men and women may sit apart, who when they enter in put upon their bodies linen garments and have their guides.'

THE SAVILE MAP

Camden's antiquarian bent led him to record that in ancient times the baths had been dedicated to Minerva – or Hercules – or both. He dismissed a popular belief that they had been discovered by Julius Caesar but accepted that the legendary battle of Mount Badon, at which King Arthur is supposed to have crushed a Saxon horde around 520 AD, took place near Bath. Around the same time that Camden visited Bath Henry Savile (1568-1617) made a fine, detailed map of the city. Savile a widely-travelled Oxford graduate, was a polymath with interests in science, heraldry, antiquarianism and painting. He was also licensed to practise medicine. This reinforces the impression given by the map itself, that it was expressly designed for spa visitors. Savile's map was the first to include detailed plans of the city's main baths. The accompanying history and description of the city emphasises the therapeutic qualities of their waters. The depiction of the former abbey church shows the nave still unroofed and the south transept open to the elements. In 1604, shortly after Savile made his map, a second major phase of rebuilding began, thanks to the generosity of 'a good Samaritan, honest Mr. Billet'. This was, in fact, Sir Thomas Bellott (1534-1611) a protégé of the great Lord Burleigh, Elizabeth's chief minister.

James Montagu, who became bishop of Bath and Wells in 1608 came up with £1,000 for the work on the abbey and supplied lead for the roof from the bishopric's own mines on Mendip. Montagu moved on to the bishopric of Winchester in 1616 but his brother, Lord Chief Justice Sir Henry Montagu (1563-1642), paid for the carving of the great west doors which completed the work of restoration in 1617. His contribution was commemorated with the Montagu arms and the inscription *Ecce quam bonum et quam jucundum est – Behold how good and pleasing it is*. Bishop Montagu bestowed one last, posthumous benefaction on the abbey when he died the following year by insisting that he be buried, not in Winchester but in Bath 'to stir up some more benefactors to that place.'

In 1608 the charitable Bellot established almshouses in Binbury Lane for up to a dozen of 'such poor diseased persons being not infected with any contagious disease as shall resort and come to the city of Bath'. A subsequent endowment of 1652 enabled a physician to be appointed to care for the inmates of 'Bellot's Hospital'. Rebuilt in 1859-64, it yet survives to serve the purposes of its founder.

A CENTRE OF HEALING

Bath's significance as a unique centre of healing was boosted in 1620 with the publication of *The Bathes of Bathe* by Thomas Venner (1577-1660) the first book written exclusively about the city's spa. Venner was Somerset-born and a university man. His book not only promoted the city but himself as a medical specialist and encouraged visitors to consult a trained medical practitioner rather than one of the many quacks and charlatans who preyed on the gullible. It was therefore appropriate that at the age of seventy-five Venner was appointed physician to a charity established by Viscount Scudamore to give free medical advice to poor strangers arriving in Bath.

In 1625 Bath's Guildhall was relocated to an island site in the Market Place, with an open-sided Market House at ground-floor level. At the same time there was a continuing general drive to upgrade the urban environment. An official scavenger was appointed to collect rubbish by cart. Property holders were required to keep the road in front of their premises in good order. 'Every person that hath a thatched house shall not mend his house with thatch but shall repair it with tile or slate.' Two-storey medieval houses were replaced with three- and four-storey residences festooned with gables and balustrades. Rebuilding, however, often proved a mixed blessing. The medieval burgage plots which had provided long rear gardens were increasingly built over and 'a multitude of chimneys arose – and there did arise so many dusty clouds in the air as to hide the light of the sun.'

A House Divided

Unlike Bristol, which was subjected to a protracted siege, Bath's exposure to armed conflict during the English civil wars was effectively limited to a single significant battle fought well away from the city. Bath was a strongly puritan city and its council was dominated by supporters of Parliament, who out-numbered the Royalists 22 to

8; but the supporters of Parliament were themselves divided between moderates and hardliners. A degree of co-operation between factions was, however, guaranteed by the fact that their respective leaders were brothers-in-law. There was a consensus that, as far as possible, it should be 'business as usual' in Bath. Markets, charities, scavenging and the water supply were all to be maintained satisfactorily. On the other hand the collection of rents often fell behind and there was little to spare for the upkeep of public buildings and facilities. Roads and bridges suffered neglect and sometimes deliberate damage.

Fighting between the Royalist supporters of Charles I and the forces of Parliament had broken out in 1642. By May of 1643 Royalist forces under the command of Ralph, Lord Hopton (1598-1652) had taken control of the south-west and were moving eastwards, towards Bath, and into Parliamentary territory held by Sir William Waller (1597-1668), one of Hopton's oldest and dearest friends but now a sworn opponent in what Waller himself called 'this war without an enemy'. Waller already had a string of victories to his credit, having taken Portsmouth, Farnham Castle, Arundel Castle, Chichester, Chepstow and Hereford and earned the nickname of 'William the Conqueror'.

Hopton's men crossed the Avon on 3 July 1643, causing Waller's forces to withdraw from positions to the south and east of Bath and to take up position on Lansdown Hill, three miles north-west of the city. Indecisive skirmishing on the fourth was followed by a full-scale engagement on the fifth. Waller's forces consisted of 2,500 horse and 1,500 foot plus an unknown number of guns. Hopton had 2,000 horse, 300 dragoons (elite, heavily-armed mounted infantry), 4,000 foot and sixteen guns, a formidable force but considerably less than the three-to-one ratio assumed desirable for a frontal assault on a defended position. Hopton's cavalry nevertheless charged uphill but, suffering considerable losses, panicked, with some 1,400 fleeing back towards the royalist capital at Oxford. The attack was, however, pressed home by Cornish pikemen led by Sir Bevil Grenville (1596-1643), a much-loved commander, who fell in hand-to-hand fighting at Waller's hastily-constructed breastworks. Waller's infantry eventually fell back to hold a wall on the crest of the hill, keeping up a stubborn fire until nightfall, when they silently withdrew back to Bath. Hopton had, against the odds, achieved his chosen objective and driven the Parliamentarians from their ground; but it had proved a pyrrhic victory. Waller's forces lost some twenty killed and sixty-odd wounded, while Hopton's suffered some two to three hundred fatalities. On 6 July, the day after the battle, a Royalist ammunition wagon exploded, wounding and temporarily blinding Hopton. The valiant Cornish contingent, utterly dismayed by the death of their charismatic commander, Grenville, refused to fight under anyone else and went home to bury him. Disabled and bereft of cavalry, Hopton was unable to exploit his success, enabling Waller to regroup and reinforce his command. Hopton fell back on Devizes, where Waller besieged him for a week until the arrival of reinforcements enabled Hopton to beat him decisively at the battle of Roundway Down, nearby. Hopton would eventually die in exile in Bruges. Waller, a tactically gifted general but lacking the energising presence of a great battlefield commander, was glad to resign his military role and survived the war, imprisonment and impoverishment to live out a peaceful retirement. The site of Grenville's death is marked by an austere neo-Classical monument put up in 1720. Ten 'Battlefield Markers', sculpted by Paul Margetts, indicate significant locations where the Cotswold Way crosses the battlefield. An authoritative and detailed account of the engagement can be found on www.battlefieldtrust.com

Following the Royalist victory at Roundway Down parliamentary forces withdrew from Bath and for the next two years Bath was occupied by a Royalist garrison. Ridden with lice, their first gift to the city was an outbreak of typhus, which carried off some two hundred victims, a high proportion of them children. The city's churches were pressed into service as hospitals and barracks. In the longer run there was much grumbling against the taxes and levies in kind imposed by the cavaliers but there was no resistance either in the form of defiance or sabotage, although three bakers were locked up for refusing to bake bread for the king's army. Many householders were forced to take in soldiers, feed them at their own expense and suffer their drunkenness, cursing, spitting, plunder and vandalism. Freedom of movement was curtailed by curfews. Luckless Twerton had to provision and quarter no less than seven different contingents in transit, ranging in number from ten to eight hundred. Combe Hay suffered eight such visitations between July 1645 and January 1646 alone. In terms of theft, confiscations and demanding drink, horses, meat and bread, 'friendly' troops differed little from enemy ones.

Military commanders on both sides continued to patronise the spa. Lord Goring came seeking relief for an ankle wound which refused to heal. General Monck (1608-70) came to convalesce from a collapse of health which caused him to resign his command temporarily. Other signs of a return to economic normality were the appointment of Bath's first postmaster in 1647-8 and, from 1652 onwards, the issuing of copper farthings by local traders to meet the shortage of small change. In 1659 the City itself began to issue its own farthings with the city arms on one side and the letters C.B. on the other.

In 1647, under pressure from Parliament, Bath's council was obliged to expel its royalist membership. This was done reluctantly and several of the expelled were reinstated within a few months. By the time Oliver Cromwell died in 1658 the leading citizens of Bath were eager to embrace a new political dispensation. In 1660 Bath became the first city in England to proclaim Charles II king and to send him an address pledging the city's loyalty to the restored monarchy.

Restoration

The revival of Bath's prosperity as a spa was promoted by a renewal of royal interest in the city. Charles II (reigned 1660-85) visited early in his reign in the hope that the waters might remedy the infertility of his Portuguese consort, Catherine of Braganza (1638-1705). Alas, it did not.

By the time the diarist Samuel Pepys (1633-1703) visited Bath in 1668 he had become a successful naval bureaucrat, able to afford to bring not only his wife and her maid, Deb Willet, but also her friend, Betty Turner, and his own chief clerk, Will Hewer. Pepys, ever the enthusiast, made an appreciative record of the bathing experience :

> Up at four o'clock, being by appointment called up to the Cross Bath; where we were carried one after another …. And, by and by, though we designed to have done before company come, much company come; very fine ladies; and the manner pretty enough, only methinks it

The King's Baths (right) and Queen's Bath (left)
by Thomas Johnson *c.* 1675

cannot be clean to go so many bodies together in the same water. Good
conversation among them that are acquainted here, and stay together.
Strange to see how hot the water is; and in some places, though this is the
most temperate bath, the springs so hot as the feet are not able to endure.

Pepys' dawn plunge was undertaken in an ineffectual effort to avoid the
crush. Had he stayed till mid-morning he might have been reassured to
see that the bath was drained down to its pebbled floor to be refilled
for the evening session.

Had Pepys wished to consult a physician during the course of his
brief stay he might have been recommended to a recent newcomer to
the city, Thomas Guidott (?1638–1706), a bumptious self-publicist keen
on establishing a national reputation for himself – despite the fact that
he never actually took his medical degree. Guidott, who was as much
a literary as a medical man, put out a steady stream of publications
in praise of the properties of Bath's waters, its antiquity as a place of
healing and the eminence and learning of its physicians. As a marketing

strategy it seems to have been remarkably successful. Not only did Guidott build up an extensive practice within the city, he also managed to establish such a reputation abroad that he was offered professorships in Venice and Leyden. He was, however, content to stay in Bath, building up an extensive collection of local antiquities and devoting his leisure hours to compiling a detailed record of the inscriptions in the abbey. Unfortunately Guidott's literary leanings also extended to writing verses so libellous that they damaged his local standing and from 1679 onwards he found it prudent to divide his time between London and Bath. In 1691 Guidott published *De Thermis Britannicis*, an account of the mineral water baths of Britain, which was subscribed to by many physicians of national repute. Guidott was back living in Bath by 1698 and was to be buried in the abbey.

A Negative Intervention – Monmouth's Rebellion

Charles II, father of a dozen acknowledged illegitimate offspring, died without a legitimate son to succeed him. As he had intended, the throne passed to his younger brother, the Duke of York, who became James II (reigned 1685-88). James's conversion to the Roman Catholic church had dismayed Britons fearful of a revival and reimposition of 'Popery'. It was, therefore, with confidence in public support that Charles II's eldest illegitimate son, James Scott, Duke of Monmouth (1649-85), a fierce Protestant, attempted to raise a rebellion and seize the throne for himself. Landing in Dorset from the Netherlands with a mere 150 men, Monmouth marched through the West Country, gathering supporters, mostly labouring folk armed only with farm implements. When Monmouth's mob appeared before Bath the corporation shut the city gates in his face. A rebel bold enough to ride forward to demand the city's surrender was shot through the head. Monmouth and his motley assemblage moved on to Sedgemoor where they were decisively defeated by regular royal troops in the last battle fought on English soil. Bath hastened to let James II know of its exemplary loyalty, not only in refusing to yield the city but also in the fact that not one Bath man had joined the uprising. This did not, however, save the city from having to erect a gallows for the public execution of four convicted rebels.

A Positive Intervention – An Heir to the Throne

In 1687 James II came to Bath on the same mission as Charles II had done. James had fathered two daughters by his first wife, Anne Hyde; both Mary and Anne, were brought up as staunch Protestants. But after the death of Anne Hyde James had converted to Catholicism and married an Italian princess, Mary of Modena. For fourteen years their union had failed to produce a surviving child, to the great relief of the nation. If Mary could produce an heir the reign of a Catholic king might prove to be not an interval to be grudgingly tolerated but a potential turning-point leading to the re-establishment of a lasting Catholic dynasty and the consequent disestablishment of the Church of England. Contrary to Catherine of Braganza's experience, Mary of Modena's visit to the Cross Bath resulted in – or at least coincided with – the onset of pregnancy. The Catholic Duke of Melfort expressed the joyous expectations of his co-religionists by commissioning a cross to surmount the Cross Bath. Consisting of three columns supporting a dome, flanked by three cherubim, with a cross on top, it was inscribed with a dedication to the Holy Trinity – just in case anyone had failed to get the point.

The birth of the future 'James III' in June 1688 precipitated a major political crisis. Leading Protestant notables intrigued to invite the Protestant Princess Mary and her husband, William, Stadholder of the Netherlands, to take the throne as joint sovereigns. The army deserted James II, who fled into exile as William and Mary headed an unresisted invasion to general rejoicing. In Bath the corporation opted to keep the Melfort cross but ordered the erasure of its inscriptions and the removal of 'all other superstitious things'.

A Female Perspective

Celia Fiennes (1662-1741) was the first woman known to have visited every county in England, often travelling quite alone. When she visited Bath in 1687 her enthusiasm for the city was, to say the least, qualified:

> … the ways to the Bath are all difficult, the town lies low in a bottom and its steep ascents all ways out of the town; the houses are indifferent, the streets of a good size well pitched; there are several good houses built for

lodgings that are new and adorned and good furniture, the baths in my opinion makes the town unpleasant, their air thick and hot by their steam, and by its own situation so low, encompassed with high hills and woods.

The discipline maintained in the baths did, however, gain her approval:

… there is a Serjeant belonging to the baths that all the bathing time walks in galleries and takes notice order is observed and punishes the rude, and most people of fashion sends to him when they begin to bathe, then he takes particular care of them and compliments them every morning, which deserves its reward at the end of the Season.

The elaborate procedures for preserving female modesty were recorded by her in detail:

… the ladies go into the bath with garments made of a fine yellow canvas, which is stiff and made large with great sleeves like a parson's gown, the water fills it up so … that your shape is not seen, it does not cling close as other linen which looks sadly in the poorer sort that go in their own … when you go out of the bath you go within a door that leads to steps which ascend by degrees … [you] let your canvas drop by degrees … which your women guides take off and the meantime your maids flings a garment of flannel made like a nightgown with great sleeves over your head and the guides take the tail and so pulls it on you just as you rise the steps and your other garment drops off so you are wrapped up in the flannel and your nightgown on the top … and so you are set in a chair which is brought into the room … the chairs you go in are … all covered inside with red baize and a curtain drawn … which makes it close and warm … then a couple of men … carries you to your lodging and sets you at your bedside where you go to bed and sweat some time as you please.

Fiennes emphasised that Bath was very much a place for pedestrians :

The places for diversion about the Bath is either the walks in that they call the King's Mead, which is a pleasant green meadow, where are walks round and across it, no place for coaches, and indeed there is little use of a coach only to bring and carry the company from the Bath for the ways are not proper for coaches, the town and all of its accommodations is adapted to the bathing and drinking of the waters and to nothing else … there are chairs as in London to carry the better sort of people in visits, or if sick or infirm, and is only in the town, for it's so encompassed with high hills few care to take the air on them; there is also pleasant walks in the Cathedral (sic) in the cloisters. Out of the Cathedral you walk into the Priory which has good walks of rows of trees which is pleasant … the Abbey … is lofty and spacious and much company walk there especially in wet weather … in that Kings Mead there are several little Cake-houses where you have fruit Sulibubs and …liqueurs to entertain the Company that walks there.

As for the cost of living:

The markets are very good here of all sorts of provision flesh and fish, especially when the season for the Company bathing and drinking lasts, great plenty and pretty reasonable; the chargeableness of Bath is the lodgings and firing, the faggotts being very small but they give you very good attendance there.

Gilmore's Bath

The Plan of Bath(see page 72) produced *ca.* 1692-4 by Joseph Gilmore 'Teacher of the Mathematicks in the City of Bristol' provides an illuminating, if idiosyncratic, overview of Bath on the eve of its great transformation into one of the architectural wonders of Georgian England. Gilmore offers a bird's eye view of Bath with an unconventional orientation which puts west, rather than north, at the top of the map. The treatment of the city's features is partly symbolic, partly pictorial. To overcome constraints of space plans of the three main baths are superimposed on the rough grazing area known as The Ham to the south-east of the city. The scale – Gilmore still uses poles and furlongs as his basic measures – is indicated by a chequered line, a pair of compasses and a couple of chubby cherubs playing with a surveyor's chain on Bathwick Meadow. A large inserted panel

at the top right-hand corner of the map reasserts the city's claim to
have been founded by Bladud in 863 BC, recounts the roles of Alfred,
Athelstan and Edgar in its history and puffs the virtues of the map's
completeness and inclusion of the city's new buildings and suburbs.
In the bottom right hand corner is a panel view of the Abbey.

The core of the city is still clearly enclosed within the circuit of its
ancient walls. Most of the intramural streets are shown close-packed
with terrace houses of three or four storeys, although many on the
north side of Westgate Street / Cheap Street are shown with large
rear gardens. In the north-west corner of the city Timber Green is
symbolically scattered with huge baulks of timber and overlooked by
a pit for cockfights. Just outside the wall a large Fives Court is marked.
There is straggling ribbon development north of the city along Broad
Street and Walcot Street. Houses on the east side of Walcot Street
have long rear garden plots running right down to the Avon. To the
west of Broad Street a large enclosed area is marked as the city's 'New
Bowling Green'.

The border of the Gilmore map, like a brochure for a modern
holiday resort, illustrates over two dozen of the city's leading lodging
houses, interspersed with views of views of such local landmarks as
two city conduits, the Guildhall, St John's Hospital, Bellot's Hospital,
the King's Bath and the churches of St Michael and St James. The
lodging-houses are imposing buildings, most three and some four
storeys high, often seeking to impress potential customers by flaunting
a selection of obtrusive architectural add-ons including oriel windows,
porticoes, balconies, balustrades, flights of steps, superfluous gabling etc.
The proprietor of each lodging is, moreover, specifically identified,
from the Mayor, Alderman Maynard, himself downwards. Alderman
Bush had two sets of lodgings, in High Street and at Bear Corner. Five
other aldermen are also identified, plus the Chamberlain and the Town
Clerk, Physician Henry Parker. Of sixteen other citizens, three were
identified as women.

Another inset panel identified Bath's inns street by street. High Street
had the most with seven. Stall Street was second with four. There were
three more in Westgate Street, two in Cheap Street and the George 'By
The Hott Bath'. Suburban establishments included two in Southgate

Street, two 'Without North Gate' and one in Broad Street. The Christopher, named for the patron saint of travellers, though much rebuilt, still stands on the High Street. The Angel on Westgate Street, opened in 1625, is also on its original site.

Sally Lunn

For many visitors to Bath their trip is not complete without a trip to Sally Lunn's celebrated teashop at No. 4 North Parade Passage to

Sally Lunn's House

sample the famous bun named after the supposed proprietor. Sally Lunn is one of Bath's best known historic characters – despite the fact that she may never actually have existed. Tradition holds that she arrived in Bath in 1680 – the date being one of the few precise 'facts' attached to her – as a Huguenot, i.e. French Protestant refugee. The persecution of Huguenots in France was certainly getting worse at this time but their mass-exodus dates from 1685 when Louis XIV revoked the Edict of Nantes which had guaranteed them toleration for almost a century. Whatever her supposed background, Sally Lunn is supposed to have found work with a local baker in Bath and then, having introduced the novel confectionery associated with her name, established her own successful business.

The earliest documented reference to the bun dates from 1780 when Philip Thicknesse, the author of *The Valetudinarian's Bath Guide* – a spoof – observed that his brother died suddenly 'after drinking a large quantity of Bath Waters, and eating a hearty breakfast of spungy hot rolls, or Sally Luns.' According to the *Dictionary of National Biography* the first recorded mention of Sally Lunn as a person did not occur until 1798, when a correspondent to the *Gentleman's Magazine* stated that 'a certain sort of hot rolls', now, or not long ago, in vogue at Bath, were gratefully and emphatically styled 'Sally Lunns' after their supposed creator. According to the Sally Lunn's House website www.sallylunns. co.uk William Dalmer, a Bath baker who certainly did exist, began advertising Sally Lunn's for sale in 1799. William Hone (1780-1842) the compiler of numerous bestselling miscellanies, who was born in Bath, gave an elaborated account of the eponymous confectionery in his *Every-day Book* of 1831 :

> The bun so fashionable, called the Sally Lunn, originated with a young woman of that name in Bath, about thirty years ago. She first cried them, in a basket with a white cloth over it, morning and evening. Dalmer, a respectable baker and musician, noticed her, bought her business, and made a song, and set it to music in behalf of 'Sally Lunn'. This compo-sition became the street favourite, barrows were made to distribute the nice cakes, Dalmer profited thereby and retired; and to this day, the Sally Lunn cake, not unlike the hot cross bun in flavour, claim pre-eminence in

all the cities in England.

Charles Dickens in *The Chimes* (1845) mentions Sally Lunns as a component of an English tea alongside crumpets and muffins. In the same year Eliza Acton included a recipe for the bun, which she called a 'rich French breakfast cake', in her *Modern Cookery for Private Families*. She also gave the confection other names – 'solemena', 'solimemne' and 'soel leme'. The eminent French chef Jules Goffe gave a recipe for 'Solilem' in his definitive *Le Livre de patisserie* (1873). Food historian Dorothy Hartley, writing in 1954, opined that the name was actually a 'Zummerzet' pronunciation of the French 'Sol et Lune' – Sun and Moon – referring to the bun's golden top and white base.

Constance Spry (1956) was tentative on the subject Sally Lunn – 'she lived, I believe, in Bath and is said to have made them for the Prince Regent' - but was very informed and opinionated on the manner of serving the bun:

> one recipe says that when baked the cakes should be sliced, toasted and buttered, shaped again into a cake and cut in quarters. Another recommends that the cake be torn open and buttered and replaced in the oven till the butter is melted. They are often sliced horizontally twice i.e. the cake is divided into three slices, toasted and buttered. But whatever way you choose it is heavy on butter.

Nowadays Sally Lunn's House serves its eponymous confection with both savoury and sweet toppings to make a substantial snack. A modern recipe for Sally Lunns can be found in Elizabeth David's *English Bread and Yeast Cookery* (1977) pp 467-469.

By 1917 *The Original Bath Guide* was stating as a matter of historical fact that 'Sally Lunn sold the tea cakes still known by her name' at 4 North Parade Passage. By the 1930s the building was marked on Bath Corporation's *Historic Map of Bath* as Sally Lunn's House. A plaque fixed to the house asserted the date of her arrival in 1680 as a Huguenot refugee. The teashop's website at the time of writing states that the original recipe was rediscovered in 1966, hidden way behind some panelling. It also asserts that archaeological investigations in 1985 revealed that the site of the house has not only been in occupation over a period of 1,800 years but that for much of this time it has been associated with the food business. Fragments of high-quality Samian tableware and of a mortar for grinding aromatic plants, taken in conjunction with the site's proximity to the Roman baths imply the possibility of it accommodating a retail food outlet catering to bathers. Its location and the remnants of a medieval oven suggest that it may have been part of the refectory and kitchen of the abbey when it was a Benedictine house.

Sally Lunn's House does not date in its present incarnation from 1485 as its plaque claims but from 1622 when a surviving building lease confirms that it was built by carpenter George Parker. The shop-front dates from the eighteenth century. Sally Lunn's hasn't always been a tea-shop. In 1937 it became the home of Miss Mabel Byng-Johnson, who lived in it as a private house, alone, although she did give tours. She also claimed to have seen the ghost of a chanting monk, praying for the repose of Roman prisoners ....

Perhaps the last word should go to Peter Borsay, author of *The Image of Georgian Bath*:

> Lunn's admission to the hall of fame, confirmed by her joining the elite to whom a tourist bus was dedicated, rested heavily on her capacity to provide a tangible link, of place and taste, between the eighteenth century and the present, and upon some astute advocacy by the owners of her erstwhile shop. She is a telling case, given the paucity of solid information about her life, of Bath's capacity to mythologize itself, and to generate living heroines from the thinnest of material.

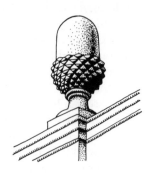

Builders of Bath

A rchitecturally speaking Bath is largely a self-made city. Although there are examples of work by eminent London architects they are few and, apart from Robert Adam's Pulteney Bridge and George Dance's façade for the Theatre Royal, of minor importance. The Woods, H.E. Goodridge and Major Davis are dealt with in the main text (see pages 106-8, 185, 198-200). What follows is a brief account of other significant Bath practitioners.

Bath, like Edinburgh, not only produced its own architects but was equally adept at keeping outsiders at bay. They failed, however, with John Strahan (died 1740), who established himself in Bristol but also laid out Avon Street (now totally rebuilt) Kingsmead and Monmouth Streets and was responsible for Beauford Square and Kingsmead Square.

The devious and corrupt Thomas Atwood (died 1775) was keen to keep local rivals at bay as well as outsiders. An 'eminent plumber', Atwood used his insider position as City Surveyor and a member of the council to get leases on Corporation land on which he built, as private speculations, The Paragon and Oxford Row on Lansdown Road. For the city he built the rather cramped 'New Prison' in Grove Street (1772). In 1775, after fifteen years of politicking and procras-tination, Atwood's plans for a new Guildhall were finally accepted and work begun when an alternative, potentially more economical, scheme was put forward by John Palmer (see below). A furious controversy ensued until Atwood was killed by falling through the floor of an old house he was inspecting. The Guildhall was eventually built by Atwood's former assistant, Thomas Baldwin, (1750-1820) – to his own plans. As City Surveyor Baldwin built the Pump Room (1786-91), rebuilt (1790) the Cross Bath and designed elegant, colonnaded Bath Street (1791) but was sacked in 1792 for failing to surrender his account books for inspection by the Corporation. The collapse of the Bath City Bank in 1793 bankrupted him but he continued in private practice for at least another twenty years. Baldwin was extensively involved in the development of the Pulteney estate at Bathwick, being responsible for Argyle Street (1787), Argyle Chapel (1789), Laura Place (1788), Great Pulteney Street (*ca.*1788), Bathwick Street (1790), Henrietta Street (1790) and the west side of Sydney Place. Baldwin's other works include Somersetshire Buildings (1782) on Milsom Street and Nos.13-15 Marlborough Buildings (1790). Baldwin's assistant John Eveleigh of No. 11, Bridge Street doubled as a surveyor, rent-collector, jobbing builder and builders' merchant, advertising in the *Bath Chronicle* that he could install chimney pieces, water closets and copper roofing – and teach architecture. After building Camden Crescent (1788) and Grosvenor Place (1791) and beginning Somerset Place (1790-1820), Eveleigh was bankrupted in 1793 and left Bath.

John Palmer (1738-1817) began as assistant to his glazier father's friend Thomas Jelly and was appointed successor to Baldwin as City Architect in 1792. Palmer's major works include St Swithin's church (1777-90) (with Jelly), Lansdown Crescent (1789-93), St James's Square (1790-94), Christ Church, Montpelier Row (1795-8), Norfolk Crescent (ca.1798) and the Theatre Royal. (He is not to be confused with John Palmer, promoter of the first Theatre Royal (see page 125) or his son, the postal reformer (see page 142).

Lansdown Crescent

Primarily a surveyor, Charles Harcourt Masters drew road maps for the Bath Turnpike Trust (1786-7) and a plan of Bath (1794) and made a model of the city at a scale of 30 feet to the inch, which he exhibited (1789-90) at his house in Orchard Street. His main architectural works were the Sydney Hotel (1796), now the

Holburne Museum, Widcombe Crescent and Terrace (*ca.*1805) and Bloomfield Crescent (*ca.*1807).

The prolific George Philip Manners began as Masters' junior partner. As City Architect he rather ruthlessly 'restored' the Abbey (1824-33), designed the obelisk in the Royal Victoria Park (1837) and built the new 'Jacobethan' Blue Coat School (1860), which dominates Saw Close. His most prominent Bath building is St Michael's, Broad Street. Manners took John Elkington Gill as his partner and he carried on alone after Manners' retirement in 1866 before taking Thomas Browne as his partner in 1874. Gill's son, Wallace, subsequently joined and eventually turned it over to Mowbray Green.

John Pinch the Elder (1769-1827) built the south range of Sydney Place (1808), Cavendish Place (1808-16), Cavendish Crescent (1817-30), St Mary the Virgin and Raby Place, Bathwick (1810-ca.1825) and the United Hospital in Beau Street (1824-26).

John Pinch the Younger (died 1849) succeeded to his father's practice in 1827 and built St Saviour, Larkhall (1829-32)

James Wilson (1816-1900) built St Stephen, Lansdown (1840-45), Kingswood School (1850-2), the Royal School (1856-58) and the massive Italianate Walcot Schools on Guinea Lane. Wilson's partner Thomas Fuller (1822-98) emigrated to Canada in 1856 after winning the competition for the Parliament Buildings in Ottawa.

The work of London architects in Bath includes:
William Wilkins, architect of the National Gallery on Trafalgar Square, built the Freemason's Hall, York Street (1817-19), which subsequently became a Friends' Meeting House. Joseph Michael Gandy (1771-1843), Sir John Soane's draughtsman, designed austere Doric House (see page 168). Sir George Gilbert Scott (1811-78), doyen of the Gothic Revival, reversed some of Manners' alterations in the course of his historicist restoration of the Abbey (1860-73) and completed the vaulting of the nave. Scott's protégé G.E. Street (1824-81), architect of the Royal Courts of Justice, built (1873-5) the chancel of St Mary the Virgin. J.M. Brydon (1840-1901) added the north and south wings and dome to Baldwin's Guildhall. Charles Voysey built (1909) the exquisite Arts and Crafts Lodge Style out at Combe Down

for T. Sturge Cotterell, owner of the Combe Down Quarries. Forsyth hails this as no less than 'the most important 20th century house in Bath'. Sir Reginald Blomfield adapted the former Sydney Hotel to become the Holburne Museum and designed the War Memorial (see page 209) at the entrance to the Royal Victoria Park. And, of course, Nicholas Grimshaw's Thermae Bath Spa (see page 232).

Bath's unique architectural heritage is displayed in detail at the excellent Building of Bath Museum, which is housed in the former chapel of the Countess of Huntingdon at the Vineyards which is part of the Paragon. The profusely-illustrated guide, written by Curator-Director, Christopher Woodward, is concise, elegant and highly informative.

For in-depth treatments see Walter Ison's classic *The Georgian Buildings of Bath* (3rd edition 1990) and *Life in the Georgian City* by Dan Cruikshank and Neil Burton (1990). A superb map of Georgian Bath has been produced by the Ordnance Survey in collaboration with the Bath Archaeological Trust and the Royal Commission on Historical Monuments of England. This definitive historical guide would make an ideal accompaniment to the walks detailed on pages 235-49.

CHAPTER SIX

The Makers of Georgian Bath

1700 – 1770

Civic Servant

'… though he is a very ugly man in his face, yet he is very much beloved and esteemed by the ladies as a witty and genteel man'.
Dudley Ryder of Beau Nash 1716

It would be only a slight exaggeration to say that first of all Richard – 'Beau'– Nash (1674-1761) invented himself and then he invented Bath. Neither achievement was self-evident from his origins. Born the son of a Swansea glass-manufacturer, Nash was educated at the grammar school in Carmarthen and went on to Jesus College, Oxford, an institution which had been purposely founded to anglicise Welshmen. Whether or not the process was necessary in Nash's case, it hardly had time to take effect, before he was sent down for womanising. This was followed by a brief interlude as an army officer, during which he demonstrated a great delight in uniforms and a great distaste for drill and discipline. Next came a spell at Inner Temple, ostensibly preparing for the legal career intended for him by his father. London, however, offered a much greater stage for display than an Oxford quad or an army parade-ground. In 1695 Nash supervised the organisation of a pageant put on by the Inns of Court in honour of William III (reigned 1688-1702). Its success gave early proof of his undoubted talent for managing social occasions and ceremony through a combination of chivvying, charm and attention to detail. The ability to take trivialities seriously would ultimately prove to be the salvation of Richard Nash.

For the next decade, however, he survived by gaming, although some of his acquaintance suspected that he might even be a highwayman, such was the disparity between the manner in which he lived and the apparently slender sources of income he could command to sustain it.

In 1705 Richard Nash decided to make an outing to Bath and stayed there for the rest of his life, dominating its society and shaping its routines for over half a century. The timing of his arrival proved especially fortunate, coming in the immediate wake of a renewal of royal patronage.

Beau Nash

William III's successor as monarch was his sister-in-law, Anne (reigned 1702-14), a devout, diminutive woman whose seventeen pregnancies had failed to secure a living heir to the throne but had wrecked her health. Seeking relief from her numerous afflictions, Queen Anne visited Bath to take the waters in 1702. Whether or not she gained any medical benefit from the experience she returned again the following year. The city was ill-equipped to receive its sovereign and her entourage. Dancing took place on a bowling-green; tea was served and cards played in a canvas booth. The Queen's own limited cultural tastes – cards, music, food, sermons and gossip – would, however, become staples of the city's social life for the rest of the century. Where the Queen led, the well-to-do and the fashionable followed and in their train came those who would live off them, quacks, conmen, courtesans, gamblers and the penniless Welsh adventurer who would, in the words of Mark Girouard, transform 'Bath from a small health resort with a social element into a large social resort with a health element.'

Little more than a wastrel tainted by scandal and a succession of false starts at serious endeavours – university, the army, the law – Richard Nash was exceptional in neither intellect nor appearance. Average in height and build, with a dark complexion, he possessed what Goldsmith called 'peculiarly irregular' features and could by no means be called handsome. What he had was style and self-belief. Nash understood the value of dressing well and made personal trademarks of his cane and white beaver hat. When he became able to afford it he travelled in the style of a great lord, driven in a post-chaise pulled by six greys, flanked by horn-playing outriders and a running footman to clear the way ahead. In a biography of Nash rushed out immediately after the Beau's death Oliver Goldsmith (1730-74) analysed Nash's improbable achievement as a triumph of societal alchemy, with Nash cast in the role of benevolent sorcerer, taking skilful advantage of Bath's self-transformation to amend the manners of its habitués into a willing acceptance of a consensual politesse:

> General society among people of rank or fashion was by no means established. The nobility still preserved a structure of Gothic haughtiness and refused to keep company with the gentry at any of the public entertain-

ments of the place. But when proper walks were made for exercise and a house built for assembling in, rank began to be laid aside and all degrees of people, from the private gentleman upwards, were soon united in society with one another.

Shortly after Nash's arrival in 1705 he was invited to become the assistant to the man responsible for organising entertainments and diversions for visitors, the Master of Ceremonies, Captain Thomas Webster. He was, like Nash, a professional gamester. Later that same year Webster was killed in a duel and Nash was elected to take his place, promising to recruit a band of musicians from London, to be paid for by subscription. Doubtless mindful of his immediate predecessor's fate, one of Nash's earliest proscriptions was a ban on wearing swords lest trivial contretemps escalate into lethal confrontations.

THE PUMP ROOM

In the very year that Nash assumed his new office the claims of medical efficacy made on behalf of Bath's spa waters by the influential physician Dr William Oliver prompted the construction of a Pump Room in which they could be consumed in surroundings of comfort and elegance. This was completed in 1706. In 1707 legislation was obtained to authorise the improvement of communications around Bath and the walkways within the town itself at the cost of some £18,000, much of which Nash helped to mobilise. A disinterested commitment to civic improvement was less evident in Nash's discreet collusion with Thomas Harrison in promoting the latter's new Assembly Room as a desirable place of resort for dancing, cards and refreshments. Kickbacks from this relationship enabled Nash to maintain himself in an increasingly lordly style.

Sensibly aware that Bath's supposed *raison d'etre* was the promotion of health, Nash frowned on excessive drinking and eating and the keeping of late hours and propagated the virtues of moderation, order and routine. As 'Arbiter Elegantiarum' Nash could be crushing in reproving breaches in his codes of dress and etiquette. Acutely aware of rank, he was nevertheless never intimidated by it and did not hesitate to confront the Duchess of Queensberry for wearing an apron to the assembly or to refuse Princess Amelia's request to extend the dancing after 11.00 p.m.

THE 'KING OF BATH'

As uncrowned' King of Bath' Beau Nash took it upon himself to welcome prestigious new visitors by making a personal call at their lodgings soon after their arrival, as when the nation's hero, John Churchill, Duke of Marlborough, victor of Blenheim, came with his duchess in 1714.

In 1716 Nash's unique social authority was explicitly acknowledged by the corporation, which granted him the honorary freedom of the city. Dudley Ryder, a young law student and future Lord Chief Justice, recorded in his diary that year, irreverently but nevertheless in plain acknowledgment of fact, that 'Gnash' was 'the life and soul of all … diversions. Without him there is no play or assembly or ball. … His sayings seem to make a great part of the conversation of others.' Writing a decade later the poet Robert Whatley likewise acknowledged 'a Power that is wholly despotick … whatever Mr. N pleases to order, every one submits to with the same Pleasure and Resignation'. Not quite everyone. In 1739 John Wesley came to preach on the sinfulness of the town's entertainments. Nash tried but was unable to prevent him from doing so. It is said that when they met Nash declared 'I never step aside for fools', to which Wesley, giving way, rejoined 'Oh, I always do'.

Nash's despotism, if such it was, was tempered with skilfully-judged gestures which managed to combine the enhancement of the city with the endorsement of his own peculiar standing within it. When the Prince of Orange came to take a cure in 1734 Nash let it be known that the commemorative obelisk erected near the Abbey to mark his visit had been put up at his initiative and expense. When the Prince and Princess of Wales came in 1738 a similar tribute was put up in Queen Square. (Nash even managed to charm Alexander Pope into composing the inscription.) In each case the royal guests reciprocated with the gift of a snuff-box, the must-have fashion accessory of the day. Nash also played a conspicuous part – the adjective is chosen advisedly – in raising funds for the establishment of the infirmary, serving as both treasurer and subsequently as a governor. Prince Hoare's picture of Nash, commissioned by the corporation, has him holding the building plans for the hospital in his right hand. The picture was exhibited between busts of

Newton and Pope, prompting one of Lord Chesterfield's better sallies:

> This picture plac'd the busts between
> Gives satyr all his strength
> Wisdom and Wit are little seen
> But folly at full length.

A would-be philanderer in his youth, Nash by middle-age had abandoned womanising beyond a little mild flirtation and the odd risqué remark, more often made to show that he could occasionally transgress the boundaries of strict propriety because he himself set them. When he was in his late sixties, however, he had a brief liaison with Fanny Murray (1729-78), the discarded teenage lover of the Duke of Marlborough's grandson, and then a longer relationship with the provocatively named Juliana Popjoy (1714-77) a former dressmaker. She, too, left him, in her case to spend the rest of her life living in a hollow tree near her birthplace, Warminster.

Although the 'rule' of Richard Nash formally ended only with his death and the pattern of daily routines that he established long outlived him, the last two decades of his life were overshadowed by scandal and the pressures of a concealed penury. Revelations of his clandestine involvement in gambling schools damaged his reputation for impartiality and were compounded by allegations of profiteering from public subscriptions. In the 1750s Nash, to whom appearance was all, was nevertheless obliged to move from St John's Close to the altogether more modest surroundings of Saw Close. He had, however, done enough for Bath for its civic leadership to decline to abandon him and in 1754 the corporation came up with a disguised subvention in the form of opening a subscription for a history of the city which Nash would write. Augusta, dowager Princess of Wales, subscribed £100. Nash never did write the proposed history and resorted instead to selling off personal possessions to keep his creditors at bay. Despite these manifest problems, to many his authority seemed undimmed. Lady Luxborough, writing in 1755, confirmed the eminence of '... our law-giver, Mr. Nash, whose white hat commands more respect and non-resistance than the crowns of some kings ... To promote society, good manners and a coalition of parties and ranks; to suppress scandal and late hours, are his views.' In consequence, she noted, such was the general prevalence of good manners and sociability that 'duchesses walk the streets here unattended'.

In February 1760 the corporation openly acknowledged Nash's plight and granted him a monthly pension of ten guineas. A martyr to gout for over a decade, Nash clung to his role as master of ceremonies at the cost of being wheeled into the Assembly Rooms. He finally died, of apoplexy, aged eighty-six, at his home in February 1761, leaving debts of some £1,200. A week later the corporation voted fifty guineas for Nash's funeral and burial in the Abbey. While he success-fully built a reputation for wit, generosity and philanthropy Beau Nash was neither a great man nor a conspicuously good one. If his sins were venal – vanity, gambling, dissimulation, self-indulgence, the pretence rather than the practice of virtue – they were also persistent. He was primarily, as Goldsmith so perceptively discerned, an early instance of a novel social type with which the twenty-first century is only too familiar – the celebrity; in Goldsmith's acute phrase 'a person so much talked of, and yet so little known'. If posterity knows him no better, at least it can scarcely ignore his name, given as it is to two streets, a cinema, a casino, a gallery and a bus tour.

A Model Squire

The Cornish origins of Ralph Allen (1693-1764) are obscure but almost certainly humble. Despite having only the most elementary education, Allen so impressed his superiors in the post office at St Columb, on the new route to Falmouth, that he was promoted to the Exeter post office in 1708 and to Bath in 1710, becoming deputy postmaster in 1712 while still not yet twenty. Allen's meteoric promo-tions coincided with a piecemeal reorganisation of England's inter-city postal system. Whereas the established system directed almost all mail, whatever its ultimate destination, via London along one of six routes, in 1696 Joseph Quash at the Exeter office began to send the mail for Bristol direct to that city. In 1700 this 'cross-post' system was extended to Chester and in 1709-10 to Oxford, via Bath, an innovation which may well have prompted Allen's transfer at that time.

Five years after Allen's arrival in Bath the city was swept up in the national crisis caused by the attempt of the exiled Stuart and Catholic pretender to the throne, James III, to dispute the succession of the Hanoverian Protestant George I, installed as monarch in 1714. Bath was suspected, correctly, to harbour many sympathisers to the Jacobite cause and the energetic George Wade (1673-1748) was despatched to the city to root out the malcontents. Allen's official position with the postal service enabled him to monitor the flow of many sorts of information and rumour and thus pass on valuable intelligence to Wade, whose friendship would prove a life-long asset. Wade, who had been made a general at only thirty-five, uncovered an underground arms cache of eleven chests of weaponry and four pieces of artillery. In 1722 he became MP for Bath and remained so until his death. Famed for building forty bridges and hundreds of miles of roads in the Scottish Highlands, Wade's (actually rather ineffectual) efforts against the supporters of Bonnie Prince Charlie in 1745 earned him a mention by name in Britain's national anthem, *God Save the King*. He died a Field-Marshal and Privy Councillor and was buried in Westminster Abbey. Wade's numerous contributions to Bath included clearing a pathway – Wade's Passage – through the muddle of houses north of the Abbey, and helping to pay for the Blue Coat School, a butchers' market and the rebuilding of St Michael's church. Marshal Wade's handsome Palladian house (of ca. 1720) stands in the Abbey Churchyard opposite the entrance to the Baths and now houses the National Trust shop.

THE GENERAL AND THE POST MASTER

Ralph Allen's management of the Bath post office proved so efficient that in 1720, in the equivalent of a modern management buy-out, he acquired the right to run the cross-post and the 'bye-way' post delivered from the line of the post roads and to nearby towns. To secure this concession Allen agreed to guarantee an annual revenue of £6,000, even though the current yield was less than £4,000. In seeking financial backers Allen found a doughty supporter in the redoubtable Wade. In 1721 marriage to Elizabeth Buckeridge, daughter of a London merchant, brought a dowry which doubtless gave a timely supplement to Allen's finances. Allen would eventually succeed in realizing an annual profit of £12,000 from his postal operations, not through any major technical or organisational innovation but through painstaking attention to detail and the ruthless elimination of fraud.

The association between the postmaster and the general was further strengthened after Wade became MP for Bath. Together the two men revived an abandoned project to make the Avon navigable to Bristol. In January 1725 Allen became the navigation project's treasurer. Later that same year Allen became a freeman of Bath and a member of its Common Council. Within three years the Avon navigation was completed, greatly reducing the freight costs of bulky goods, such as building materials.

PRIOR PARK

In 1726 Ralph and Elizabeth Allen moved into a house near the abbey. In 1728 he bought from Elizabeth's brother the land on which he would build a magnificent mansion, Prior Park, and which would additionally give him access to the building stone of Combe Down. This gave Allen a near-monopoly of the supply of the fine stone which would be needed for the expansion of the city. It also enabled him to become a major local employer. And, thanks to the new navigability of the Avon, the stone could be shipped downriver for use in Bristol and beyond. Thanks to this secondary source of income Ralph Allen, who was already on the way to becoming very rich, became extremely rich, enabling him to acquire a portfolio of properties, to entertain lavishly and to donate to charity on a munificent scale. Allen gave to Bath's new hospital not only all the building stone needed for its construction but £1,000 as well.

At Prior Park Ralph Allen entertained a wide circle of cultured and influential acquaintance, not least Bath's distinguished MPs Prime Minister William Pitt the Elder (1708-78) and the spectacularly heroic Field Marshal Ligonier (1680-1770). The most eminent poet of the age, Alexander Pope (1688-1744), advised on the distribution of Prior Park's garden features. Bath's leading painter, William Hoare (see page 163), was a constant visitor. The novelist Henry Fielding (1707-54) took the amiable, public-spirited Allen as the model for his Squire Allworthy in *Tom Jones* (1749) and dedicated *Amelia* (1751) to him.

After Fielding's death Allen took on the responsibility for his family and paid for his children's education.

In 1742 Allen served as Mayor of Bath. When 'the Young Pretender', 'Bonnie Prince Charlie', son and successor of the exiled Stuart king James III ('the Old Pretender'), attempted another Jacobite coup in 1745, Allen raised and financed a volunteer militia of a hundred men in support of the Hanoverian cause. In 1749 he became a Justice of the Peace. From 1750 onwards Allen passed his summers in a house he had built at Weymouth. In 1758 he added Claverton Manor to his holdings. Allen died in 1764 and was buried at Claverton.

Building Bath

'His Buildings, already erected in this City, have been of so great Benefit to this Place in particular, and to the country in general, that while they remain standing Monuments to the World of his Taste in Architecture, they will with grateful Hearts be looked on by our latest Posterity, as the Works of that great Benefactor, and the name WOOD, the Restorer of Bath, will always be sacred here.' *Bath Journal* 18 February 1754

If Richard Nash reformed Bath's manners and Ralph Allen promoted its prosperity, John Wood (1704-54) established both the framework and the style in which the city was to be transformed from a ramshackle market town to a city which set the architectural standards of the age. Born in Bath, the son of a local builder, Wood received an elementary education at the Blue Coat School and presumably learned the basics of the building trade before leaving for London as a teenager. Over the course of the ensuing decade he worked as a joiner and surveyor in London and Yorkshire before returning to the city of his birth in 1727 to restore the Hospital of St John and to build a residential complex, Chandos Buildings, for the fabulously wealthy Duke of Chandos. Crammed onto the site of the former St John's almshouse, the houses were poorly-arranged internally and ill-lit. Despite this inauspicious beginning Wood harboured grandiose ambitions for the development of his native city, notwithstanding that the death of George I (reigned 1714-27) and accession of George II (reigned 1727-60) caused many speculators to draw back from making commitments until the new regime had bedded in. Wood envisaged building to the north-west of Bath's surviving medieval walls, on land belonging to Mr Gay, a London medical man, and to the south-east of the Abbey, on land which had been inherited by the Duke of Kingston.

John Wood's vision of a future Bath was profoundly shaped by his deeply-held and highly eccentric understanding of the nature of its origins and past. Wood, who was an enthusiast for the newly-imported 'craft' of Freemasonry, completely accepted the Bladud myth, convinced himself that 'Bath, like Alexandria, was founded for the capital Seat of a famous King' and proposed to re-establish its supposed Roman grandeur on a scale that would have made even Mussolini gasp for breath. In his *Essay Towards a Description of Bath* (1742) Wood recalled how 'I proposed to make a Grand Place of Assembly, to be called the Royal Forum of Bath; another place, no less magnificent, to be called the Grand Circus; and a third Place, of equal state with either of the former, for the practice of Medicinal Exercises, to be called the Imperial Gymnasium.' The corporation, scarcely surprisingly, would have none of such nonsense. Undeterred, Wood went ahead on his own, leasing land from Gay at the city's margin to lay out Queen Square. Wood's personal contribution as developer was the overall conception of building a terrace of separate houses so that it had 'the outside Appearance of one magnificent Structure' – in other words, a palace. The actual work of construction and the internal planning of the individual properties (not Wood's strong points) were delegated to local builders who as sub-lessees joined him in risking their own capital in the pursuit of profit, a business arrangement Wood would have seen in operation when working on the Duke of Chandos' projects in and around Cavendish Square in London. Queen Square, begun in 1728, was completed by 1736. It was Wood's first attempt at town planning and epitomised his beliefs about the relationship between architecture and the social order – ' … the Intention of a Square in a City is for People to assemble together; and the Spot whereon they meet, ought to be separated from the Ground common to Men and Beasts, and even to Mankind in general, if Decency and good order are to be observed in such Places of Assembly'.

The success of Queen Square encouraged Wood to revive his notion of building a forum where the abbey's orchard had once stood. All that was completed were two lengthy terraces of lodgings, prosaically dubbed North and South Parade. Wood, meanwhile, was also engaged in building Prior Park for Ralph Allen and with Allen's support, won the commission to design a new Exchange for Bristol. This, in turn, was so successful that Wood was asked to design a combined Exchange and Town Hall for Bristol's great rival, Liverpool. Nor did Wood's busy building schedule (he had also taken on providing a new nave for Llandaff Cathedral) inhibit a prodigious literary output elaborating his archaeological and architectural theories. *The Origin of Building, or, The Plagiarism of the Heathens Detected* (1744) was followed by *Choir Gaure Vulgarly called Stonehenge, Described, Restored and Explained* (1747) and a *Dissertation upon the Order of Columns and their Appendages* (1751). In 1753 Wood bought the land to build what would become the earliest circus in England. The foundation stone was laid the following year but that was as much as Wood saw achieved, leaving it to his namesake son to bring his vision to fruition. Asthmatic, irascible and obsessive, Wood died, not yet fifty, and was buried at St Mary's, Swainswick, three miles north of city.

Impatient Patients

In 1746 John Russell, fourth Duke of Bedford (1710–71), temporarily exhausted by his duties as First Lord of the Admiralty and Lord Lieutenant of Bedfordshire, surrendered to the admonitions of his physician and agreed to take the waters at Bath, in particular hoping that it would relieve the gout which was already a torment, although he was only in his early thirties. His father, suffering the same complaint in his twenties, had likewise tried the waters, sending for his Italian musicians and favourite horse and greyhound to relieve the tedium. The fourth duke, who also took his favourite mount, was to experience similar boredom, as a letter to his wife revealed :

> As you seem desirous of knowing what I do with myself, I will tell you, as well as an idle Bath life can be described in writing. In the first place I get up early in the morning, sometimes before 7 o'clock, and drink the waters or bathe in their respective turns, so as to be able to be at the coffee house at breakfast at 10 o'clock. This morning after breakfast I rode out.

Other mornings I saunter about this town till I am footsore and then lounge, till the time of dressing, in the bookseller's shop … Two or three people generally dine here, always Lord Fane (which, by the by, is the only comfortable thing I have yet mentioned). After dinner one glass of Bath water, a very short walk and then home to write letters or read. Now comes the gaiety. At close of the evening I sit down to Guinea Whisk (whist) either with Lord Winchelsea or Lady Bell and have made a shift already to win 16 guineas. How long they will last God knows … After the lightest of suppers and one glass of Bath water, I get to bed soon after

The Pump Room

11. . Does not this agreeable life make you wish to be here?

Riding on the downs was one of the Duke's most favoured distractions. The gout afflicted his feet so severely that they were 'not yet got strong enough to bear a great deal of walking on these hard, hot pavements'. It was therefore with no small relief, as of relinquishing yet another duty done, that the duke returned to Woburn and his duchess.

Writing twenty years later the aesthete Horace Walpole (1717-97) experienced an even greater ennui:

> The waters do not benefit me so much as at first, the pains in my stomach return almost every morning... This ... is not near so great a disappointment to me as you might imagine, for I am so childish as not to think health itself a compensation for passing my time very disagreeably ... health does not give one the sort of spirits that make one like diversions, public places and mixed company ... I shall depart on Wednesday, even on the penalty of coming again ... I am not at all in love with their country, which so charms everybody. Mountains are very good frames to a prospect, but here they run against one's nose; nor can one stir out of the town without clambering. ... The place is healthy, everything is cheap and the provisions better than ever I tasted. Still I have taken an insuperable aversion to it, which I feel rather than can account for....

BOOSTING BATH

'You never can go, my dear Mother, where you
So much have to see and so little to do.'
The New Bath Guide

Asked to name the most significant poets of eighteenth-century England few people nowadays are likely to name Christopher Anstey (1724-1805) but at one point he was all the rage and it was Bath that made him so. A Cambridge don and the son of one, Anstey resigned his Fellowship on inheriting the family estate at Trumpington, outside Cambridge, where he lived the life of a country gentleman and literary dilettante, producing the first translation into Latin of Thomas Gray's celebrated *Elegy written in a Country Churchyard*, which contains some of the best-known lines in English literature ('Full many a flower is born to blush unseen'.)

First driven to Bath by a 'bilious fever', Anstey revisited it every year throughout the 1760s and found in the posturings of its visitors an ideal subject for gentle satire, tempered by emollient flattery. The result, first published in 1766, was the *New Bath Guide, or Memoirs of the B-r-d (Blunderhead) Family, in a series of Poetical Epistles*. Herewith a few lines of Anstey in public relations mode :

> Of all the gay places the World can afford,
> By Gentle and Simple for Pastime ador'd,
> Fine Balls, and fine Concerts, fine Buildings and Springs,
> Fine Walks, and fine Views, and a Thousand fine Things,
> Not to mention the sweet Situation and Air,
> What Place, my dear Mother, with Bath can compare?
> Let Bristol for Commerce and Dirt be renown'd,
> At Sal'sbury Pen-Knives and Scissors be ground;
> The towns of Devizes, of Bradford and Frome,
> May boast that they better can manage the Loom;
> I believe that they may: - but the World to refine,
> In Manners, in Dress, in Politeness to shine,
> O Bath! – let the Art, let the Glory be thine.

Composed on the other side of the country from Bath, in Trumpington, and first printed in Cambridge, the *New Bath Guide* was an instant smash hit. That habitually waspish critic Horace Walpole wrote gushingly to a literary friend –

> It is a set of letters in verse, in all kinds of verses, describing the life at Bath, and incidentally everything else, but so much wit, so much humour, fun, and poetry, so much originality, never met together before … the man has a better ear than Dryden or Handel … There is a description of a milliner's box in all the terms of landscape … a Moravian ode and a Methodist ditty, that are incomparable and the best names that ever were composed.

Characteristically Walpole later denigrated Anstey but never retracted his views about the merits of the poem. Thomas Gray himself was equally complimentary – 'It is the only thing in fashion.' Enthusiastic reviews appeared in *The Critical Review*, the *Monthly Review* and the *Gentleman's Magazine*. Tobias Smollett (see below) almost certainly drew on it when composing *Humphrey Clinker*; he was himself definitely in Bath in 1766-7 when the book was the sensation of the day. Five editions were printed in the first year of publication. After the second edition Dr Johnson's astute publisher friend Dodsley paid Anstey £250 for the copyright. Ten years later he had made so much money out of it that he gave it back to Anstey as a gift. With characteristic generosity Anstey donated a proportion of his windfall to Bath's General Hospital.

In 1770 Anstey settled permanently in Bath with a view to securing the best possible education for his eight (finally thirteen) children and became one of the Crescent's earliest residents. The *New Bath Guide* remained popular for well over half a century, going through over forty editions, and as late as 1830 was thought to merit a version with illustrations by the celebrated caricaturist George Cruickshank (1792-1878). Anstey continued to write verse, producing among other works *A Serious Alarm to the People of Bath* (1772) and, in *Bath Guide* vein, *The Election Ball* (1776); but none of his later compositions came near to repeating the success of the *New Bath Guide*.

William Hoare's painting of Anstey, done soon after the publication of *The Election Ball* shows the poet at his desk, with a quill pen in hand, staring at the onlooker, as if pausing for inspiration, while one of his daughters tugs at his coat to draw his attention to her doll, which sports a hairstyle and head-dress of preposterously monstrous proportions, an ideal target for an Anstey arrow. Anstey was also painted by Gainsborough and Lawrence and has a monument in Poets' Corner at Westminster Abbey. He was buried at Walcot church.

'... a mob of impudent plebeians'

Published only a few months before his death *The Expedition of Humphrey Clinker* is regarded as the most accomplished work of the Scottish novelist and physician Tobias Smollett (1721-71). It describes, by means of letters written between the various characters, an extended journey from Wales to London to Scotland and back again. The description of Bath given in the letter from the main character, Matthew Bramble, to his friend and doctor, Lewis, occurs therefore near the beginning of the narrative and is noteworthy for its bilious tone and dismissive judgments on the manners, the architecture and the company of the spa. After passing through Gloucester, Clifton and Bristol, the party arrive at Bath, where Matthew's husband-hunting sister, Tabitha, fastens on Sir Ulic MacKilligut. Matthew, however, is repelled by the city as '*a sink of profligacy and extortion*', and pours out his disgust to Lewis:

> I find nothing but disappointment at Bath; which is so altered, that I can scarcely believe it is the same place that I frequented about thirty years ago … this place, which Nature and Providence seem to have intended as a resource from distemper and disquiet, is become the very centre of racket and dissipation. Instead of that peace, tranquility and ease, so necessary to those who labour under bad health, weak nerves and irregular spirits; here we have nothing but noise, tumult and hurry; with the fatigue and slavery of maintaining a ceremonial, more stiff, formal and oppressive, than the etiquette of a German elector. A national hospital it may be but one would imagine that none but lunatics are admitted …

Having rubbished the outcome of Nash's civilizing mission, Matthew moved on to Wood's architecture:

> The Square, though irregular, is, on the whole, pretty well laid out, spacious, open and airy; and, in my opinion, by far the most wholesome and agreeable situation in Bath, especially the upper side of it; but the avenues to it are mean, dangerous and indirect.

Bath's crowning architectural glory is subjected to verbal demolition in detail:

> The Circus is a petty bauble, contrived for shew, and looks like Vespasian's amphitheatre turned outside in. If we consider it in point of magnificence, the great number of small doors belonging to the separate houses, the inconsiderable height of the different orders, the affected ornaments of the architrave, which are both childish and misplaced, and the areas projecting into the street, surrounded with iron rails, destroy a good part of its effect upon the eye; and, perhaps, we shall find it still more defective,

if we view it in the light of convenience. The figure of each separate dwelling-house, being the segment of a circle, must spoil the symmetry of the rooms, by contracting them towards the street windows, and leaving a larger sweep in the space behind.

Bramble/Smollett then proceeds to give Wood posthumous instruction in what he should have done:

If, instead of the areas and iron rails, which seem to be of very little use, there had been a corridor with arcades all round, as in Covent-garden, the appearance of the whole would have been more magnificent and striking; those arcades would have afforded an agreeable covered walk, and sheltered the poor chairmen and their carriages from the rain, which here is almost perpetual.

The climactic passages of Bramble's diatribe are reserved for the people Bath attracts. Whereas many foreign visitors to Georgian England were impressed by the openness and mobility of a society which rewarded energy and enterprise, Smollett's narrator sees Britain's thrusters and boosters as proof that the country is going to the dogs and the social order itself in peril of dissolution:

Every upstart of fortune, harnessed in the trappings of the mode, presents himself at Bath, as in the very focus of observation – Clerks and factors from the East Indies, loaded with the spoil of plundered provinces; planters, Negro-drivers and hucksters from our American plantations, enriched they know not how; agents, commissaries and contractors, who have fattened in two successive wars, on the blood of the nation; usurers, brokers and jobbers of every kind: men of low birth and no breeding, have found themselves suddenly translated into a state of affluence, unknown to former ages; and no wonder that their brains should be intoxicated with pride, vanity and presumption. Knowing no other criterion of greatness, but the ostentation of wealth, they discharge their affluence without taste or conduct, through every channel of the most absurd extravagance; and all of them hurry to Bath, because here, without any further qualification, they can mingle with the princes and nobles of the land.

The bottom-feeders of the social pond are identified as the female dependents of the City slickers of the day, for whom special venom is reserved:

> Even the wives and daughters of low tradesmen, who, like shovel-nosed sharks, prey upon the blubber of those uncouth whales of fortune, are infected with the same rage of displaying their importance; and the slightest indisposition serves them for a pretext to insist upon being conveyed to Bath, where they may hobble country-dances and cotillions among lordlings, esquires, counsellors and clergy. These delicate creatures ... cannot breathe in the gross air of the Lower Town, or conform to the vulgar rules of a common lodging-house; the husband, therefore, must provide an entire house or elegant apartments in new buildings.
>
> Such is the composition of what is called the fashionable company at Bath; where a very inconsiderable proportion of genteel people are lost in a mob of impudent plebeians, who have neither understanding nor judgment, nor the least idea of propriety and decorum; and seem to enjoy nothing so much as an opportunity of insulting their betters.

So much for social mobility.

A Literary Lioness

The flamboyant figure of Justice which presides over Bath's handsome Guildhall is more amazon than abstraction. Designed by the Bath artist Robert Edge Pine (1730-88), it was probably modelled on Catherine Macaulay (1731-91), a redoubtable republican whose eight volume *History of England* astonished the male literary establishment of her day. Born into the wealthy Sawbridge family of Kent, Catherine was self-educated and self-contained, content apparently with spinsterhood until, at the relatively advanced age of twenty-nine, she married a Scottish 'man midwife', George Macaulay. Their happy marriage lasted but six years until his early death in 1766, leaving Catherine with an infant daughter, Catherine Sophia, to bring up. With her late husband's encouragement Catherine had already embarked on the historical project which would dominate her life. Covering the period 1603-1714, her *History* chronicled the confrontations between

Crown and Parliament which issued in the 'balanced' constitution of Hanoverian England. She herself looked forward to an even more democratic form of government and proclaimed her opposition to both slavery and capital punishment. As an historian she revealed herself as an unashamed defender of England's experiment with republican government under the Cromwellian Commonwealth – 'the brightest age that ever adorned the page of history'. She later became an ardent supporter of the cause of Britain's rebellious American colonies and won the warm regard of many of its leaders. Apart from her *History* she also wrote commentaries on Hobbes, a refutation of Burke's criticisms of the French Revolution and a treatise on the necessity of female education.

The first volume of the *History*, published in 1763, was received with a mixture of admiration and condescension, its radical sympathies less alarming to reviewers than the fact that they were expressed by a woman. The populist John Wilkes and the arch-conservative Dr Johnson both came to loathe her, while her admirers ranged from the elder Pitt to Mirabeau. The poet Thomas Gray thought she had produced 'the most sensible, unaffected and best history of England that this country has ever produced', a judgment endorsed by Horace Walpole. Subsequent volumes appeared in 1765, 1767, 1768 and 1771. By the time she had completed the fifth volume of the *History* Catherine Macaulay was so broken in health by her exertions that it was deemed advisable in 1774 for her to repair to Bath, where she settled at Alfred House, the residence of a doting dotard, the Revd. Dr Thomas Wilson (1703-84), Rector of St Stephen, Walbrook, London. Following the death of his wife in 1772 Wilson had all but abandoned his London parish in favour of 14 Alfred Street, opposite the new upper Assembly Rooms. The forceful Mrs Macaulay and her pretty child filled a void in the old man's life and he soon determined to make her his heir. The widow Macaulay, meanwhile, attracted such a circle of admirers that artists tried to cash in on her celebrity by painting portraits of her to adorn their showrooms. Pine, who shared Mrs Macaulay's republican principles, produced at least two versions, including a full-length depiction of her, set in a landscape of Roman ruins. Quill pen in hand, draped in vaguely 'classical' costume, she leans on the five volumes of her *History* thus far completed and gazes purposefully away from the viewer. In her other hand is a letter addressed to her patron Dr Wilson. A plinth inscription proclaims her conviction – 'Government – A Power Delegated for the Happiness of Mankind'. Joseph Wright (see page 162) chose instead to produce a double portrait of *Dr Thomas Wilson with his adopted Daughter Catherine Sophia Macaulay*, in which the venerable clergyman expounds a text to the attentive child. Mrs Macaulay was also painted by Gainsborough and Cipriani and included in Richard Samuel's group portrait of *The Nine Living Muses of Great Britain*.

Catherine Macaulay's cult of personality reached its pinnacle in 1777 when 'a numerous and brilliant company' convened at Alfred House to mark her birthday in an assemblage which lasted until two a.m. Six gentlemen hailed her with six poems specially composed for the occasion and subsequently published in volume form. Dr Wilson presented her with a gold medal. The author's personal physician, the notorious quack James Graham, (1745-94) presented her with a copy of his *Works*. In the same year Wilson installed a stylised marble statue of Mrs Macaulay as 'History' in his London church, until his neglected parishioners indignantly obliged him to take it away. Doubtless many felt vindicated by the humiliation of their absentee priest the following year when Mrs Macaulay suddenly married James Graham's brother, a stripling of twenty-one and, as the mere assistant to a sea surgeon, entirely beneath her in social standing. At a stroke the alliance destroyed both the author's relationship with Dr Wilson and her quasi-regal status in Bath. The newly-weds left Bath at once and for good. After America achieved its independence they made a triumphal tour there, lasting almost a year and including a stay of ten days with George Washington at his plantation home, Mount Vernon. The marriage appears to have been very happy. James Graham moved on to London where he became Gainsborough's neighbour at Schomberg House in Pall Mall. Volumes 6 and 7 of the *History* were published in 1781, Volume 8 in 1783.

Although Catherine Macaulay's *magnum opus* was overshadowed by other contemporary efforts, she was a meticulous scholar, making use of primary sources with commendable objectivity as she worked her way through state papers, memoirs and her personal collection of some five thousand tracts, pamphlets and sermons. When an archivist cavilled at showing her all of the often sexually explicit correspondence between James I and his favourite the Duke of Buckingham Mrs Macaulay swept aside his objections with the magisterial observation that 'a historian is of no sex' and insisted on reading the lot. A feminist *avant la lettre* , she behaved not as though women would eventually achieve equality with men but as though they already had. In her *Vindication of the Rights of Women* Mary Wollstonecraft hailed Mrs Macaulay as quite simply 'the woman of the greatest abilities that this country has ever produced.'

A Literary Lightweight

It was perhaps fortunate for Lady Anna Miller (1741-81) that Smollett was dead by the time she set herself up as Bath's most pushy and pretentious literary hostess. As it was she earned the complete contempt of metropolitan critics like Horace Walpole and Dr Johnson and was satirized in print as 'the Bath Sapho'. Having inherited a hefty fortune, Anna had married an impoverished Irish cavalryman who proceeded to build a house at Batheaston so extravagant that the couple had to retire for a while to France to recover their finances. In 1770-71 they toured Italy together. On their return Lady Miller inaugurated a fortnightly salon at their Batheaston home, where guests were invited to toss their original compositions into an antique urn the Millers had brought back with them. Unearthed at Frascati, it was rather improbably claimed to have belonged to Cicero. The authors of the best three efforts at each soirée were crowned by the hostess with a wreath of myrtle. In 1775 a selection of these offerings was published under the title of *Poetical Amusements at a Villa near Bath*. It sold out in ten days. In 1776 Anna published, anonymously, the letters that she had written home to a friend, describing her travels. Produced in three volumes they enjoyed such success that a two volume version was published the following year. Further volumes of *Poetical Amusements* appeared in 1776,1777 and 1781. Despite occasional contributions by such talents as Anstey and Garrick, the overall literary standard was fairly dismal, a failing brushed aside by Lady Miller with the explanation that 'they originated amidst the hurry of plays, balls, public breakfasts and concerts'. At least the profits were donated to charity. Anna died at Hot Wells, Bristol, leaving a son, a stunningly beautiful daughter of ten and a husband who became a London club bore. Lady Miller was buried in Bath Abbey (see page 60).

At least one of Lady Miller's circle might have won Smollett's approval as a useful member of society. A Norfolk Quaker by birth, a shopkeeper by trade, and a dabbler in poetry by preference, Edmund Rack (?1735-87) settled in Bath around 1775 and in 1778 founded what became the Bath and West of England Agricultural Society, himself serving as its first secretary. In 1779 he became a founder member of the Bath Philosophical Society, serving it also as its first secretary. Despite poor health and impoverishment, Rack also completed a topographical survey of Somerset, which was published posthumously.

Aristocrat, Autocrat

Married at twenty-one, Selina, Countess of Huntingdon (1709-91) was initially content to produce a brood of four sons and three daughters and to play the part of a conventional Lady Bountiful. In 1739, however, she took to religion in a serious way by becoming one of the earliest converts to Methodism. The loss of two of her sons to smallpox in 1743, the death of her husband in 1746, release from family responsibilities as her other offspring grew up and got married, all combined to intensify her commitment to a Calvinist Christianity which she became determined to bring to others of her rank. And quite how they might have got it otherwise is difficult to imagine, as the Methodism practised by John and Charles Wesley was explicitly aimed at bringing the marginal and the outcast – miners, fisherfolk, itinerants - back to the bosom of the church. The countess, by contrast, aimed at the aristocracy. Intent, as she saw it, on confronting the devil in his own backyard, Selina targeted the communities in which the elite gathered for convivial diversion. In 1761 she sold her jewellery to fund the building of a chapel in Brighton. Bath's rival spa, Tunbridge Wells, was similarly favoured. But Bath itself was the jewel in the crown of her crusade. Erected 'to protect the residents from the evils of Bath society', the Countess of Huntingdon's Chapel at the Vineyards was opened for worship in 1765. The first sermon was preached by George Whitefield (1714-70), who was famed for both easy eloquence and a squint which led his gaze to roam accusingly at random over the congregation, inducing frissons of guilt wherever it appeared to rest. Whitefield regarded the countess as 'all aflame for Jesus' and, more accommodating to her imperious manner than the Wesleys, he remained her close collaborator until his death. The countess, while devoting much of her energies to the seminary she had founded, continued to take a close personal interest in her outpost at Bath. In 1781 she sacked the minister for allowing laymen to preach in the chapel.

The sceptical and disdainful Horace Walpole attended a service at the Huntingdon chapel the year after its opening and found more to approve in the architecture than the preacher – John Wesley himself – as he confided in a characteristically waspish letter to a friend:

> My health advances faster than my amusement. However, I have been at one opera, Mr. Wesley's. The chapel is very neat, with true Gothic windows (yet I am not converted); but I was glad to see that luxury is creeping in upon them before persecution … very neat mahogany … red cushions for the parson and clerk … scarlet armed chairs … a balcony for elect ladies … Wesley is a lean elderly man, fresh-coloured, his hair smoothly combed … Wondrous clean but as evidently an actor as Garrick.

Walpole was well qualified to comment on the architecture, himself being *the* pioneer of the 'Gothic Revival' which would take almost another lifetime to hit Bath with full force.

The Countess of Huntingdon's Chapel was the first ecclesiastical use of Gothic in Bath. The roadside frontage is a villa which served occasionally as a residence for the Countess but mainly as a manse for the incumbent preacher. As it incorporated a dwelling house this made the complex technically a private chapel, beyond the jurisdiction of the Anglican church authorities. The galleried chapel to the rear is an unashamedly theatrical preaching-box in which the pulpit, fronted by a massive eagle worthy of a Roman legionary, dominates a stage-like stepped altar. A Sunday School was added to the chapel in 1842.

By the time of her death the 'Countess of Huntingdon's connexion' consisted of a network of some sixty chapels in Britain, plus outreach activities in America and Sierra Leone. It survives to this day as an Evangelical enterprise with some twenty-plus congregations in the UK. The chapel in Bath was taken over by a Presbyterian congregation in 1932 and passed to the United Reformed Church in 1972. Worship ceased in 1981. Acquired by the Bath Preservation Trust for restoration, in 1992 it reopened as the Building of Bath Museum, devoted to telling the story of the city's Georgian development. With the history of the chapel and its sponsor side-lined to a single subsidiary display, it serves as an illustration of how nowadays it is architecture, rather than the architect of the universe, which is deemed worthy of reverence.

A RIVAL ESTABLISHMENT

The Octagon chapel was built (1765-7) on the garden of the banker William Street for the Revd. Dr Dechair as a proprietary chapel – i.e. one in which worshippers paid for the privilege. The poor were, therefore, by definition excluded. Individual places could be booked by the season at rates varying for six to ten shillings. Reached via a passage off up-market Milsom Street, the chapel was intended for the fashionable and the fastidious. The architect was Timothy Lightholer, better known as a carver and often confused with his brother Thomas Lightholer who turned his decorative skills to forging coins. The pulpit was an imposing double-decker. The octagonal shape of the building was intended to emphasise the centrality of the sermon to worship by maximising the congregation's ability to both hear and see the preacher. The organist was the renowned William Herschel (see page 201). The altarpiece was painted by Bath's Michelangelo William Hoare (see page 163). Its subject, *The Pool of Bethesda*, showing Christ as a healer, was clearly appropriate for a health resort. Hoare was paid £100 and granted a free seat for life, not to mention having the benefit of a free display of his handiwork placed permanently before the gaze of those best able to afford it. An early press advertisement asserted that the Octagon chapel was 'the only safe place of worship in Bath with no risk to health as there are no steps to climb and no bodies buried below.' Featuring 'recesses, fireplaces, carpeted floors and every accommodation and refinement of luxury', the chapel struck the clerical diarist Parson Woodforde (1740-1802) as 'a handsome building, but not like a place of worship'. Bath's upper crust disagreed and flocked to the Octagon so that the members of the congregation were, in the words of Johnson's sometime hostess Mrs Thrale 'packed like seeds in a sunflower'.

Worship at the Octagon was discontinued in 1895. During the Second World War it became in the words of the architectural historian Bryan Little, 'in its capacity of food office one of Bath's best-known, most visited buildings.' The chapel was then used as a showroom for antiques and from 1981 to 2005 as the headquarters and gallery of the Royal Photographic Society. The RPS has relocated to Fenton House, 122 Wells Road (www.rps.org). The keyboard and pipes of the majestic Snetzler organ once played by Herschel can be seen at the Herschel Museum of Astronomy.

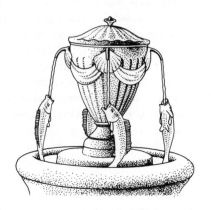

Playing the Part

'Plays are like mirrors made for men to see
How BAD they are, how GOOD they ought to be.'

Bath's theatrical history begins with occasional performances in the Guildhall or in the courtyards of the city's larger inns. Touring troupes visited Bath in Elizabethan times and in 1674 the city corporation contributed part of the costs of 'the players in the Town Hall'.

Bath's first theatre was built in 1705 by George Trim, a local clothier and a member of the corporation, at the cost of £1,500. Located at the top of Parsonage Lane, it was, despite the bravado with which the coats of arms of its sponsors were painted on its walls, distinctly cramped. There was only one box and that was only big enough for four persons. As demand for elite entertainment was strictly seasonal, there was no question of a continuous year round programme. Many performances were put on at the behest of private individuals for their personal guests. On one occasion, a performance ordered by the Countess of Burlington, the entire audience numbered just seventeen.

Probably the high point of Bath's early theatrical history was the performance in 1728 of the smash-hit *The Beggar's Opera*, by John Gay (1685-1732*)*. This was a quite new form of entertainment, in which the leading characters were neither gods nor kings, fairies or fops, but drawn from low life, the hero a highwayman, the love interest a couple of tavern molls. In mockery of the contemporary craze for Italian opera, *The Beggar's Opera* incorporated dozens of the popular street ballads of the day, making it, in effect, the first British 'musical'. Premiered in London by the impresario John Rich(1682-1761), *The Beggar's Opera* was to become the greatest commercial success of the entire century, making 'Gay rich and Rich gay.' Even if Bath's theatre was still only a small-scale, part-time business, it is significant that it was the first place outside London to stage Gay's triumph – and under the personal direction of John Gay himself.

After Trim's theatre was demolished in 1737 to make way for the Mineral Water Hospital, Bath's actors variously found accommodation beneath Lady Hawley's Assembly Rooms (a.k.a. Simpson's), at the Globe Inn, at the George Inn and at 'The New Theatre' in Kingsmead Street, an optimistic designation for a space just fifty feet long and half that wide. Despite the limitations of these venues players put on not only Shakespeare but those works of their own day which contemporaries regarded as new 'classics' Farquhar's *The Constant Couple*, Steele's *The Conscious Lovers* and Addison's *Cato*. The best the company could hope for, apparently, were total takings of thirty pounds a night – of which a third went to Lady Hawley, who also took another quarter in respect of the use of scenery and costumes and a further £2.10s for music, candles, playbills and attendants. The £10 left over had to be divided between up to a dozen actors.

In 1747 John Hippisley advanced a proposal for the building of a theatre truly worthy of Bath –

> Theatrical performances, when conducted with Decency and Regularity, have always been esteem'd the most rational Amusements, by the Polite and Thinking Part of Mankind. Strangers, therefore, must be greatly surpris'd to find at Bath Entertainments of this sort in no better Perfection than they are, as it is a Place, during its Seasons, honour'd with so great a Number of Persons, eminent for Politeness, Judgment and Taste; and where it might reasonably be expected (next to London) the best theatre in England.

Hippisley had plausible credentials for advancing such a project. He was a Somerset man by birth, a talented player of comedy, a dramatist and a proven entrepreneur, having run a coffee-house in London and built a theatre in Bristol. He underlined the impossibility of improvement under existing constraints of space : 'The present Play-House, or rather Play room, is so small and incommodious that 'tis impossible to have Things done better in it than they are. The

Profits arising from the Performance, as now conducted, will not support a larger, or better, Company of Actors … '. Hippisley clinched his argument with the withering observation that 'nothing can be more disagreeable than for Persons of the first Quality and those of the lowest Rank, to be seated on the same bench together…' as was virtually unavoidable in the current circumstances.

Hippisley himself died in 1748, before his Bath venture could come to fruition, but in 1750 his projected theatre, funded by local businessman John Palmer and built to the designs of local architect Thomas Jelly, at last opened in Orchard Street with a performance of *Henry IV Part I*. In 1756 Orchard Street finally absorbed the company of its predecessor and rival 'New Theatre'. Rebuilt in 1767, in 1768 the Orchard Street establishment was granted a patent by George III to become the Theatre Royal, the first provincial establishment in England to be so honoured. The building was altered and extended again in 1775-6, doubling its capacity. Orchard Street was destined to become the launch-pad for some of the most luminous theatrical talents of the late Georgian and Regency periods.

'The Bath Roscius'

Although he became known as 'the Bath Roscius', in deference to the most celebrated actor of ancient Rome, John Henderson (1747-85) was actually born just off London's Cheapside. Stage-struck from an early age, he took David Garrick as his model but allegedly irritated the great man by daring to mimic him all too successfully to his face. Unable to secure access to the London stage Henderson, initially appearing under the pseudonym Courtney, made his debut at Bath in 1772, as Hamlet. Within a fortnight he was appearing as Richard III and within the next two months had played a further eight roles and was appearing under his own name. He welcomed the pressure –

> The continual practice I am in here is of great advantage to me – I once thought it a hardship to be forced upon so many characters. I think so now no longer, being convinced that every part I play, however unsuited to me, does me good. In London it would do me harm for this reason: there are computed to be thirty different audiences in London, here there

are but two; and those who see me at a disadvantage one night, see me at an advantage the next.

Gainsborough (see page 165) soon became one of Henderson's great friends and supporters, painted him, advised him to continue to model himself on Garrick and teasingly warned him of the perils of over-eating. The playwright Richard Cumberland (1732-1811) kept Garrick informed of Henderson's progress and commented shrewdly on his strengths and weaknesses – 'Nature has not been beneficent to him in figure or in face; a prominent forehead, corpulent habit, inactive features'– but these were more than offset by 'great sensibility, just elocution, a perfect ear, good sense' and what would perhaps nowadays be called an acute sense of dramatic timing – 'the most marking pauses (next to your own) I ever heard' – plus astonishing powers of memory. It was still more than five years before a London manager finally offered Henderson an appointment but he made a triumphant debut as Shylock and was spoken of as second only to Garrick. Fate decreed that Henderson should never surpass or succeed his unwilling mentor. 'The Bath Roscius' was accidentally poisoned to death by his wife, though the knowledge was successfully kept from her. Despite the relative brevity of his London stage career Henderson was laid to rest in Westminster Abbey's Poets' Corner.

Mrs Siddons
Between 1778 and 1782 Sarah Siddons (1755-1831), who became the leading tragedienne of her age, served as a member of the Theatre Royal's permanent company. Henderson had seen her in Birmingham in 1774 and had written to John Palmer that she was 'an actress who never had had an equal, nor would she have a superior'. Notwithstanding such an accolade, Mrs Siddons' first appearance at Drury Lane in 1775 was not a success and her years in Bath gave her the opportunity to rebuild her confidence and to re-establish a reputation. First appearing in October 1777 in Vanbrugh's *The Provok'd Husband*, Mrs Siddons played over two dozen different roles in her first season and, over the course of the four subsequent years, over a hundred more, an astonishing repertoire for a performer in her twenties.

Palmer worked her unsparingly – 'after the rehearsal at Bath, and on a Monday evening, I had to go and act at Bristol … and reaching Bath again … I was obliged to represent some fatiguing part there on the Tuesday evening.'

Summoned to London in 1782, Sarah Siddons ended her farewell performance in Bath with a valedictory address to her appreciative audience, composed in verse by herself and teasingly entitled *Mrs Siddons's Three Reasons*. Flattering her audience and thanking them for their loyalty, she excused her desertion to the capital with a brilliant *coup de théâtre* – producing on stage her own three children, whose upkeep demanded that she pursue the more generous rewards of the metropolis.

> Stand forth, ye elves, and plead your mother's cause;
> Ye little magnets, whose soft influence draws
> Me from a point where every gentle breeze
> Wafted my bark to happiness and ease –
> Sends me adventurous upon a larger main,
> In hopes that you may profit by my gain.

While Mrs Siddons went on to conquer London, Mr Siddons, her handsome actor husband, a versatile but lightweight player, whom she had married in defiance of her family, gave up the stage entirely and remained in Bath, declining into poor health and dying in 1805.

Robert Elliston

Bath also kick-started the career of Robert Elliston (1774-1831), one of the foremost comic players of the day and a daring impresario with, ultimately, more chutzpah than prudence. Intended for the clergy, Elliston, a Londoner, was sent to St Paul's school but in 1791 ran away to Bath and made his first stage appearance at Orchard Street in a minor part in *Richard III*. This was followed by a two year apprenticeship with a touring company, playing a different part every night. Returning to Bath in 1793 Elliston married a dancing teacher, Elizabeh Rundall, with whom he had ten children. For the next decade they were happy and settled while he built a solid reputation, particularly for playing romantic comedy. In 1804 London beckoned and he departed to embark on a spectacular career in theatrical management which ended in bankruptcy and alcoholism.

Bigger and Better

By 1800 the Theatre Royal had become too small and had to be abandoned. The shell still stands but only the remnants of stage boxes recall its theatrical incarnation. In 1809 the building was converted to become a Roman Catholic Chapel. In 1866 it was converted into a Freemasons' Hall.

In 1805 the Theatre Royal company moved into a new and larger home in Beauford Square, opening with *Richard III*. The façade and decoration of the building were designed by the City of London Surveyor and Professor of Architecture at the Royal Academy, George Dance the Younger (1741-1825), a regular visitor to Bath for his 'habitual winter cough'. Supervision of the construction was entrusted to City Architect John Palmer (1738-1817), who had been responsible for designing the actual structure. The moving spirit behind this metamorphosis was William Wyatt Dimond (?1750-1812). Apprenticed as an engraver, Dimond had early abandoned his craft to make his debut as Romeo at Drury Lane in 1772. After two brief sojourns in Bath he then returned to play opposite Mrs Siddons from 1779 to 1782, excelling in light comedy roles. Having married advantageously, Dimond was able to settle in Norfolk Crescent. In 1786 he began to share in the management of the Theatre Royal and in 1795 became the senior manager. As such he proved to be both popular and effective, achieving not only the transition to new premises but managing to attract such stars as Mrs Jordan, Elliston, Charles Kemble, Joseph Grimaldi, William Macready and, on her final tour in 1811, Mrs Siddons. Dimond knew how to ring the changes in his programme, reviving old favourites like *The School for Scandal* and *The Beggar's Opera* and introducing novelties like a patriotic panorama of the Battle of Trafalgar or a season of Italian opera. At the climax of a gratifyingly successful career Dimond was felled by a stroke on Christmas Eve. An excellent actor, a more than competent manager and a respected member of the City Corporation, he was buried in Bath Abbey.

After Dimond the Theatre Royal went through a bad patch – for about half a century. Although local businessmen and the local press continued to value it as an asset to the city, theatre as a form of entertainment came under increasingly hostile attack in, to use Mac Hopkins-Clark's apt phrase, 'a city overflowing with retired clergymen, Nonconformists and hypocrites.' 'Respectable' people increasingly favoured dinner-parties and musical evenings in their own homes as opposed to going out. As Bath ceased to attract the social elite on a seasonal basis the Theatre Royal programme plunged relentlessly down-market to feature farces, pantomimes and animal acts. Classic works were dumbed-down and bowdlerised. When the London actress Fanny Kemble (1809-93) came to Bath in 1830 she noted condescendingly – 'My fellow labourers amuse me a great deal; their various versions of Shakespeare are very droll.'

Managers at the Theatre Royal succeeded one another with bewildering rapidity. Dimond's son William gave up the battle when his mother died in 1823. Mr Charlton, the former stage-manager, managed to have gas footlights installed before he was sacked in 1827. Mr Bellamy, an actor from the company, installed gas lighting before he, too, went, in 1833. His successor, Mr Banett, lasted one season. Mr Woulds, a company member since 1811, staggered on till 1839, at the cost of personal bankruptcy, his marriage and a term in prison for failing to maintain his family. Mr Davidge installed the dramatist Edward Stirling as stage-manager in his absence and lasted the one season. Two local men, Mr Newcombe and Mr Bedford, gallantly stepped forward and lasted just over one month. Another outsider cleared off leaving the company underpaid by £350. Mr Hooper managed to last from 1842 to 1845, when the management was taken over by William Macready's widow. After her death in 1845 her son-in-law, James Chute, finally began to turn things round. Initially cutting back on performances and reducing prices, he introduced the work of new playwrights, like Bulwer Lytton, Sheridan Knowles and Dion Boucicault, and himself mounted a spectacular production of *A Midsummer Night's Dream*. By 1862 the number of performances per week had increased from two to five – and then, on Friday 18 April, the whole theatre burned down, destroying with it all the costumes, scenery and stock of scripts.

Thanks largely to the initiative of Jerom Murch (see page 196), the city of Bath managed not only to rebuild the theatre but to take over its ownership from the descendants and heirs of the original founding trustees. Less than twelve months after its destruction a renascent Theatre Royal opened on the same site with a production of *A Midsummer Night's Dream*, starring fifteen-year-old Ellen Terry (1847-1928) as Titania. The rebuilt interior was the work of C.J. Phipps (1835-97), who had been born and trained in Bath. Following his success in reconstructing the Theatre Royal, Phipps came to specialise in theatrical architecture, building more than a score of theatres in London alone. It was Phipps's decision to move the main entrance of the Theatre Royal round to the Saw Close, adapting Beau Nash's residence, built in 1720, to serve as the foyer.

Chute left in 1868, to be followed by four managements in less than ten years. Then came Mr Neebe and stability. Neebe had managed theatres at Exeter and Weymouth and was a whizz at marketing. He sold tickets in three guinea books, arranged for special excursion trains to be laid on to bring families to the annual pantomime and most daring of all, opened a theatre bar. On stage Neebe found a sure-fire winner in the new comic operas of Gilbert and Sullivan. By the time Neebe left in 1884 Bath's theatre was at last a paying proposition and capable of sustaining performances all year round, although at the cost of losing its own resident stock company of players. William Lewis, owner of the *Bath Express* and *Bath Herald*, took over in 1885 and subsequently brought in C.J. Phipps to redecorate the theatre and modernise the lavatory arrangements. When Lewis died in 1900, his son Egbert took over. The Theatre Royal was extensively refurbished again in 1902 when a fire-proof curtain was installed. In 1905 the theatre's centenary year – and the bi-centenary of theatre in Bath – was marked by a farewell performance by the giant of the English stage, Sir Henry Irving (1838-1905). The Theatre Royal managed to survive the challenge of the cinema, before which so many provincial houses folded. Fortunately spared destruction by bombing, it prospered during the entertainment-starved days of World War Two.

In 1979 the management of the Theatre Royal was re-formed on a charitable basis. The obtrusive rooftop flytower was added in 1982 as part of another programme of upgrading. The adjacent Ustinov Studio Theatre was created in 1997 as a bijou space for experimental performances. A Shakespeare festival was inaugurated in 1998. In 2005, as part of its bicentennial celebrations, the Theatre Royal staged a celebratory production of Sheridan's *The Rivals* and established the Egg Theatre for children. Its regular programme also includes festivals devoted to Puppets, Children and the Peter Hall Company. Part of the ground floor of the Theatre Royal building is occupied by the Garrick's Head public house. Over the entrance is a bust of Garrick, by local Bath sculptor Lucius Gahagan (see page 163), dating from 1831.

The Pavilion Music Hall in Saw Close occupied the site of an eighteenth-century carrier's stables and yard. Opened for music and dancing in 1886, it was remodelled in 1894-6 as the Lyric Theatre of Varieties. By the 1930s it was known as the Palace Theatre. In 1956-7 it became the Regency Ballrooms, then subsequently a bingo hall.

Positively Last Performance
In the North Choir Aisle of the Abbey an oval medallion frames the portrait relief of the Irish actor James Quin (1693-1766), who died at his lodgings at 8 Pierrepont Street. Vain, arrogant and quarrelsome – he had killed a fellow actor in a duel - Quin could also be generous and left £100 to his landlady, Mary Simpson, and £50 to the painter Thomas Gainsborough. Quin had had a stage career of almost forty years and was regarded by the hyper-critical Horace Walpole as the greatest actor of his day. By more general agreement he was certainly the greatest Falstaff. Quin himself, however, on first seeing David Garrick, opined that, if the newcomer's naturalism was as successful as it seemed to be, his own mannered declamatory style had been wrong all along. As a contemporary wit observed, Quin was incapable of absorbing himself into a part :

> Nature, in spite of all his skill, crept in –
> Horatio, Dorax, Falstaff – still 'twas Quin

Garrick and Quin were certainly regarded as rivals by London audiences but Quin at least had the satisfaction of attaining for his last season the highest income ever earned by an actor - £1,000. He also had an additional, and unique, distinction to his credit, having been appointed elocution teacher to the future George III.

Retiring to Bath, Quin became a regular guest of Ralph Allen's at Prior Park. Inclined to gluttony – he eventually weighed some twenty stones - Quin made a regular Friday ritual of a massive meal at the Three Tuns in Stall Street, on one occasion downing six bottles of claret and informing the friends who carried him home that he was not to be woken until Sunday – in time for lunch. Quin also repaired his relationship with Garrick – who composed the epitaph on his monument:

> Here lies, James Quin; deign, reader, to be taught,
> Whate'er thy strength, of body, force of thought,
> In nature's happiest mould however cast
> To this completion thou must come at last.

All in Harmony

Bath's reputation for high standards of musical performance goes back at least to the seventeenth century. The diarist Samuel Pepys, himself a keen amateur composer, recorded in 1668 how, recovering at his lodgings after taking the waters, he was entertained – 'And by and by comes musick to play to me, extraordinary good as ever I heard at London almost any where: 5s.'

The music most accessible to the majority of the population of Bath was provided by the 'city waits' or town band. The waits were in attendance on the city corporation on celebratory or ceremonial occasions, such as the announcement of military or naval victories or the anniversary of the royal accession or the birthdays of members of the royal family. From 1733 onwards it was agreed that they should receive a retainer of four guineas per year. A more regular income came from welcoming or serenading distinguished visitors to the city. While many were doubtless happy enough to tip the performers for providing this mark of distinction the practice was clearly open to abuse and in 1774 it was formally ordered that they should 'desist from playing at Lodging-houses, to the great disturbance of the sick and others who resort to this place'. Repetitions of such offence, it was warned, would lead the magistrates to treat offenders as 'vagrants or extortioners'.

The Bath Orchestra, initially recruited from London by Beau Nash, provided background music at the Pump Rooms in the mornings and played at balls in the evenings. Wealthy visitors could afford to entertain their friends with private concerts, either in their lodgings or in one of the larger inns, like the Three Tuns, which had a large dining-room capable of serving as a concert room. A more informal mode of musical entertainment was to be found in the various all-male clubs which sprang up in the last quarter of the eighteenth century for the singing of 'glees' and 'catches', repetitive compositions, often of a humorous or boisterous nature, whose performance was usually accompanied by much drinking. One of the most popular – *Anacreon in Heaven* – was sung to more than twenty different sets of verses until Americans took it up as the tune for *The Star-Spangled Banner*.

Bath frequently figured on the itinerary of foreign virtuosi visiting England. The Italian violin maestro Francesco Geminiani came to Bath as early as 1718 and again in 1721. When the violinist Franz La Motte and the oboe player J.C. Fischer performed in 1779 in a concert lasting from 6.30 until 10 they drew an audience of eight hundred, including 'sixty of the Nobility … and several foreigners of distinction'. The Italian *castrato* and composer Giusto Ferdinando Tenducci (*ca*.1735-90) visited Bath in 1781 to perform before a select audience at a 'little private concert arranged in the picture rooms of Mr. Beach'. Tenducci had performed at Bath on previous occasions and had been painted by Gainsborough (see page 165). While marvelling at Tenducci's voice, members of his audience, which included the arch-gossip Horace Walpole, must have been, to say the least, intrigued by his colourful past – imprisoned for debt, a convert to Protestantism, married (!) and claiming to be the father of two (!!), twice imprisoned for his marriage, divorced and massively indebted – the occasion must have provided its privileged participants with enough scandal to last for weeks. Shortly after his Bath appearance Tenducci announced his renunciation of the concert platform in favour of teaching and published his *Instruction of Mr. Tenducci to his Scholars*. Its frontispiece is probably the mezzotint based on Beach's portrait of the singer.

In 1789 Bath thrilled to the brilliant black violinist George Bridg-etower (1779-1840), then a wondrous prodigy of just ten years old, rumoured (inevitably) to be the grandson of an African prince. Bath's own child prodigy was Jane Miles (*ca*.1762-1846). Born Jenny Guest, daughter of a Bath tailor, she was the pupil of Linley, J.C. Bach and Rauzzini (see below). By the time she was six her keyboard skills were judged worthy of a poem in the *Bath Chronicle*, which later hailed her as 'the British Caecilia'. Fanny Burney (1752-1840), daughter of the eminent musicologist, Dr Charles Burney (1726-1814), heard

Jane Miles in Bath and thought her the most accomplished performer she had heard outside London. In 1783 Jane Miles published a set of six sonatas whose five hundred subscribers included members of the royal family. She was subsequently appointed music tutor to the royal princesses Amelia and Charlotte.

The Abbey was fortunate to have, for over thirty years, a fine organist in Thomas Chilcot (died 1766) and, from 1740, a fine new organ. Chilcot organised performances of oratorios for charitable fund-raising events but the general standard of choral singing does not seem to have been high. According to an anonymous complainant to the *Bath Herald* in 1796 the main problem was that the recruits from the Blue Coat School had no sooner begun to respond to training than they were put out to apprenticeships and replaced with yet another intake of 'squalling boys'.

As a highly desirable social accomplishment music figured on the curriculum of many of the city's educational establishments. Susan Sibbald, a pupil with the Misses Lee's in the 1790s had music lessons three times a week, the school itself possessing no less than three pianos. Giving instrumental or vocal tuition to visitors provided a welcome source of income to Bath's resident cadre of professional musicians. Hiring out instruments was a minor industry in itself. In March 1799 Lintern's music shop had two hundred harpsichords and pianos hired out 'and as fast as they were return'd from one family they were wanted by another'.

A Musical Dynasty

Thomas Linley (1732-95) fathered a talented musical dynasty cursed by personal tragedy. Of his twelve children only three would survive their father. Born in Wells, the son of a carpenter, as a child Thomas Linley heard Thomas Chilcot play and at once determined to become a musician. Chilcot took him on as a pupil, after which Linley studied in Naples and became a virtuoso on the harpsichord. Returning to Bath, Linley established himself as the city's foremost teacher of singing and took over the Assembly Room concerts, promoting especially the works of Handel. In consequence he was invited to produce oratorios at Drury Lane. Initially Linley kept on his Bath home at No.

5 Pierrepont Street. But theatrical success soon lured him to London permanently. In 1775 Linley's son-in-law, the dramatist Richard Brinsley Sheridan (1751-1816) wrote *The Duenna*, for which Linley and his eldest son, also Thomas, provided the music. *The Duenna* ran for seventy-eight nights, a huge hit by the standards of the time and led directly to Linley's appointment as musical director at Drury Lane.

Thomas Linley the Younger (1756-78) proved a child prodigy on the violin, performing in public from the age of eight. After studying for three years in Italy, where he gained the friendship of Mozart, he returned to Bath to become leader of the Pump Room orchestra at seventeen. Dr Charles Burney warmly recommended him as 'a Charming Performer' and the city's most preferred teacher on the instrument. Thomas Linley's tragic death in a boating accident left his father a broken man.

Little is known of Maria Linley (died 1784) beyond the fact that she sang at the Bath concerts, died young and, on her deathbed, recovered briefly from a series of paroxysms to sit upright and give a faultless rendition of '*I know that my Redeemer liveth*'. Another singing daughter, Mary (1758-87) died before thirty, leaving three young children; Gainsborough painted Mary with the most famous of her sisters, Elizabeth.

Elizabeth Linley (1754-92) was summoned to sing before George III in London when she was just nineteen. Her peerless voice was matched by a beauty which won the praises of the ageing lecher John Wilkes and the effetely asexual Horace Walpole. A bishop, no less, hailed Elizabeth Linley as 'the connecting link between angel and woman.' Richard Cosway (1742-1821) painted her in miniature. Even more to the point, perhaps, Sir Joshua Reynolds (1723-92) painted her as St Cecilia, the patron saint of music, and then cast her as the Virgin in his version of the Nativity. Pursued by several unwanted suitors, including the Duke of Clarence, Elizabeth Linley eloped with the playwright Sheridan, initially against the wishes of both her father and his. Once married, as Mrs Sheridan Elizabeth renounced the public stage to keep her husband's accounts, review scripts submitted to him for production and help to research his political speeches. Her early death deprived Sheridan of a formidable helpmeet.

Rauzzini

'In private life few men were more esteemed; none more generally beloved ... In Mr. Rauzzini, this city has sustained a public loss.'
Bath Chronicle 1810

Handsome, gifted Venanzio Rauzzini (1746-1810) had come to fame in his native Italy as a *castrato* of eighteen, singing female roles in the Roman carnival season of 1764. Entering the service of the music-mad Elector of Bavaria, Rauzzini was soon performing in Venice, Vienna and Munich, where Charles Burney was much impressed with his excellence as a singer, actor, composer and performer on the harpsichord. The blessings of looks and talent are not, however, always unmixed and in 1772 Rauzzini was advised to flee to Italy if he did not wish to accept the advances of 'an exalted personage ... deeply and hopelessly enamoured of him'. It Italy Rauzzini created the role of Cecilio in Mozart's *Lucio Silla*, leading the composer to create the virtuoso solo *Exsultate, Jubilate* for him. Rauzzini made his London stage debut in 1774, gaining the immediate approbation of Garrick. Over the next few years the newcomer composed and performed in operas, sang at philanthropic concerts and provincial festivals at Salisbury, Oxford and Winchester and established a reputation as a private teacher. From 1777 onwards Rauzzini appeared in a series of winter subscription concerts at Bath.

By 1781 Rauzzini was in sole charge of Bath's concert programme. In that same year he was twice hired by William Beckford (see page 183) to perform for his guests at Fonthill and decided to make Bath his permanent home. In the summers, however, Rauzzini resided at Perrymead Villa, Widcombe, where Haydn visited him in 1794. While continuing to perform and to compose prolifically Rauzzini devoted much of his energy to training rising stars like Mrs Elizabeth Billington (1768-1818). Rauzzini's pupils responded to his commitment with loyalty and affection. When the tenor Michael Kelly (1764-1826) stayed with his 'old friend and master' at Perrymead a few years after Haydn, he found that the singers 'Madame Mara and Signora Storace' were already Rauzzini's guests. Kelly noted with interest that his host could entertain lavishly thanks to the profits from a concert programme which cost him little 'as it was almost an article of faith among the profession to give their services free. I have known Mrs. Billington renounce many profitable engagements in London … and … travel to Bath and back to London as fast as four horses could carry her, without accepting the most trifling remuneration.'

Rauzzini died at his home at 13 Gay Street and was buried in the Abbey where a tablet was erected in his memory by his 'affectionate pupils Anna Selina Storace and John Braham.'

CHAPTER SEVEN

Apogee

1770 – 1837

Urban Improvements

'Within the last fifty years the city of Bath has so considerably increased in size and the number of its inhabitants, that it is become one of the *most agreeable* as well as *most polite* places in the kingdom; owing chiefly to the elegant neatness of its buildings, and the accommodations for strangers, which are superior to those of any city in Europe.' *New Bath Guide* 1800

In the eighteenth century building booms tended to alternate with outbreaks of war. Wars sucked men and money out of the economy and created uncertainty about the future, making men of enterprise hesitate to undertake large-scale projects. During the Seven Years War (1756-63), therefore, the only major projects in Bath were the completion of the Royal Circus and Bladud buildings, which were already under way, and the beginning of Milsom Street and George Street. Between the ending of that war and the outbreak of hostilities in the American colonies, by contrast, major completed projects included the Royal Crescent, the Paragon, the Assembly Rooms, Pulteney Bridge and the Guildhall, whose size and generous internal arrangements reflected the wealth commanded by the city corporation. Apart from the council room there was a separate court room, with an office off it for the mayor, a banqueting room, a suite of three rooms for the town clerk and his assistants, a records room and an office for the City Surveyor, plus a kitchen suite and a flat for a resident caretaker. It had originally been intended to include a covered market at street level but this was built adjacent instead. In addition to this a New Prison was built at Grove

Street, the Theatre Royal was enlarged and the Baths improved. During the American war (1776-83) the only achievements were the erection of a tennis court on Julian Road and the building of St Swithin's church. The ending of that conflict was followed by another renewed outburst of construction with the development of the Bathwick estate, the passage of an Improvement Act by Parliament, the making of Lansdown Crescent, Bath Street and Grosvenor Gardens and the initiation of the new Pump Room, St James's Square and Grosvenor Place.

NEW CRESCENTS, CIRCUSES AND SQUARES

In little more than a decade the number of houses in the city increased by more than forty per cent. Horace Walpole caught the prevailing mood neatly when he observed in 1791 that 'Bath shoots out into new crescents, circuses and squares every year.' The coming of war with the revolutionary regime in France ended the boom. Two of Bath's three local banks failed. Over the course of the French wars (1792-1815). Sydney Gardens, opened in 1795, constituted what one might term the only inessential project of the age. The *New Bath Guide* of 1801 enthused effusively over their attractions. Laid out over sixteen acres, they were:

> interspersed with a great number of small, delightful groves, pleasant vistas and charming lawns, intersected by serpentine walks, which at every turn meet with sweet, shady bowers, furnished with handsome seats, some composed by nature, others by art. It is decorated with water-falls, stone and thatched pavilions, alcoves; the Kennet and Avon canal running through, with two elegant cast-iron bridges thrown over it, after the manner of the Chinese: a sham castle planted with several pieces of cannon, bowling greens, swings, a labyrinth formed by enclosed pathways … and a grotto of antique appearance … four thatched umbrellas are placed at equal distances from each other … to serve as shelter from sudden rain and storms.

The original intention of the developers of Sydney Gardens was to use them as the focal point for a group of residential terraces but this was scotched by the building slump and only the southern ones were ever built.

Sydney Gardens

Writing in 1807 the poet Robert Southey (1774-1843), who had passed much of his childhood in Bath and remained fond of the city, declared that 'it is plain that Bath has out-grown its beauty. Long suburbs extend now on every side of the city, and the meads on the opposite side of the river, which, when the Parades were built, justified the motto on one of the houses, *Rus in Urbe*, are now covered with another town.' Southey was, of course, seeing the city at a particular juncture when, as he noted himself, one of the Crescents (probably Norfolk) was a 'melancholy new ruin', its developers broken by the 'sudden check .... given to all such speculations when the last war broke out.'

The building of places of worship was not, however, subject to the same commercial constraints as house-building and may well have provided welcome employment for the city's craftsmen. A Dissenting chapel was completed in 1795 and Laura Chapel on the Bathwick estate in the same year. Christ Church, Julian Road was opened to worship in 1798. Equally, one might say, the building of the new theatre (see page 128) was safe from the risks associated with housing speculations.

The pace of construction and urban improvement picked up again with the coming of peace in 1815. In addition to the building of Cavendish Crescent and Raby Place, five new churches were put up, Cleveland Bridge was built and the Royal Victoria Park laid out. The opening of The Bazaar, The Corridor and Jolly's (see page 174) signalled the return of free-spending times. The introduction of gas-lighting in 1819, only two years after its introduction to the streets of London, was another indication of progressiveness, as was the replacement of the traditional constabulary with a professional police force in 1836.

John Palmer

What Ralph Allen was to Bath in the first half of the eighteenth century John Palmer (1742-1818) was in the second. John Palmer senior (1702-88) built up a modest business empire consisting of a tallow chandlery, a brewery and maltings and the Orchard Street theatre (see page 125). In 1776 John Palmer junior took over management of the theatre and in 1779 took over another one in Bristol. Securing these interests involved Palmer in much travelling to and from London; managing them made him acutely aware of the shortcomings of a postal system still bedevilled with delays, abuses, inefficiencies and theft. With Prior Park as an ever-present reminder of the fortune that Ralph Allen had made out of postal reform, Palmer determined to emulate his predecessor by instituting a similarly innovative scheme. Palmer's proposal was to abolish the system of reliance on unarmed post-boys riding tired hacks and to replace them with purpose-built mailcoaches, protected by an armed guard and capable of achieving eight or nine miles an hour. Passengers might be carried inside these coaches, but not outside. Departures from London would be in the early evening rather than at midnight and would no longer wait for government documents if they were late. Exempted from paying tolls on turnpike roads, the mailcoaches would also be accorded priority over other vehicles.

In 1782 the Hon. J.J. Pratt, MP for Bath, put Palmer's scheme before William Pitt the Younger, (1759-1806), then Chancellor of the Exchequer. As custodian of the national purse Pitt was even more attracted by the prospect of increased postal revenues than by the promise of faster, more reliable deliveries. After confronting the inevitable opposition from the operators of the current postal system, a trial was run on the London-Bath-Bristol route in August 1784. Within three weeks the service was extended to four other provincial cities and then rapidly extended throughout England and Wales and subsequently to Scotland, Ireland and France. The start-up costs for the scheme proved to be less than half of what had been anticipated. Postal revenues rose over 40 per cent in less than three years. Costs per mile fell. Speed of delivery improved. Between 1784 and 1792 no coach was robbed or even stopped. By 1788 320 towns and cities which had previously had deliveries three times a week had the benefit of a daily service. By 1792 the entire coaching fleet had been upgraded with new vehicles.

Despite this brilliant success, Palmer became entangled in disputes with the postal authorities over his role and remuneration and was eventually pushed out, but with the compensation of a pension of £3,000 per year. Twenty years later, in 1813, in belated recognition of the proven value of the mailcoach service, he was granted a further one-off payment of £50,000. The nation's commercial interests had, in the interim, shown its appreciation by showering Palmer with silverware, commemorative medallions and the freedom of no less than eighteen British towns and cities.

The ending of Palmer's postal preoccupations enabled him to increase his involvement in Bath's civic life. A common councilman since 1775 and an improvement commissioner since 1789, he became a turnpike trustee in 1793, an alderman in 1795, served as mayor in 1796 and again in 1809 and as MP for the city four times between 1801 and 1807. Palmer's gifts to the city included a silver cup for racing donated in 1791, and silver cups presented to the local Volunteer unit in 1805. He was buried in the Abbey with full civic honours. Contrary to expectations, however, no public monument was raised in his memory.

'Potter to Her Majesty'

Like Chippendale, Sheraton and Spode, the name of Josiah Wedgwood (1730-95) became synonymous with a range of finely crafted products which bore the unmistakable imprint of his personal genius. A master of both the aesthetic and scientific aspects of producing style-setting ceramics, Wedgwood was also a virtuoso at marketing. Having established showrooms in London and Dublin, what more natural than to set another one up in Bath? Stock could be supplied from Etruria, the Wedgwood works at Burslem, via the newly-opened Trent and Mersey Canal and Staffordshire and Worcestershire Canal, to Stourport where consignments could be transhipped for onward movement down the Severn to Bristol. Shipments could take up to six weeks but were far cheaper than by road. The management of the new Bath outlet was entrusted to William and Ann Ward, in-laws of Wedgwood's business partner, Thomas Bentley. The first premises were in recently-built Westgate Buildings, a terrace of thirteen units on the then expanding west side of the city. Other occupants of Westgate Buildings included a wine-merchant, next door, and, at No. 2 the painter Solomon Williams, who charged a shilling to people looking for 'an agreeable hour's amusement' in perusing his output of portraits and landscapes. Wedgwood came in person to supervise the fitting out of the showroom, which was officially opened in September 1772.

A PRESTIGIOUS SHOWROOM

The top end of the Wedgwood showroom's trade was geared to the taste of the fashionable and wealthy and was inevitably highly seasonal. Sales to such customers might range from entire dinner services to decorative items like vases, busts and bas-reliefs and giftwares such as cameos, medallions, lockets, bracelets, seals and snuffboxes. The leisured lifestyle of the city was likewise reflected in the sale of inkpots and paintboxes. While many selected from items on display others might order goods, often customised with their coat of arms, to be made at Etruria and shipped direct to their homes in London or the country. A secondary stream of revenue was derived from the sale of humbler, household items such as teapots, basins, dishes, lamps and candlesticks. Decorated flowerpots were also sold in large numbers to bring colour to the city's window-ledges and balconies. Some of these domestic goods might be sold to the less affluent visitors to Bath but in a city of coffee-houses, lodging-houses, inns, there was always a substantial local demand for cups, plates, tureens, mugs, jugs, ewers, washbasins and chamberpots.

Disappointing sales figures induced Wedgwood to relocate the showroom to a more central location with greater potential for a passing trade and in September 1774 the Wards reopened at a prestigious corner site on the corner of Milsom Street and Green Street. Sales increased gratifyingly but in 1779 the showroom moved again to a less prominent but cheaper location at No. 22 Milsom Street, which was further up the road and on the opposite side. In 1792, after twenty years in business the Wards were ready to retire. Their premises were taken over by a Mr Ellen who added glassware and porcelain to the range of stock so that the showroom ceased to be an exclusively Wedgwood outlet. Mr Denner, the Wards' shopman, opened up a rival establishment, initially off Abbey Churchyard and then in Burton Street. In their few remaining years of retirement the Wards doubtless basked in the success of their daughter Ann, who had married a London lawyer and, as 'Mrs Radcliffe' scored a sensational success in 1794 with her 'Gothick' fantasy *The Mysteries of Udolpho* – which Jane Austen would so mercilessly satirise in *Northanger Abbey*.

The Social Round

If building projects fluctuated decade by decade, Bath's well-established social round continued on its measured course of water-drinking, promenading, shopping, gaming, theatre-going and attendance at church, chapel and dances.

The twice weekly formal evening ball at the Assembly Rooms began at six, most men arriving on foot, ladies still coming by sedan chair. Some arrivals paid on the door but most would have taken out a subscription for the season. Heating was provided from four blazing fireplaces, lighting from five chandeliers, each bearing forty candles, and another eighty candles in wall brackets, the illumination multiplied by reflections from mirrors. Three tiers of benches ringed the dance floor. A dozen musicians played from a raised gallery. A regular turn-out ran to five or six hundred people, though not all would dance. Many of the older persons made straight for the card tables in side rooms. Mothers might take to the benches to scan the company for marital prospects for their offspring. From six until eight only minuets were danced. Formal dress was strictly required of all dancers, infringements courting the censure of the Master of Ceremonies and risking the ignominy of ejection. After eight o'clock minuets gave way to country

The Assembly Rooms

dances. At nine there was a break for tea, coffee and light refreshments in the tea-room and an interval of recovery for the musicians. When the company returned to the ballroom the country dances were resumed. The evening ended promptly at eleven. For those who really did like dancing there were also two weekly cotillon or 'fancy' balls, where no minuets were danced. On other evenings the rooms were used for private concerts or parties. During the day they were open for cards and conversation and, in inclement weather, a constitutional stroll.

From the days of Beau Nash the Assembly Rooms had been open to anyone who could afford the entrance fee or subscription, dressed decently and behaved properly. In 1816, doubtless in an attempt to restore a supposedly eroded exclusiveness, the committee of the Upper Rooms decreed that henceforth 'no Clerk, hired or otherwise, in this city or neighbourhood – no person concerned in retail trade – no theatrical nor public performer by profession, shall be admitted.' Doubtless it would have been inconvenient to remember that Bath's first purpose-built Assembly Rooms, Lindsey's, had been promoted as a commercial speculation by Henry Thayer, a London apothecary and that the Upper Rooms themselves had been underwritten by a consortium led by Benjamin Colborne, a Bath apothecary.

JANE AUSTEN'S BATH

Jane Austen's association with Bath has spawned a minor industry. The author, who certainly wrote with an eye to posterity, would doubtless still have been quite taken aback by the extent and fervour of the admiration her works now command. Bath provides a major setting for the action in two of her novels and is referred to in all of them, although by no means always to its advantage. Wickham, in *Pride and Prejudice*, escapes to Bath from an unhappy marriage to waste money he does not have. In *Emma* Philip Elton uses the city as a hunting-ground for a wife. In *Sense and Sensibility* the cad Willoughby seduces Eliza Williams in Bath, leaving her pregnant.

Jane Austen's own five years residence in the city represented a less than happy passage of her life, relieved only by the fact that she spent much of her time not actually being in Bath but on extended excursions to coastal resorts. Indeed, in October 1808 she would write gleefully to her sister Cassandra 'It will be two years tomorrow since we left Bath for Clifton, with what happy feelings of escape.' Perhaps the most telling evidence of her attitude to living in Bath is the fact that so little survives in the way of personal correspondence from her period of residence. This may be either because her normally prolific output was curtailed – for whatever reason – or because her sister Cassandra subsequently culled it to conceal – what? From the whole period of Jane Austen's period of residence in Bath only five letters survive and three of those were businesslike missives dealing with the consequences of her father's death. No letters at all survive for the entire period from June 1801, the month after her arrival, to September 1804.

When Jane Austen arrived to take up permanent residence in Bath she already knew the city well. She first visited the city in 1797 and came again as recently as May 1799 when she had stayed for some weeks at 13 Queen Square with her mother and brother Edward. Her letters record a vacation punctuated with modest indulgences like visits to the Orchard Street theatre, firework displays in Sydney Gardens, dancing at the Assembly balls and taking long country walks out to villages like Charlcombe or Weston.

In December 1800 the Reverend George Austen, Jane's scholarly and supportive father, announced that he was to relinquish his parochial duties and retire to Bath, where Jane's mother had a brother and sister-in-law already established. Unmarried and still entirely dependent on her parents, Jane had no option but to accompany them.

That Jane Austen arrived in Bath with less than positive feelings was quite as much a consequence of what she was leaving behind as of what she was coming to. The Rectory at Steventon in Hampshire had been her home since birth. Vacating it meant parting from a wide circle of friends, neighbours and relatives and abandoning a domestic routine which had allowed her the space and time to follow her vocation as a writer. Like many couples reorganizing their lives for retirement George Austen and his wife combined relocating their place of residence with a degree of down-sizing. The extensive library of books, from which Jane's education had been largely derived, was sold off, as was Jane's own beloved piano. Much familiar furniture was also left behind.

A MINOR SCANDAL

The household to which the Austens were to be initially attached in Bath while they looked for a home of their own to rent was less than congenial for Jane. The Austens had always been pinched for money but their in-laws were wealthy, placing Jane in the despised role of a poor relative. Her aunt, Mrs Leigh-Perrot, was, moreover, a bossy and interfering woman who had but recently become notorious after being accused of purloining lace from Smith's haberdashery on the corner of Bath Street. Accusations, enquiries, an arrest and a subsequent court case stretched the episode over some seven months until it became clear that the staff of the bankrupt business had in fact conspired to set up Mrs Leigh-Perrot by themselves adding in the item in question to a parcel of her purchases with a view to blackmailing her. The value of the lace being above twenty shillings the charge made against Mrs Leigh-Perrot was one of Grand Larceny, which carried the death penalty or at the least a sentence of transportation to a penal colony in Australia. As it turned out after a trial of seven hours the judge's summing up led the jury to vote an acquittal in just fifteen minutes. The relief of vindication was, however, clouded over by continuing publicity in the form of local press coverage and a detailed pamphlet recounting the whole affair, published in April 1800 by the opportunistic Richard Cruttwell, printer of the *Bath Chronicle* and proprietor of a 'Patent Medicine Warehouse' on St James's Street. Jane Austen would have been all too aware that any sort of scandal, even one of which the subject was proved to be wholly innocent, still jeopardised the standing of not only the victim but of anyone associated with them.

As it turned out, the Austens' arrival began quite auspiciously. Although Jane described Bath seen from Kingsdown as 'all vapour, shadow, smoke and confusion', she received a warm welcome at No. 1 The Paragon and was even allocated a room all to herself. Retail therapy – for which Bath was eminently equipped – afforded another source of comfort in the form of a new white straw bonnet and a gown made up to order by a professional dressmaker. A further relief was the discovery that the local prices of provisions were by no means as high as had been feared. At Steventon the Austens had supplied almost all of their own needs but lodgings in Bath did not come with a handy kitchen garden. House-hunting proved dispiriting as a succession of properties was dismissed as too small, too damp or too near the Leigh-Perrots. In the end the Austens were fortunate to secure, at an attractively low rental, a property, 4 Sydney Place (later Terrace), opposite fashionable Sydney Gardens and away from the noise of the city centre. While the house was being redecorated the family repaired to the seaside at Sidmouth where Jane may have encountered an unnamed stranger who seems to have piqued her interest and whom her sister Cassandra considered to be the only man who was ever worthy of her. Unfortunately he was inconsiderate enough to die shortly afterwards, so that particular avenue of escape was closed for ever.

AN OVERNIGHT ENGAGEMENT

Jane, still unmarried at twenty-five, may have hoped that a husband might be found in Bath, a city renowned for matchmaking. It was, moreover, not only a much larger place than her own home village but one whose population of eligible men was constantly renewed by visitors – although admittedly many of these would be either already married or engaged or to be avoided as unscrupulous adventurers, wastrels and idlers. As it turned out Jane's best bet, at least in practical terms, was turned down by Jane herself. In December 1802 an engagement was announced between Jane and the rich and respectable Harris Bigg-Wither. The engagement lasted overnight and the following morning, to general embarrassment, Jane renounced her best prospect of security and motherhood. He was, indeed, younger than her. He did stutter. She had known him for ages. Perhaps she – or both of them – had been egged on by his sisters or Cassandra, who would naturally have been keen to see Jane, a fortnight off twenty-seven, finally 'settled'. Perhaps Jane, so eminently aware in her writing of the relationship between money and matrimony, still hankered for romance or at least a true meeting of minds.

Once the Austen family had finally settled in to their new home Jane could begin writing again. Much of the novel that would eventually be published as *Northanger Abbey* (the working manuscript was entitled *Susan*) is set in Bath and Jane's new situation would enable her to update the draft, begun in 1798, to incorporate any recent changes in the city. Like Jane herself the heroine, Catherine Morland, experiences the necessity of establishing a new routine but as a temporary rather than a permanent resident, – 'Every morning now brought its regular duties, shops to be visited; some new part of town to be looked at; and the Pump Room to be attended, where they paraded up and down for an hour, looking at everybody and speaking to no one.' Catherine and her family live on prestigious Great Pulteney Street while the Thorpe family with whom they become entangled live on George Street. Snobbish, scheming General Tilney has his lodgings on Milsom Street, where the vulgar chatterbox Isabella Thorpe goes shopping.

Like *Northanger Abbey*, *Persuasion*, the other novel to appear posthumously, also drew heavily on Bath for its settings, in some instances reprising the same locations such as the Pump Rooms and the shops on Milsom Street. The Musgrove family patronise the celebrated White Hart Inn, where Catherine and her benefactors, the Allens, initially arrive in Bath. Heroine Anne Elliot's trusted elder confidante, Lady Russell, lodges in Rivers Street, kindly Admiral Croft (see page 155) and his wife on Gay Street. *Persuasion* would, however, be written, in 1815-16, with Bath in grateful retrospect.

Early in 1803 *Susan* was sold to a London publisher for £10. Although he would advertise it as a forthcoming publication it would not in fact be published until 1818, after the author's death. Jane may have begun work on *The Watsons* around 1803, perhaps encouraged by the sale of *Susan*. Initially the action was set in a Sussex coastal resort then switched to Dorking, perhaps an indication of the author's uncertainty of direction. Jane failed to persevere with it and it remained an uncompleted fragment. Echoing the author's own personal situation, *The Watsons*, she subsequently confessed, was too full of 'guilt and misery' for her to finish it.

In 1804 the Austens went to Lyme Regis, returning to 27 (then 3) Green Park Buildings on a six month lease, although the residence had once been dismissed from their consideration as too damp. Christmas was overshadowed by the news – received on Jane's birthday - of the death from a riding accident of her best friend, Anne Lefroy. Just over a month later Jane's father died on 21 January 1805. He was buried in St Swithin's, Walcot in the new church built on the site of the one in which he had been married to Jane's mother. Further reduced in circumstances the surviving members of the Austen family moved to a smaller residence at 25 Gay Street. By now taking tea with friends becomes doubly welcome as it meant their own 'Tea & Sugar will last a great while'. Jane added new sleeves to an old dress but without much conviction that the effort was worth it. After the customary summer break away they took lodgings in down-market Trim Street in cheap, cramped rooms with no 'aspect' to look out on. By the summer they had decided to move on, initially staying in the Bristol resort suburb of Clifton before settling in Southampton for two years. In 1809, thanks to Jane's brother, Edward, who had been taken up by rich relatives, they were finally able to return to rural Hampshire, making Chawton Cottage their permanent home.

Counter-Revolution on Great Pulteney Street

While Jane Austen has become a major icon and a minor industry, the name of Hannah More (1745-1833) is now all but forgotten. But when Jane Austen lived in Bath she was still a literary unknown, while Hannah More took up residence there as an established celebrity. Born on the fringe of Bristol, Hannah More at first followed the family trade of teaching before taking the whole nation as her classroom. Her first literary effort *The Search after Happiness* was a didactic drama for the edification of her pupils, published in Bristol when she was just seventeen. When it was published in London eleven years later it made her a national name, running to twelve editions by 1800. A regular patron of the theatre herself, in 1775 More had the satisfaction of having Garrick stage her drama *The Inflexible Captive* at the Theatre Royal. In the same year she made the first of thirty-five annual visits to the capital, where she became a prominent member of the formidable female circle known as the Bluestockings. Convening in the spacious salons of their leading lights, the Bluestockings eschewed cards, alcohol and politics in favour of tea and serious conversation. Any male admitted to their company could consider himself flattered and it was through them that More became acquainted with Dr Johnson, Edmund Burke and Sir Joshua Reynolds. As early as 1779 Hannah More was being depicted alongside Catherine Macaulay in a group portrait as one of *The Nine Living Muses of Great Britain*.

During the 1780s More became an evangelical and a member of the anti-slavery movement. This brought her the friendship of the slaver-turned-vicar, John Newton, composer of the abolitionist anthem *Amazing Grace*, and of William Wilberforce, leader of the parliamentary campaign for abolition. Moving in such high-minded and influential circles gave her ample material for her next major publication *Thoughts on the Importance of the Manners of the Great to General Society*. Published in 1788, this went through no less than eight editions within two years. The second printing sold out in six days, the third in four hours.

In 1789 Hannah and her sisters moved into No. 76 Great Pulteney Street, where they would remain until 1801. This doubtless proved an estimable vantage-point for More's next pronouncement *An Estimate of the Religion of the Fashionable World*, which would go through five editions. During her residence in Bath More turned her facile pen to a new agenda. From composing tomes for toffs she switched to pamphlets for plebs. The onset of revolutionary republicanism in France traumatised the propertied classes in England with nightmare visions of mobs, massacres and mass-executions in their own green, pleasant and deferential land – tumbrils trundling along Milsom Street? a guillotine in Queen Square? Hannah More set out to provide the embattled stakeholders of the existing order with the intellectual ammunition to controvert the subversive notions of alien, atheist agitators. Her counterblast to Tom Paine's *Rights of Man*, was a dialogue between a mason and a blacksmith, ridiculing Paine's ideas. Published as *Village politics: addressed to all the mechanics, journeymen and day labourers in Great Britain*, it appeared in 1792 under the pseudonym of 'Will Chip, a country carpenter'. Between 1795 and 1798 in collaboration with other writers Hannah More was responsible for the monthly publication of 114 Cheap Repository Tracts, of which she wrote forty-nine herself. Anxious aristocrats and beleaguered bourgeois bought 700,000 within the first four months of their appearance, over two million in their first year, distributing them among their servants, tradesmen and tenants. Perhaps surprisingly the Tracts also sold well in the newly-independent United States and – less surprisingly - were despatched to the slave plantations of the West Indies and the freed slave colony of Sierra Leone. The entire enterprise was masterminded and managed from the More ménage on Great Pulteney Street and later permanently institutionalised in 1799 in the form of The Religious Tract Society.

The social anxiety that Hannah More was addressing manifested itself locally in Bath with the building of Christ Church, Julian Road. Designed by local architect John Palmer (no relation to his namesake) and consecrated in 1798, this was the first instance in England of a free church erected primarily for the families of the labouring poor and members of the servant classes, who were too poor to afford pew rents.

More returned to type in 1799 with the publication of her *Strictures on the Modern system of Female Education* in which she took a swipe at both the sentimentalism of Jean-Jacques Rousseau and the rationalism of proto-feminist Mary Wollstonecraft (1759-97). Claiming the moral high-ground as her accustomed territory, More set out her case that it was the education and conduct of the female portion of a nation's population that would prove decisive in determining its future moral state. After removing from Bath to Wrington in 1801, More continued to bombard the public at intervals with further hefty exhortations in the form of works on *Practical Piety* (1811), *Christian Morals* (1813) and *Moral Sketches* (1819). *Practical Piety* ran through twelve editions in a decade, *Moral Sketches* through seven in a couple of years.

Hannah More finally died at eighty-eight, seriously rich from writings which over the course of more than half a century ran to eleven volumes. She bequeathed some £30,000 to charities and religious societies. A four volume memoir of her life and letters appeared within a year of her passing. Lauded by the Victorians but dismissed by subsequent generations as a sanctimonious, snobbish reactionary, Hannah More nevertheless transcended the constraints of both gender and birth to achieve a degree of cultural authority unprecedented for a middle-class woman of her day. She was buried beside her sisters at All Saints', Wrington.

Living Off Letters

Jane Austen's novels never made her rich and she found life in Bath rather a struggle. Not so the Reverend – and self-styled 'Doctor' – John Trusler (1735-1820), a prolific writer with an eye to the main chance. In 1769 Trusler hit on the idea of sending a circular to every parish priest in England and Ireland offering them three years' supply of weekly sermons printed up to look as though they were handwritten. This proved to be such a profitable wheeze that Trusler was able to set up a highly lucrative printing and bookselling business in London while himself retiring to Bath, where he churned out titles year after year. Trusler was particularly adept at abridging other people's work and produced versions of Captain Cook's account of his explorations, Blackstone's classic commentaries on English law, a chronology of English history and a compendium of the Bible.

His main stock-in-trade however, was catering to the needs of people who lacked his own bumptious certainty and he enjoyed great success with books of etiquette and table manners, a *Compendium of Useful Knowledge* and a treatise on *The Way to be Rich and Respectable*. Trusler's *Practical Husbandry* was subtitled the *Art of Farming, with certainty of gain*; first issued in 1780, it ran to a fifth edition, published in Bath in the year of the author's death. Perhaps Trusler's most characteristic work was *A Sure Way to Lengthen Life*, which also ran to five editions. The author could certainly claim to speak with authority, dying at Villa House, Bathwick in his eighty-fifth year.

Bath Salts

In Jane Austen's *Persuasion* vain, foppish, spendthrift Sir Walter Elliot is obliged by his own ill-management to lease out his ancestral home in order to live more economically in Bath. Elliott looks down on his tenant, the good-hearted Admiral Croft for his bluff manner, simple dress and weatherbeaten looks. The reader is left in little doubt, however, which character has the author's approval. Jane Austen's own brothers were in the Royal Navy and any thinking Briton knew that the navy was the bulwark of the nation's freedom. What Elliot and his ilk despised was the fact that the navy was also the instrument of ambition. While the British army was still organised on principles of aristocratic privilege, the navy offered at least the possibility of a career in which talent mattered more than lineage. Drive, luck and the patronage of a successful senior officer all counted but sheer professionalism was the essential prerequisite. And whereas a life in the military could whittle away a fortune thanks to the pressure to purchase promotion, drink heavily and gamble recklessly, the navy – especially in wartime – offered the possibility of fabulous wealth. Enemy ships taken more or less intact yielded prize money to the officers and crew responsible for their capture. A captain on £200 a year might collect as much as £40,000 – two *centuries* salary ! – sufficient to buy a fine house in London and an estate in the country, to marry off one's daughters, set one's sons up for life and still leave more than enough for a long and honourable retirement – including free-spending visits to Bath. Although Admiral Croft's financial status is not divulged in detail, he can not only take over Sir Walter Elliot's country home but also afford a Bath address which raises him considerably in that supercilious snob's estimation. And, as the Admiral and his wife promenade they are invariably able to pause from time to time to chat with 'a little knot of the navy'.

It was Admiral Sawyer (1731-98) who secured the greatest ever single prize taken at one stroke when in 1762 he took part in the seizure of the Spanish treasure-ship *Hermione* off Cadiz. The luckless captain of the *Hermione*, homeward-bound from Peru, didn't even know that Spain and Britain were at war. Sawyer came away from the encounter with £65,053 13s 9d to his credit. Equally to his credit, rather than opt for an easy life ashore, he chose to serve on for another thirty-three years, until failing health compelled him to retire to Bath, where he died three years later.

Admiral Lord Rodney (1718-92) stayed at 14 Gay Street in 1782 after his victory at the Battle of the Saints, which foiled a Franco-Spanish invasion of Jamaica. For capturing nine ships and the enemy admiral Rodney was rewarded with a pension of £2,000 and a peerage.

Admiral Lord Howe (1726-99), who stayed at Great Pulteney Street in 1794, 1795 and 1798, had, while serving as treasurer of the Navy, entirely – and most unusually – refused to profit from the large sums which passed through his hands. (It was quite normal to lend out cash not immediately required for disbursement and pocket the interest.) Despite the forbidding manner which earned him the nickname of 'Black Dick', Howe won the devotion of his crews. In 1794 at the beginning of the wars against revolutionary France, Howe won the victory off Ushant known as 'the Glorious First of June'. The British took six ships and George III came out to the fleet in person to present Howe with a diamond-hilted sword. As widely respected for his integrity as for his bravery, in March 1797 Howe was, at the personal request of the king, drawn out of a well-earned retirement at Bath to mediate successfully between the Lords of the Admiralty and the leaders of the naval mutiny at Spithead. It was his last service to his country. Plagued, like so many of his contemporaries, by the agonies of gout, Howe, in the absence of his regular physician, consented to a new-fangled treatment – electricity – which killed him stone dead

Howe's near-contemporary and neighbour at 34 Great Pulteney Street was Admiral Alexander Hood (1726-1814), who had served under Howe. Unlike Howe, Hood was an unduly cautious commander who owed his eminence to not making mistakes. He owed his handsome fortune to a handsome countenance and an advantageous marriage. Hood's grandson, Arthur Hood (1824-91) was born in Bath and also attained the rank of admiral.

Admiral Duncan (1731-1804) spent much time in Bath in the 1760s recovering from service in the Caribbean. He returned after the hard-fought battle of Camperdown at which he had smashed the Dutch fleet. Bath was among many British cities which made him an honorary freeman. Between 1796 and 1801 Duncan was several times in residence at 44 Great Pulteney Street.

Although the naval career of Arthur Phillip (1738-1814) was inter-rupted by more than a decade of peaceable retirement as a country gentleman, he was nevertheless entrusted with command of the 'First Fleet' which sailed in 1788 to begin the settlement of Australia as a penal colony. Confounding the reservations of his seniors, Phillip rose to the challenge, heading off more than one near-mutiny, holding the reluctant colonists together through long months of near-starvation, and establishing friendly relations with local aboriginal leaders, despite having been speared by one of them. This triumph was bought at the cost of broken health and Phillip was permitted to retire and take up residence at 19 Bennet Street. His most enduring memorial is, of course, the city of Sydney, which he founded, but he is also memorialised in Bath Abbey and in the church at Bathampton where he is buried. An annual memorial service is held on his birthday, 11 October.

In the junior days of his service Sir Henry Trollope (1756-1839) was a buccanneering commander in the 'Hornblower' mould until gout undermined not only his constitution but his sanity. Retiring to Bath, he became obsessed with an irrational fear of burglars, turned his bedroom into a veritable armoury and one day locked himself in there and blew his brains out.

HORATIO NELSON

Britain's most famous admiral came to Bath not to retire but to recuperate, either physically or mentally. In December 1780 Horatio Nelson (1768-1805) stayed in the house of an apothecary at 2 Pierrepont Street to recover his health after a dramatic but debilitating period in Nicaragua, when yellow fever had virtually wiped out his command. His own left arm was dead white, numb and alarmingly swollen. The prescribed remedy was a demanding regimen which challenged Nelson's fortitude – 'I have been so ill since I have been here that I was obliged to be carried to and from bed with the most excruciating tortures … I am physicked three times a day, drink the waters three times and baths every other night, besides not drinking wine, which I think the worst of all.' By January 1781 he was recovered enough to see a heavily pregnant Mrs Siddons (see page 126) at the Orchard Street theatre. By April he was fit enough to leave.

Nelson came back again on his temporary retirement from active service in 1787, newly married, for a sojourn of several months before retiring to his native Norfolk on half pay for the next four years. In February 1797 Nelson was back in Bath again after his victory at Cape St Vincent. Newly promoted to the rank of admiral, he was given the freedom of the city. His delighted father, who came each year for a restorative cure, wrote that 'the name and services of Nelson have sounded throughout the city of Bath, from the common ballad-singer to the public theatre'; his son was 'universally the subject of conversation'. Nelson came back in September of the same year to recover from the amputation of his right arm after the assault on Tenerife. The wound had not yet healed and he needed drafts of laudanum to sleep. Despite the attentions of a physician, a surgeon and an apothecary, it failed to improve, raising fears of the need for a further amputation. Acknowledging that the expertise of the local medical establishment lay in treating rheumatic, skin and liver diseases, Nelson removed to London for more skilled assistance than Bath could afford.

When, during Nelson's last visit in 1798, he went to the Orchard Street Theatre, the audience rose to hail him with a spontaneous rendition of *Rule, Britannia*. Nelson was posthumously honoured in the naming of Nelson Place, Nelson Villas, Nelson Street and Nile Street.

'Blessed Asylum'

While Bath's old salts could usually rely on a goodly substance to console them as they battled against decrepitude, gout, boredom or the bottle, there was another large class of worthy, ageing persons, with long records of service to others, which, if seldom hazardous, were usually selfless. These were the widows and spinsters who, apart from such vivid exceptions as Jane Eyre, flit as virtual shadows through the pages of nineteenth-century fiction. Frequently through the death of those male relatives who might otherwise have protected them, sometimes as victims of bankruptcy or fraud, such unfortunates, as widows or spinsters, were reduced to the category of 'distressed gentlewomen'. Thanks to the careful researches of local historian Elizabeth White the story of a rare but successful venture to aid such genteel victims of circumstance has been skilfully recovered.

Despite its name Partis College is not an educational institution. Standing discreetly back from the Newbridge Road in Weston, some two miles from Bath's city centre, it was founded by Mrs Anna Partis (1758-1846) in memory of her lawyer husband, with whom she had initially begun the venture. A wealthy but childless widow, Mrs Partis lived simply herself, without male servants or even a carriage. Her 'blessed asylum' would absorb some £70,000 of her fortune in building costs, salaries and endowments; she also gave away at least £26,000 to other good causes.

Built between 1820 and 1824, Partis College, now a Grade I listed building, consisted of three blocks of houses, facing onto a common green but with separate, individual garden plots behind each residence. The first intake of residents was admitted in 1825, although the institution was not formally opened until 1826. Governance was invested in a board of trustees, all male, which initially included a lord, four baronets, a knight and two clergymen. Mrs Partis until her death screened applicants personally. Most were recommended by friends or friends of friends, their applications supported by written testimonials of character and circumstances – in one case sixty letters of recommendation. Most applicants had been governesses, teachers, companions, in some sort of medical or domestic occupation or engaged in missionary work. Two-thirds were turned down. Ten houses were set aside for female dependents of Anglican clergy, ten for those of professional men and officers in the armed services and ten for those of mercantile occupations. The rules of the institution were few, simple, straightforward and humane. Applicants had to be aged fifty or more, committed members of the Church of England and possessed of an income of £20 to £30 per year. If accepted, they would receive a pension of £30 a year, a house, rent free, which they were required to furnish themselves, and a maid, whom they would pay. Apart from attendance at chapel and a ten o'clock curfew residents were free to come and go as they pleased. They could have friends stay with them and go away on holiday for up to two months a year. The usual humiliations to remind recipients of alms of their dependent status – communal meals and uniforms – were conspicuous by their absence. Pets were not allowed. Inmates who became so frail that they required constant attendance were compelled to return to relatives but kept their pension. One lived at the College for over forty years, several passed the thirty year mark; the average tenure was seventeen years.

Looking the Part

Over a hundred and fifty artists worked in Bath in the eighteenth century, more than in any other British city outside London. A few, like Charles Jagger (*ca*.1770-1827), were locally born. The Barkers and the Hoares were to establish local artistic dynasties. Several more came from the surrounding region - Samuel Collins (?1735-68) from Bristol, miniaturist Joseph Daniell (*ca*.1760-1803) from Bridgewater, Ozias Humphrey (1742-1810) from Devon and Jonathan Spilsbury (1737-1812) from Worcester. Others, like Thomas Worlidge (1700-66) and Charles Gill (?1742-*ca*.1828), divided their time between Bath and London. Thomas Beach (1738-1806), like Gill a pupil of Sir Joshua Reynolds, based himself in Bath during the winter and spent summers touring the West Country to paint clients in their country houses. The Flemish portraitist Adriaen Carpentiers (fl.1739-78) made Bath one of several stopping-places on his annual itinerary. A few artists, like Thomas Gainsborough (1727-88) and Sir Thomas Lawrence (1769-1830), were to use the city as the launch-pad for careers that took them to the forefront of the nation's artistic life. Samuel Collins, by contrast, fled from Bath to Dublin to escape scandal and debt. Robert Edge Pine (*ca*.1730-88), after seven successful years in Bath, emigrated to newly-independent America, where he painted George Washington and established a flourishing portrait practice in Philadelphia. James Sharples (*ca*.1751-1811), who also numbered Washington among his sitters, settled in New York. Ozias Humphrey (1742-1810) and Thomas Hickey (1741-1824), inspired by the tales of retired India merchants and soldiers, tried their luck out East.

Whatever the precise pattern of their careers, artists came to Bath from all over Europe to take advantage of the buoyant local demand for art. The accomplished sculptor Giuseppe Plura (fl.1749-56) came from Italy, Elias Martin (1739-1818) from Sweden, his pupil Jacob Spornberg (fl.1768-ca.1840), who specialized in profiles, from Finland, the enamellist Christian Friedrich Zinke (1683-1767) from Dresden and Andreas Mussard (fl.1724-65), who specialized in painting children, from Geneva. Charles Christian Rosenberg (1745-1844), an Austrian, who became known as 'Rosenberg of Bath', advertised that he could knock out a 'likeness' after 'a sitting of one minute only', on a price range extending from 7/6 to a guinea, and also, for a shilling a season, allowed clients to use his facilities for checking changes in their weight and height. Finally the city also had its own coterie of talented amateurs.

Despite the plethora of artistic talent resident in the city, some of the best known, and best, views of the city itself were produced by Thomas Malton the Younger (1748-1802), a London-based draughtsman who stayed only briefly in Bath in 1780. A pioneer of the aquatint process, Malton excelled in depicting architectural and topographical views with the greatest accuracy. In later life he taught perspective drawing to such rising talents as Girtin and Turner.

In 1784 the famed landscape architect Humphrey Repton (1752-1818) produced a lively depiction, in pencil, ink and watercolour, of *Taking the Waters at the Pump Room, Bath*, now in the Victoria Art Gallery. The London caricaturist Thomas Rowlandson (1756-1827) gently satirised the spa's social round in a celebrated print series, *Comforts of Bath* (1798), with more emphasis on the grotesque than the gracious.

To gain the best access to their potential market artists tended to establish themselves near the Pump Rooms or the Abbey. Gainsborough's first house was immediately opposite the south-west door of the Abbey. Robert Edge Pine and François-Germain Aliamet were near neighbours in Hetling Court. Just round the corner Joseph Hutchison (1747-1830) and Thomas Beach lived at No.1 and No. 2 Westgate Buildings respectively. Other artists settled on the more fashionable thoroughfares. Joseph Wright of Derby (1734-97), one of the few major talents to fail in Bath, stuck it out for two fruitless years on expensive Brock Street, between the Circus and the Crescent. Although he charged only a third of the rate demanded by Gainsborough, Wright lacked his rival's easy manner and was judged old-fashioned in style.

Bridge Street and Trim Street, both running east-west, afforded painters the crucial north light required for their painting-rooms but at lower rents than were required on Alfred Street, where Thomas Lawrence started out, or at Edgar Buildings, where William Hoare (1707-92) established himself. George Roth, James Hewlett (1768-1836), William Hibbart (1727-1808), Peter Ogier (fl.1793-1800) and Thomas Walmsley (1763-1806) were all located along Bridge Street in the last two decades of the eighteenth century. Trim Street was home to Elias Martin, Solomon Williams (1757-1824) and the Irish sculptor Lawrence Gahagan (1756-1820). Once firmly established, artists could, like Gainsborough, move up-market and uphill.

The Hoares

Born in Suffolk and trained in London, William Hoare (1707-92) spent nine years studying in Italy, where he shared lodgings with the eminent sculptor Peter Scheemakers (1691-1781) and was a fellow pupil of the Venetian portraitist Pompeo Batoni (1708-87), who remained a lifelong friend. Hoare also made lasting friendships with several aristocratic young 'Grand Tourists' who would later become influential patrons. Failing to find success on his return to London, in 1738 Hoare settled in Bath. The newcomer soon won the important local endorsement of Ralph Allen (see page 103), becoming an habitué of the Prior Park circle where, undetected, he once made a furtive but full-length pencil sketch of the stunted and deformed poet Alexander Pope. Almost inevitably Hoare also made portraits of Allen, Christopher Anstey, Beau Nash and Nash's successor as Master of Ceremonies, Samuel Derrick. By 1742 Hoare had so far established himself as to paint a joint portrait of two of the city's most eminent medical practitioners, Dr William Oliver and Dr Jeremy Peirce, in the supposed process of examining three patients, a man, a woman and a boy, each exhibiting symptoms of one of the diseases which the Bath Hospital specialised in treating – paralysis, rheumatism and skin afflictions. Two of the patients are shown wearing the brass badges which gave free admission to the baths. On the wall in the background hangs an elevation and plan of the Hospital, which is where the picture, Hoare's gift, still hangs. Almost forty years later Hoare would paint and likewise donate a memorial portrait of the Hospital's late Treasurer, Bristol banker Daniel Danvers. He also gave works to the Guildhall and an altarpiece, *The Pool of Bethesda*, to the Octagon Chapel (see page 121). This may have been inspired by Hogarth's mural of the same theme at St Bartholomew's Hospital in London. Like Hogarth, Hoare combined charitable impulses with skilful self-promotion; like Hogarth he was also a governor of London's Foundling Hospital. William Hoare's social acceptance in Bath as a gentleman, as well as an artist of talent, was signalled by his election to the posts of Hospital Governor and Visitor. Hoare's standing outside Bath is attested by his election, at the special request of George III himself, as one of the forty founding members of the Royal Academy. Hoare accumulated a goodly income from painting politicians while they were visiting Bath to take the waters, most notably William Pitt the Elder and members of the Pelham family. He also painted many portraits for the Hoare banking family (no relation) which can be seen at Stourhead. Hoare's self-portrait in oils is in the Victoria Art Gallery. In 1828, long after Hoare's death, Sir Francis Chantrey (1781-1841) sculpted a wall-monument with portrait medallion of Hoare for Bath Abbey. Another monument is in the church at Walcot where he is buried.

'A tall, handsome and agreeable person, somewhat skilled in music,' Prince Hoare (1711-69), William Hoare's younger brother, studied sculpture with Scheemakers before settling in Bath around 1740. His most prestigious commissions were portrait busts of local worthies, like Ralph Allen, or distinguished visitors, like the fourth Earl of Chesterfield. Between 1742 and 1747 Hoare toured Italy, perfecting the art of copying from the antique. Returning to Bath, he made a marriage which gave him such a good income that his professional career became little better than dilettantism. The best known of his later commissions was the statue of Beau Nash which can still be seen in the Pump Room. At his death Prince Hoare left the contents of his studio to William's son, who had also been named Prince in compliment to him.

Thomas Gainsborough

Born in Sudbury, Suffolk, Thomas Gainsborough (1727-88) trained in London at the St Martin's Lane Academy and initially established a studio in Hatton Garden but, having married and started a family, returned to East Anglia, settling in Ipswich, where he built up a portrait practice among the gentry. The fact that Gainsborough's wife was the illegitimate daughter, but only child, of the fabulously wealthy third Duke of Beaufort implied, however, that the artist was unlikely to remain content with provincial obscurity.

By the autumn of 1758 Gainsborough had become established enough for his arrival in Bath to be noticed in the *Bath Advertizer*. Staying for six months to test the market, Gainsborough was sufficiently encouraged to bring his family to settle permanently in the city, taking a seven year lease on a house in Abbey Street in 1760. It was a large property, big enough to house not only his wife and two daughters, but also to provide both a studio and a show room with a blank wall over twenty feet long, rooms for taking in lodgers and another, opposite the exhibition room, where his sister, Mary Gibbons (1713-90) opened a shop selling millinery and perfumes. Eventually no less than ten members of Gainsborough's extensive family would follow him to Bath to gain their livelihoods as lodging-house keepers and milliners, indirectly capitalising on his standing and connections.

Bath was to suit Gainsborough very well for over a decade, as he prospered so much from what he himself called 'picking pockets in the portrait way' that his house was nicknamed 'Gain's borough'. Unlike many of his contemporary competitors he never found it necessary to advertise his services in the local press. Apart from affording him a steady flow of well-heeled clients, Bath also offered Gainsborough the companionship of other artists, had a number of good print dealers and afforded access to several remarkably fine collections of paintings, as at Stourhead and Corsham and, most notably, the Van Dycks at Wilton House, near Salisbury. As an advertisement of his own virtuosity Gainsborough produced a reduced size copy of Van Dyck's famous *Pembroke Family* at Wilton to hang in his own exhibition rooms, knowing that many visitors would have seen the original.

In 1761 Gainsborough sent his portrait of Robert Craggs Nugent,

MP for Bristol, (now on loan to the Holburne Museum) to the second exhibition organised by the Society of Artists in London. Other important subjects painted by Gainsborough included his patron Sir William St Quintin, the retired Shakespearean actor James Quin (see page 131) and Georgiana, the future Duchess of Devonshire. Indeed, demand for Gainsborough's attention drove him to overwork (and excessive drinking) which became life-threatening in 1763, when he took to his bed for five weeks with a 'most terrible fever' and the *Bath Journal* even announced his death. The shock appears to have made him take stock of his life and re-order his priorities, both professional and personal. In 1767 he took out a second lease on his 'House in the Smoake' to retain it as a studio and 'shew' room while his enterprising sister took over the rest as a lodging house. Gainsborough himself removed with his family to a newly-built house, No. 17 Royal Circus in 1768. He could well afford to. As keenly oriented to the market as his sister, Gainsborough had been able, over the course of the decade since his fishing expedition of 1758-9, to raise his price for a head from five guineas to twenty and the charge for a half-length portrait from eight guineas to forty.

In the same year as Gainsborough moved to the Royal Circus he became one of the forty founding members of the Royal Academy, established in London under the presidency of Sir Joshua Reynolds. Perhaps an equal accolade was the fact that Gainsborough was also, like Hoare, one of the few who did not reside permanently in the metropolis. By 1771 Gainsborough was charging thirty guineas for a head, sixty for a half-length and a hundred guineas for a full-length portrait. In the same year, his dashing depiction of the Master of Ceremonies of the Upper Rooms, Captain William Wade, painted for the Royal Academy's Summer Exhibition, was presented by the artist to the Assembly Rooms, where it can still be seen. Eventually, however, the pull of the capital proved too strong and in 1774 Gainsborough removed from Bath to a home on Pall Mall.

Thomas Lawrence

Five years after Gainsborough left Bath, his eventual successor as Britain's favourite portraitist arrived. Thomas Lawrence (1769-1830) was born in Bristol but at the age of four his family had moved to Devizes, where his father kept the Black Bear inn. Lawrence's childish good looks and precocious talent for drawing soon attracted the attention of prestigious passengers passing through the thriving Wiltshire market town en route to Bath. Fanny Burney wrote to a friend about the 'most lovely boy of ten ... not merely the wonder of the family but of the times for his astonishing skill in drawing.' Sir Joshua Reynolds confirmed the child's genius. David Garrick opined that Lawrence would one day have to choose between painting and the stage. Although Lawrence's parents were understandably proud of his talents and promise and eager to thrust him forward, they neglected his schooling and, considering that they were themselves in business, singularly failed to train him how to handle money or to organise the routines of daily domestic life. Lawrence, one might say, was polished, rather than educated.

In 1779 Lawrence's father went bankrupt. Henceforth the boy would be the family's main support. Initially Lawrence senior had the idea of taking his little prodigy on tour, like a sort of Mozart with a sketch-pad rather than a piano, but, after a trial run in Oxford, opted instead to settle at No. 4 Alfred Street, Bath. By the age of fourteen Thomas Lawrence was able to charge three guineas for a half length portrait in pastel, which was, according to his earliest biographer, 'at that time and for Bath a very extraordinary sum'. Pastel was an ideal medium for a young man of slender means working under pressure. In skilled hands it could yield impressive results quickly but did not require the artist to have a studio. Instead he could work wherever people were likely to gather, which was in itself a simple but effective mode of direct marketing. As pastel, unlike oils, required no time to dry out, both client and onlookers could be gratified by seeing a finished product in a matter of minutes.

Bath proved to be far more important than simply an economic lifeline for the Lawrence family, providing the young artist with the sort of social contacts and cultural stimulation that could never have been found in Devizes. Lawrence was taken into the family circle of the scholarly physician Dr William Falconer and became a good friend of Prince Hoare. At the Theatre Royal Lawrence was aroused by the great Mrs Siddons (see page 126) with whose daughters he would later become romantically entangled. Patrons and admirers were pleased to allow him to browse in their collections of prints and engravings, igniting the ambition to become a collector himself

Thomas Lawrence left Bath in 1787 to attend the Royal Academy Schools in London where he soon proved so far in advance of his contemporaries that he dropped out having, within two years of quitting Bath, been bidden to Windsor to paint the Royal Family. Elected a full Academician at the earliest permitted age, Lawrence would go on to receive a knighthood, the Legion d'Honneur, the Presidency of the Royal Academy and burial in St Paul's Cathedral. Suave, reserved, hardworking, kindly and gracious, Sir Thomas Lawrence would prove as hopeless with money as his father had been and would die deeply in debt. A fellow artist, Benjamin Haydon, epitomised Lawrence knowingly in his diary – 'his manner was elegant but not high bred … He had smiled so often and so long that at last his smile wore the appearance of being set in enamel.'

The Barkers

Benjamin Barker of Pontypool, a painter of animals and decorator of japanned goods, brought his family to settle in Bath in 1783. The talents of his eldest son Thomas Barker (1767-1847) soon attracted the attention of William Hoare and won the patronage of the wealthy coach-builder Charles Spackman (1749-1822), who paid for the young Thomas to spend four years in Rome. After briefly trying his hand in London, Barker returned to Bath and remained in the city for the rest of his life. On Sion Hill the London architect J.M. Gandy (1771-1843) designed Doric House for Barker, including a thirty foot gallery for showing the artist's work. In 1803, the year of his marriage, Barker contributed to the first set of lithographs ever to be published in Britain. In 1813 he produced his own series of forty *Rustic Scenes*, which were printed by D.J. Redman of Bath. Barker was almost certainly also responsible for the landscape illustrations in Henry Bankes's *Lithography, or, The Art of Making Drawings on Stone*, published by Redman that same year as the first ever British treatise on the art. In 1814 painter and printer again collaborated on thirty-two lithographs of *Landscape Scenery*.

Although Barker did paint portraits and occasional 'scriptural subjects', he became best known for landscapes and more particularly bucolic scenes featuring gypsies, shepherds etc. 'The Woodman', in an engraved version by the celebrated Bartolozzi became widely popular. Barker scenes were reproduced on Staffordshire pottery, Worcester china, Manchester cottons and Glasgow linens, but the artist never attempted to claim any copyright. He nevertheless accumulated a considerable fortune and was able in late middle age to indulge in large-scale personal projects. One was a massive fresco on a wall of his gallery depicting *The Massacre of the Inhabitants of Chios by the Turks*, an implicit endorsement of the then current struggle of the Greeks for independence from Ottoman rule. Another was a depiction of a scandalous contemporary event *The Trial of Queen Caroline* (on a charge of alleged adultery) in which Barker was able to include numerous portraits of eminent men of the day, enabling viewers of the picture to play celebrity I-Spy. These ventures however failed to revive Barker's career and although he retained imposing Doric House until his death, he departed this life surrounded by pawnbrokers' tickets. Apparently undeterred, all four of Barker's sons became artists.

Walter Sickert

Born in Germany of Danish-English-Irish ancestry, Walter Sickert (1860-1942)was a protégé of Whistler, a friend of Degas and, briefly, Sir Winston Churchill's tutor in painting, notwithstanding his own pronouncement that 'any fool can paint, drawing is the thing'. Endlessly restless, Sickert lived variously in Dieppe, Venice, Kent and Camden Town and spent the summers of 1917 and 1918 in Bath. In 1938 he moved into St George's Hill House at Bathampton and devoted his last years to painting views of his garden and the city of Bath. Pulteney Bridge was a favourite subject. Sickert gave his last public lectures at Bath School of Art in 1939. Examples of his work can be seen in the Victoria Art Gallery. Sickert's work can also be seen in more than two dozen galleries in seven countries. At his death in 1942 his worldly wealth was reckoned at £145. His pictures nowadays sell for tens of thousands. Sickert is buried at Bathampton. Although he did once paint a series of pictures inspired by the 'Jack the Ripper' murders the suggestion that Sickert actually was the Ripper is a ludicrous fantasy.

Bath School of Art

Bath School of Art was founded in 1852 as one of seventeen provincial establishments set up after the Great Exhibition of 1851. Bombed out in 1942, it relocated in 1946 to Corsham where it was known as the Bath Academy of Art. Until 1966 the institution was headed by Clifford and Rosemary Ellis, who were prolific designers of bookjackets. They attracted such talents as Terry Frost, Claus Oldenburg and Jim Dine. In 1972 the institution returned to Bath and is now part of Bath Spa University.

Dressing the Part

'a round, plump, coarse-looking dame ... all her aim is to appear an elegant woman of fashion, all her success is to seem an ordinary woman ... with fine clothes on.' Fanny Burney of Lady Anna Miller

As a resort of the fashionable Bath was necessarily a centre of fashion. The giant canvas of George Byam and his wife Louisa, which can now be seen in the Holburne Museum, was first painted by Thomas Gainsborough *ca.* 1762. Three or four years later the Byams arranged for the artist to repaint their portrait to include their new daughter, Selina. Fashion had moved on in the intervening period, so both adults were repainted in different clothes.

Specialist Suppliers

By the eighteenth century Bath had abandoned large-scale cloth production in favour of satisfying the demand for individualised consumption. The Bath historian Richard Warner noted in 1801 that 'The clothing manufacture for which the city was once famous is extinguished ... the baubles of fashion form at present the most considerable articles of trade.' This view was endorsed a decade later by a French visitor Louis Simond – 'Half of the inhabitants do nothing, the other half supply them with nothings – a multitude of splendid shops, full of all that wealth and luxury can desire, arranged with all the arts of seduction.'

Convention required persons of gentle status to wear different clothes for mornings, afternoons and evenings, as well as specific dress for travelling, riding, dancing or mourning. When the heroine of *Northanger Abbey* arrives in Bath she devotes her first few days of residence to 'learning what was mostly worn' before daring to appear in public. Maintaining visitors, residents and the servants of both to an appropriate sartorial standard was a major source of occupation, giving employment not only to shopkeepers, hairdressers, shoe-menders and their assistants but also to a wide range of specialised garment makers and providers of expert services, such as the cleaning of furs and feathers, the dyeing of silks or the outfitting of funerals. These trades in turn provided a market for local makers of pins, brushes, baskets and baggage.

Many fashion retailers boasted of royal, metropolitan or foreign connections. In the late eighteenth century the milliner Mrs Goldsmith claimed to be from London's Old Bond Street, as did Riviere the jeweller's of Milsom Street. Edward Rain was a 'French and Italian shoemaker', Mr F.Albrecht a 'French staymaker'.

Advertisements in the *Bath Chronicle* make it clear that in the pre-railway days much business could be generated by importing London goods in bulk – as in a consignment of a hundred dozen kid gloves; or by offering imitations of the latest Parisian modes – 'La Redincote a l'Indienne' or 'La Robe a la Tippo Sahib'; or novelty items like the 'elastic wig', the 'Circassian vest' for improved posture or 'shamoy' (chamois) leather socks 'for prevention of chilblains'.

Individuals in the fashion trades often worked from their own homes and tended to be highly specialised. They were often willing to travel to clients, like Mr Marsh, the staymaker who was 'happy to wait on ladies not more than twenty miles from Bath'. Some shops specialised in a specific category of fashion item, as in the Bengal Warehouse. Most establishments, however, tended to carry a range of allied products. Cameron's of Milsom Street, a ladies' hairdressing salon, also dealt in perfumery, feathers and flowers, all adjuncts to the elaborate coiffeurs of the late eighteenth century.

Purveyors of fashionable clothing often sold accessories such as umbrellas, canes, whips and spurs and, most notably, an extensive selection of exotically-named products allegedly beneficial to health or beauty – 'Alfred's Excellent Composition' for removing superfluous hair from the face and arms, 'Royal Prussian Paste' 'to prevent skin being chapped, pimpled, sunburnt, freckled etc.', 'G. Steart's Vegetable Liquid' hair tonic and 'Donna Maria's Beautifier and Restorer of Relaxed Bosoms'. A whole range of products was marketed under the soubriquet of 'Lady Molyneux', including a 'dentifrice tooth powder'

Riding and Walking Dress, 1799

and an 'Italian paste' for whitening skin, both obtainable from Richard Cruttwell, the printer of the *Bath Chronicle*.

In Business – and Out of It

Shops catering to the *fashionistas* of Georgian Bath clustered on Milsom, Stall, Gay, George, Bath and Bond Streets, North Parade and Wade's Passage. No. 3 Milsom Street, opposite the ultra-fashionable Octagon chapel (see page 120), appears to have been a specially favoured site. In 1780 a Mr Taylor sold petticoats there; by 1782 the occupant, Bally, was selling hats, hosiery and haberdashery. He was followed by Charles Abbott, who added lace and gloves to the mix. By

1788 he had been superseded by a Mr Green. In 1793 Abbott was back. In 1794 Green was once again the proprietor. Fashion and fortune, in other words, often proved short-lived partners. The columns of the *Bath Chronicle* were replete with announcements of businesses moving or closing as a result of the death of a partner, the dissolution of a partnership, the foreclosure of a lease or a simple lack of demand.

In 1770 James and Peter Ferry of Gallaway's Buildings were obliged to organise a 'closing-down sale of silks at a quarter cheaper than anywhere else in England'. Another sale of silks, by William Smith & Co. in 1787 was allegedly occasioned by their 'quitting Bath latter end of April. Their engagement in London will not admit a longer stay'. Milliners Dorest and Vasey of 5 Churchyard folded in 1789 – 'because of declining business all goods to be sold at prices below cost'. In 1792 donations were requested 'for a poor widow who supported herself in embroidery business, now out of fashion …'.

Top and Bottom

While the top end of the market was the province of attentive specialists with fancy names, the lower end was catered for by suppliers geared to kitting out the city's vast army of footmen and maids, hence the existence of a Ready Made Dress Warehouse, Cheap Lace Warehouse and Cheap Hat Warehouse, Samuel Slack's busy Bath Street business in 'cheap India muslins' and Thomas Harding's offer of 'fine hats and stout livery for servants, warranted to keep out the cold'.

Bath's nineteenth-century decline as a centre of fashionable resort was not matched by any decline as a centre of fashion. An observer noted approvingly in 1887 that: 'The shops of Bath are a revelation to the stranger and give token of the fact that Bath is still the centre of fashion and luxury not only to the fashionable visitors but to the whole of the West of England. Kings of Milsom Street would do credit to the Rue de Rivoli or Regent Street for sustained splendour and gorgeous raiment.'

Jolly Good Company

Jolly's was destined to become not so much a shop as an institution in Bath. It began in 1823 as a 'seasonal branch' of Jolly's Bazaar of

Margate. Proprietor James Jolly soon re-established the venture as a 'Parisian depot' in New Bond Street and then in 1831 re-opened in new premises in Milsom Street, under the management of his son, Thomas (1801-89). Promising 'Economy, fashion and variety', Jolly & Sons traded on a strictly cash only basis and refused to offer discounts. This proved no barrier to success and the shop was extended in 1834, complete with the sort of imposing plate-glass frontage which was still a novelty in London. Thomas travelled regularly to Paris and the great silk-producing city of Lyons to buy stock. By 1851 Jolly's was employing no less than sixteen male staff and forty-two female assistants. In 1852 Thomas, who still had the original Margate business, opened another branch at College Green, Bristol. Thomas Jolly went on to serve twice as mayor of Bath and to remain on the council until his eighties. His son William Cracknell Jolly (1828-1904) would serve as mayor in 1894. W.C. Jolly maintained the firm's strong links with the French silk industry and extended the imported stock to include Belgian lace and Irish linens. He also enlarged the main store in 1879, refurbished it again in 1888 and by the 1890s had established a profitable mail order business with some 14,000 postal customers. There was also an agency in Bombay to serve the needs of the memsahibs of the British Raj. The Jolly family continued to maintain a major interest in the business into the twentieth century, when the store was awarded a royal warrant by the formidably imperious Queen Mary, consort of George V. Jolly's was acquired by Dingle's of Plymouth in 1965 and subsequently became part of the House of Fraser, although still trading under its original name.

Hidden History

By the mid-eighteenth century about a third of all the apprentices serving their indentures in Bath were involved in the clothing and shoemaking trades. Bath may not have had multi-storey factories to draw attention to its manufacturing but in 1831 it had over five hundred adult males employed in making shoes and boots, plus three hundred and fifty in tailoring. A substantial percentage of the almost three thousand employed in retailing would also have been in clothing-related businesses.

Mechanisation would reduce the number in tailoring from a peak of 453 in 1841 to 308 by 1901, in shoe-making from 605 to 202. These declining figures for male employment were offset by increases in the female labour force. In 1831 some 10 per cent of the city's female workforce was employed in making cloth or clothing, by 1901 the figure was just under 17 per cent. Between 1841 and 1901 the number of staymakers rose from 75 to 233, despite the fact that from the 1870s onwards large-scale factory production was established by Bayers, down by the river and Drew, Son & Company with premises in Gascoyne Place and Trim Street. By 1911 textiles and dress-making employed over 2,000 women in Bath, including 859 as dressmakers, 255 as staymakers, 232 as milliners, 223 as tailoresses and 117 as shirt-makers or seamstresses. In 1921 Bath's combined male and female labour force in the textiles and dress sector was just over 2,500; by 1931 it was under 2,000, by the 1970s, down to 800.

Heritage of Style

Given this history, both of consumption and production, it is entirely fitting(!) that Bath should have become home to an outstanding museum devoted to the history of dress. Bath's Fashion Museum was the creation of the remarkable Doris Langley Moore (1902-89). Born in Liverpool and educated at convent schools in South Africa, she became one of the world's leading authorities on Lord Byron and managed to acquire the Albanian chieftain's costume he wore in Thomas Phillips iconic portrait of 1814. Doris Moore's first publication was a translation of twenty-nine Greek odes; others included romantic novels, handbooks of household management and pioneering studies in the history of fashion. She also devised a ballet, based on Spenser's *Faerie Queene*, which gave Moira Shearer her first role and for which William Walton supplied the music and Robert Helpmann the chore-ography. A compulsive shopaholic with a particular weakness for hats, Doris Moore established what was originally called the Museum of Costume, based on her own collection. Initially housed in Kent, then in Brighton, it moved to Bath in 1963 and is housed in the basement of the Assembly Room in Bennett Street. (See www.fashionmuseum. co.uk for details of opening hours and admission charges)

CHAPTER EIGHT

Afterglow – Victorian Bath

1837 – 1901

For Bath the long reign of Victoria (1837-1901) represented an era of continued growth but relative decline. The city remained a favoured location for retirement. The American Nathaniel Hawthorne, who usually wrote affectionately of the England he characterized as *Our Old Home* (1863), was brusquely dismissive of Bath as 'the great metropolis of that second-class gentility with which watering-places are chiefly populated.' The poet Swinburne was kinder, but even his wistful *Ballad of Bath* evokes a sleeping city 'like a queen enchanted who may not laugh or weep … guarded from change and care':

> City lulled asleep by the chime of passing years
> Sweeter smiles thy rest than the radiance round thy peers;
> Only love and lovely remembrance here have place
> Time on thee lies lighter than music on men's ears;
> Dawn and noon and sunset are one before thy face.

Advances in medicine offered alternative therapies to 'taking the waters' and popular belief attributed great virtues to the novelty of taking 'sea air'. The advent of the railway stimulated the growth of new industries and occupations in Bath and brought new types of visitor to the city. But railways also boosted the growth of rival resorts like Brighton, Bournemouth and Eastbourne. In the face of such novel challenges Bath sought both to revitalize its therapeutic facilities and to capitalize on the heritage appeal of its literary associations and its architecture.

Pickwick's Bath

Charles Dickens' *The Posthumous Papers of the Pickwick Club* was published in instalments in 1836-7. Chapters 35-37 give an account of Mr Pickwick's sojourn in Bath. Pickwick and his party of four depart from the White Horse Cellar on Piccadilly by coach at 7.30 a.m. The coach, to the astonishment of Mr Pickwick's valet, Sam Weller, has the name Pickwick painted on the side. (Dickens had, in fact, appropriated the name of his eponymous hero from one Moses Pickwick, the Bath-based proprietor of an extensive network of coach-lines.) The Pickwickians' travelling companions are a Mr and Mrs Dowler. Dowler is an apparently fierce ex-army officer who undertakes to introduce the innocents to the niceties of life in Bath. Putting up at the White Hart, opposite the Pump Room, Mr Pickwick and his party are introduced by Mr Dowler to 'a charming young man of not much more than fifty', sporting gold accoutrements in the form of an eye-glass, snuff-box, rings, tiepin, watch, watch-chain and seals and a gold-topped cane, the whole complemented by shiny buttons, highly-polished boots, the stiffest linen, 'a wig of the glossiest, blackest and curliest' and teeth 'in such perfect order that it was difficult at a small distance to tell the real

Gurney's Steam Coach, London to Bath, *c.* 1835

from the false.' Such was the appearance of Bath's supposedly current Master of Ceremonies – Angelo Cyrus Bantam of Queen Square, who welcomes them effusively to 'Ba-ath'. Bantam invites Dowler to see that Pickwick and his friends sign the register of distinguished visitors which will be opened in the Pump Room at 2.00 p.m. He also informs them that there will be a ball that evening and emphasizes that 'The ball nights in Ba-ath are moments snatched from Paradise; rendered bewitching by music, beauty, elegance, fashion, etiquette and – and – above all, by the absence of tradespeople, who are quite inconsistent with Paradise…'. When, that evening, Mr Pickwick innocently refers to the Dowager Lady Snuphanuph as a fat, old lady Bantam reproves him with the declaration that 'nobody's fat or old in Ba-ath'. In the event Mr Pickwick's evening turns into a social disaster when Bantam ushers him into a game of cards with the Dowager and two other ladies and Pickwick proves quite unequal to the concentrated ferocity of their play.

Having decided to stay in Bath for two months the Pickwick party join forces with the Dowlers to take the upper half of a house in Royal Crescent. Here Pickwick happens on a fantastical written re-working of 'The True Legend of Prince Bladud', which explains the origins of the local hot spring as the perpetual upwelling of Bladud's tears after the pagan gods capriciously granted his wish to stay in Bath forever and buried him underground. Sam Weller takes the waters but once, disliking what he calls 'their wery strong flavour o' warm flat-irons.' He also spends an evening with 'the select footmen of Bath', demolishing 'a boiled leg of mutton with the usual trimmings'. In the course of this he encounters a Mr Whiffers who has, on singular occasions lowered himself by consenting to eat salted butter and consenting to carry a coal scuttle up to the second floor but when faced with a meal of cold meat, resigns his well-paid position in disgust. Meanwhile a farcical incident in the early hours of the morning involving Mr Winkle, a sedan chair and Mrs Dowler, results in rousing Mr Dowler to such ire that Mr Winkle, fearing a duel, flees to Bristol, 'which struck him as being a shade more dirty than any place he had ever seen.' Dowler is soon revealed as an abject coward and Mr Winkle acquires an amorous involvement which brings Pickwick over to Bristol, at which point Dickens loses interest in Bath and, noting that the rest of their stay there 'passed over without the occurrence of anything material' has the whole party return to London forthwith.

Dickens himself first came to Bath in 1835 as a young reporter for the *Morning Chronicle*; and stayed at the Saracen's Head in Broad Street. In 1840 he spent three days with the writer Walter Savage Landor (see page 190). During this stay the novelist found the original of the malicious Quilp in 'a frightful little dwarf named Prior, who let donkeys on hire'. He also formed the first conception of what would be, to contemporaries, his most compelling character – Little Nell, the heroine of *The Old Curiosity Shop*, whose death would bring Dickens' readers to tears on both sides of the Atlantic. Dickens would subsequently return to Bath to perform with his amateur company in theatricals at the Assembly Rooms and to give one of his sell-out evenings of readings.

On the Eve of the Railway Age

In the very year that Brunel's Great Western Railway at last connected Bath with London a judicious and lengthy review of some eighty printed pages analysed and summarized the city's standing as a spa. *The Spas of England*, a survey in two volumes, was the work of A.B. Granville MD, FRS (1783-1872) – which makes him sound very proper and rather stuffy. He was, in fact, a decidedly romantic and fascinating character. Born Augustus Bozzi in Milan, Granville was related to the Bonapartes and had been variously a student revolutionary, an actor and a surgeon in the Royal Navy, adopted his mother's Cornish surname, converted to Anglicanism and become a British subject. He had studied under Volta and was a friend of Dalton and Canova. The French scientist Gay-Lussac entrusted him to bring the first sample of iodine to Britain, the Latin American revolutionary Bolivar entrusted him with confidential despatches. As a physician Granville specialized in obstetrics and paediatrics, but also found time to write expertly about sewerage, quarantine and the embalming of Egyptian mummies.

Granville's first point was that by 1840 ten times more people were visiting Bath than in the days of Beau Nash but 'those who use its mineral resources are infinitely fewer in number' – despite the Corporation's expenditure of £120,000 on modernizing the baths and improving their facilities. In Granville's opinion:

> ...this falling off of Bath as a medical resource of great power in the treatment of disease, is unjust and unmerited; for England possesses not a more powerful Spa, nor an agent of the class of mineral waters more calculated to do away with the necessity of removing to a foreign watering-place for the successful treatment of some of the most obstinate cases of disease.

The first cause of decline identified by Granville was the greed of local physicians who justified their constant demand for fees by prescribing medications or bleeding which simply interfered with the effect of the waters – which meant that the patients might as well have saved their money, stayed at home and paid their usual doctor to dose them. The second cause identified by Granville was the growth of the city itself:

> There are now upwards of 60,000 permanent residents, who of course never once think of the mineral springs; and .... have surrounded the springs with extended lines of houses and streets and public buildings and squares – the best of all of which they themselves occupy. Strangers, therefore, are unwilling to plunge, when looking after health and tranquility, into the turmoil and confinement of a large city, in the most crowded and busy part of which the springs and the baths are hemmed in.

Unsurprisingly Granville, as a medical man himself, thought that the waters should only be used under close medical supervision, either externally or internally.

> Bath water used as a bath, stimulates the skin and strengthens the muscles ... it will render supple stiff joints, animate paralytic limbs and quicken the circulation to such a degree indeed as to require caution in its use, and render it necessary to discriminate well the nature of the patient's constitution ere the bath and its various degrees of temperature are recommended.

Properly utilized, the waters should prove efficacious especially for the treatment of paralysis, chronic rheumatism and gout. As for internal consumption – 'the water must be drank (sic) at the fountain's head and always early in the morning, and not in bed; nor at a late hour in the day, as patients at Bath are constantly doing ... by the latter practice the very peculiar effects of Bath water are constantly frustrated.'

Granville therefore proposed changing the main 'season' from autumn and winter to summer so that people would find it easier to get up at the crack of day, have far less risk of catching cold and be more inclined to complement the effect of the waters by taking healthy exercise outdoors. The usual sojourn of a fortnight or three weeks, moreover, was quite inadequate – 'a full course should consist of at least five or six weeks.'

In Granville's view Bath still had everything going for it in terms of attractions and facilities –

> No place offers better or more numerous resources ... whether for out-of-door amusements, motives for exercise, or attractive objects for distant excursions, on the one hand; or, on the other hand, for in-door pleasing as well as useful occupation, such as libraries, subscription rooms, balls, fetes and even society ... it stands prominently forward as almost unique, both with regard to facilities of procuring excellent house-room and for the supply of good food ... Living in Bath is very reasonable and there are excellent markets for all sorts of provisions ... Mountain water, beautifully transparent and pure ... is abundantly supplied ... Fuel is cheap ... The city of Bath is profusely lighted with gas at night. The streets are very well paved and kept clean ... With vehicles and other means of conveyance, Bath is proverbially well supplied ... For mental recreation ... Bath possesses resources equal to those of a small capital.... by simply inviting all those who may have visited the foreign baths ... and who have not yet seen the English 'Spa of Spas' (as I trust it will soon again become), to proceed thither in numbers as soon as Sir Isambard, the magician, shall, with his *Great* Western wand, have brought Bath within three hours of the metropolis and so judge for themselves of its superiority and importance.

Beckford's Tower

An English Eccentric

Considering that it was built for a recluse, at one hundred and fifty feet Beckford's Tower is an obtrusive monument to a towering ego. Novelist and bibliophile, composer and collector, painter and poseur, William Beckford (1760-1844) claimed to be descended from Edward III – and *all* the signatories of Magna Carta. He inherited a million pounds and an income of £100,000 a year and managed to get through most of it in the course of what the original edition of *The Dictionary of National*

Biography baldly dismissed as 'a wasted life'. Normally restrained in its judgments, the *DNB* excoriated Beckford as 'wilful, extravagant and capricious', condemning him as 'neglectful of his genius, his private affairs and his responsibilities as a citizen'. But even the *DNB* conceded that Beckford had been 'the most brilliant amateur in English literature'. The art historian Kenneth Clark dubbed him 'one of the first men in England who could afford to be eccentric on the grandest scale'.

Born the son of a Lord Mayor of London and heir to extensive slave plantations in Jamaica, Beckford received a haphazard private education which imbued him with a passion for architecture and Arabic and, in the words of one of his academic admirers, 'a penchant for fooling about with the forbidden'. Beckford met Voltaire, witnessed the demolition of the Bastille and took advantage of the panic-stricken flight of French aristocrats from the Terror to acquire their family treasures at knock-down prices. He also bought the library of Edward Gibbon, the famed author of *The Decline and Fall of the Roman Empire* – acquiring 7,000 volumes for just £950. Beckford's other possessions included works by Bellini, Claude, Poussin, Rembrandt and Hogarth and a Japanese coffer once owned by Cardinal Mazarin.

In his early twenties Beckford wrote his most celebrated work, the oriental fantasy *Vathek*, in a non-stop frenzy of three days and two nights – in French. A homosexual incident with a teenage aristocrat then made it prudent for Beckford to spend the best part of a decade in Switzerland and Portugal. When he returned to the family seat of Fonthill in Wiltshire he spent a quarter of a million pounds on rebuilding it as a Gothic palace on a monumental scale – which fell down. Obliged by the collapse of his fortunes to sell off Fonthill and most of its contents, in 1823 Beckford removed to Bath. It was perhaps a slightly surprising choice since he had written as recently as 1817 'Bath does not please me.' The Gothic Abbey, naturally appealed to him – 'a great spectacle' – but the rest of the city he dismissed as 'incredibly dingy and wretched'.

20 LANSDOWN CRESCENT

Beckford acquired 20 Lansdown Crescent and began collecting all over again, acquiring No. 1 Lansdown Place West across the lane, and then No. 19 adjoining, to house his overflow. He also bought up the farms to the rear of his residence to create a mile long pleasure garden and ride leading up to the hill where, in 1827, his classically-inspired retreat was completed to the designs of local architect H.E. Goodridge. Its spectacular belvedere afforded the eccentric dilettante panoramic views over five counties. A contemporary guide enthused over its interior décor as being of 'almost regal splendour and magnificence.' Professor Pevsner, however, writing in the 1950s would – unusually – characterize the Tower as 'crazy ... bleak and sinister'.

Although Beckford failed in his original ambition to have his tower serve as his mausoleum, he was eventually buried beneath it. Beckford's Tower is now a museum and education centre, open to visitors at weekends and on Bank Holidays from Easter until October. Beckford's life has been most recently chronicled by Timothy Mowl in *William Beckford – Composing for Mozart*.

H.E. GOODRIDGE AND HIS WORKS

Beckford's architect, Henry Edmund Goodridge (1797-1864), the son of the builder of Bathwick, built up a successful independent practice in Bath, with a drawing-office at 7 Henrietta Street. His own residence, Montebello (later Bathwick Grange) was built between 1828 and 1830 on Bathwick Hill and was noted for its landscaped garden. From 1848 until his death he lived in another nearby villa of his own design, Fiesole, now a youth hostel. Goodridge was also responsible for the Argyle chapel (1821), the Corridor (1825), the six Greek Revival linked villas of Woodland Place (1826) and semi-detached villas of Woodhill Place opposite, the Cleveland Bridge and its tollhouses (1827), Cleveland Place East and West (*ca*. 1827-30), Holy Trinity, Combe Down (1832-5) and the Eastern Dispensary (1845). This latter was praised by *The Builder* as an ingenious model to be imitated nationwide. Goodridge lies in Lansdown Cemetery in the shadow of his most notable composition. The Percy (now Elim Pente-costal) Chapel in Charlotte Street (1854) was built by Goodridge in collaboration with his son, Alfred Samuel Goodridge who carried on his father's practice.

God's Wonderful Railway

The Great Western Railway (GWR), running from Temple Meads station, Bristol to Paddington station in London, was the single-handed creation of Isambard Kingdom Brunel (1806-59), voted second only to Churchill in a BBC poll of the 'Great Britons' of all time. The son of a French émigré, Brunel assisted his father in completing the first tunnel ever to run under a river, the Thames, between Rotherhithe and Wapping, designed the spectacular Clifton suspension bridge at Bristol, built the first transatlantic steamer, the *Great Western* and the *Great Eastern,* which was five times bigger than any ship ever built before. Brunel's *Great Britain*, built and now once more berthed at Bristol, was the ever first iron-hulled, screw-propeller steam-powered ocean liner. A man who combined demonic energy, with uncompromising vision and ground-breaking technical skills, Brunel walked and surveyed every foot of the GWR route himself, creating Britain's flattest, fastest inter-city route. Brunel's approach to Bath, skirting the city to the south in a lengthy curve, enabled him to site the station close to the city centre without slicing through it, which would have caused much greater expense and disruption than proved necessary. Approaching from the east London passengers pass a huge but stylish retaining wall, running through Sydney Gardens, to protect the Kennnet and Avon Canal.

Controversially the railway was originally built to a non-standard 'broad' gauge of 6 ft and ½ inch which Brunel's advanced mathematical education had convinced him would enable trains to achieve higher speeds with greater stability than the 4ft 8 ½ inch 'standard gauge' used over the rest of the British network. This made it impossible for through traffic to run from other companies' systems onto the GWR network until it finally adopted standard gauge in the 1890s.

Visitors who come to Bath from London by rail will cross the Thames at Maidenhead over the flattest single-span brick arch ever built and pass through the Box tunnel, which cost the lives of over a hundred men. Initially anticipating that trains would not be able to go fast enough to reach Bristol in a tolerable time Brunel planned for a refreshment and comfort stop to be made at Swindon. Here he designed the horseshoe-shaped bar for the station refreshment room as the most efficient way of serving the maximum numbers of customers in the shortest possible time. It was later widely adopted by Victorian public houses. Swindon became the engineering headquarters of the GWR and the archetypal modern 'railway town'. There is an extensive museum there devoted to the GWR and Brunel's career.

A NEW SERVICE

The Bristol to Bath section of the GWR opened on 31 August 1840, when an eight coach train, drawn by the locomotive *Fireball*, arrived at Bath at 8.33 a.m. The through service to London opened the following year on the completion of the Box tunnel. Queen Victoria personally endorsed the service with a fourteen mile run from Slough into Paddington, Brunel himself attending the locomotive. At Bath Station the novel service was finely adjusted to the social hierarchy of the day with separate stairs for first, second and third class passengers to reach the platforms, where they were separated into their respective pens while waiting for the next train. Ironically in view of Brunel's own addiction to chain-smoking cigars, smoking was prohibited on both the platforms and the trains. Arrivals in Bath could have their bags delivered to their accommodation by station staff. Bath residents could order their coal from the same source.

BATH STATION

Bath station, a twenty arch viaduct between two river crossings, was designed by Brunel himself, the viaduct featuring a 'gateway' reminiscent of St John's College, Cambridge. Originally there was a station entrance on the south side as well as the north. Today's platforms are much longer than the earliest ones. The original glazed roof was replaced by a canopy in 1897. Hydraulic lifts to each platform were installed by 1885, though only those on the west-bound platform survive. The glazed forecourt canopy also dates from the 1880s. Manvers Street, running north towards the city center was intended to be a *gran via* but developed piecemeal. The Royal Hotel and the Manvers Arms (later Argyll Hotel) were designed to give architectural anchorage to sweeping terraces. In Barry Cunliffe's words 'Brunel made a carefully considered attempt to integrate his railway with the architecture of the

city. That the approach is now a dismal failure is no fault of his.'
   Bryan Little was similarly complimentary:

> Brunel's castellated work near the station is scarcely local to Bath, for
> Brunel was architecturally a Romantic and everywhere an enthusiast for
> Gothic, but his work at Bath is notable and a good reminder of his taste.
> The loopholes and battlements just west of the Great Western station lead
> us on to a whole Cathedral's worth of Perpendicular tunnel and culvert
> arches all the way to Saltford.

Bath's second station was a more obtrusive affair. Queen's Square
station was built in 1869-70 as the terminus of a spur line off the
Midland Railway's main Birmingham-Bristol through route. In 1874 it
was linked in with the Somerset and Dorset Joint Railway Company's
line, giving it access to the south coast. The name was changed to
Green Park station in 1951. The last train ran in 1966. After years
of dereliction the station was bought by Bath City Council in 1974
and, with co-financing by Sainsbury's, restored in 1982-4 to create a
brasserie, shops, farmers' market and car park.

   The Great Western Railway achieved levels of speed and efficiency
which, even by twenty-first century standards, must command respect.
As early as the mid-1840s services were already running at over forty
miles an hour, making Bath little more than two hours distant from the
capital. This made possible the emergence of an entirely new type of
visitor to Bath – the day-tripper. To meet the demands of such a novel
newcomer a new type of guidebook was required, omitting the usual
advice on lodgings, provisions, servants etc. required by temporary
residents in favour of an emphasis on orientation, topography, potted
history and sight-seeing directions. In 1857 an anonymous author,
writing under the pseudonym 'Indicator', published *A Guide Through
and Round Bath : For the Use of Such as are Desirous to See, Of the Place –
the Most Possible, in a Time – the Least Possible.* This was followed in 1858
by the more crisply titled *Bath : What to See and How to See It.*

Industry

In 1811 Louis Simond had observed somewhat facetiously that Bath had 'no trade, no manufactures, no occupations of any kind, except that of killing time, the most laborious of all.' That was only mildly witty and scarcely true. Bath had, in fact, besides its large cohorts of servants and shopkeepers, substantial classes of builders, printers and makers of clothes, footwear, furniture and household goods. But it did not suit the image of the visitor-oriented city to emphasise the fact. As the nineteenth century wore on, however, it became increasingly more difficult to deny, much less disguise, it.

Following the completion of the Kennet and Avon Canal in 1810 and the advent of the Great Western Railway in 1840-41, Bath began to develop a distinct industrial quarter to the west of Manvers Street and the station. The immediate vicinity, Broad Quay, as might be expected, attracted businesses devoted to processing bulky raw materials, including stone and grain and the Pickwick Iron Works, as well as a dealer in marine stores, coach-builders and Marshall and Banks Steam Dye Works. Larger-scale businesses, requiring more space, established themselves along the Lower Bristol Road and along the bank of the Avon towards Twerton. By the 1840s sixty-seven steam-powered looms were employing some eight hundred hands at Twerton Mills. Foremost among incomers was the engineering firm of Stothert and Pitt, who specialized in making heavy cranes. Already employing a labour force of 540 by 1851, in 1857 they moved from their foundry in Southgate Street to occupy the Newark Works on Lower Bristol Road, where they remained until closure in 1987. The Pitman Press moved to Lower Bristol Road in 1859 and remains there as LIBERfabrica.

HOUSES FOR THE WORKERS

To house the more favoured and skilled employees of these industrial enterprises rows of terraced artisan cottages were built within walking distance of their place of work. Often plain to the point of austerity for many they nevertheless represented a considerable advance on the attic, court or mews into which Bath's working poor had traditionally been decanted. Bryan Little's classic *The Building of Bath* contains an illustration of Locksbrook Terrace as it stood in 1947. Locksbrook Terrace no longer stands. The expansion of Bath's manufacturing base can be gauged from the fact that the city had forty-six exhibitors at the Great Exhibition of 1851. Bristol, two and a half times larger had sixty-five.

Apart from diversifying the city's economic base, the growth of local industry also supplied many of its basic needs, most notably for building materials, beer and bread flour. Stothert's manufactured many of the new iron bridges which spanned the Avon. Even more to the point industrial employment tended to be relatively immune to the seasonal fluctuations which affected the city's visitor-oriented service sector, thus providing a welcome element of income stability to a significant section of the resident population.

Victorian industrial development may have done little to beautify Bath but it did not, for the most part, intrude itself upon the city's visitors. Gibbs's *Bath Visitant* assured readers in 1835 that 'Bath is not a city of trade. No manufactures worthy of notice are carried on within its limits'. This was disingenuous but because Bath's industrial parishes were peripheral to its fashion-conscious centre the fiction of an industrial vacuum was not difficult to maintain.

Men of Letters

The final Bath sojourn of Walter Savage Landor (1775-1864) was meant to be a calm retirement after a life of largely self-inflicted troubles. Landor was asked to leave both Rugby *and* Oxford. An outstanding Latinist, he antagonized teachers at both institutions by refusing to compete for prestigious prizes for Latin verse composition. He was turned down for a militia commission on account of his rabid republicanism – which didn't last. He fell out spectacularly with his father – but was more than content to inherit his fortune and set up in style in Bath in 1805. Here he lived for three years, with a fine carriage and two men-servants, indulging in casual affairs and mismanaging his own. This was followed by a quixotic foray to Spain to fight the French. Back in Bath in 1811 he announced one evening at the Assembly Room 'that's the nicest girl in the room and I'm going to marry her.' And he did. The fact that Julia Thuillier had no fortune was for Landor a positive incentive to marriage. She stuck it out for twenty-four years. Most of this time was passed in Italy.

Landor – minus Mrs Landor – finally returned to settle in Bath in 1838. He had, over forty years, established a literary reputaion which won him the admiration of Southey, Coleridge and Lamb, and, in his old age, of Dickens and Browning as well. Living in Bath Landor developed a particular fondness for Widcombe, expressing his fervent wish to be buried in the churchyard of St Thomas a Becket. It was not, alas, to be. A typical act of unconsidered generosity rebounded to involve him in losing a libel case which forced him to flee back to Italy, virtually penniless. Fortunately the kindness of Robert Browning and other admirers saved him from penury but could not grant him the last resting-place of his wishes.

A CRICKETING HISTORIAN

James Pycroft (1813-95) was the first historian of English cricket. He claimed to have been responsible as an undergraduate for inaugurating the annual Oxford and Cambridge cricket match and at twenty-two published a technical treatise entitled *Principles of Scientific Batting*. Pursuing a triple career as clergyman, schoolmaster and author, Pycroft enjoyed sufficient success with his Greek and Latin Grammars and an English reading course that ran to four editions that he was able to give up his clerical duties in his forties, retire to Bathwick and devote his days to writing and his favourite sport. A stalwart member of the Lansdown cricket club, Pycroft displayed no exceptional talent in the field but was acknowledged as the nation's leading expert on the rules and traditions of the game. Pycroft's pioneering history of cricket first appeared in 1851 and by 1887 had reached its ninth edition. He also published a comprehensive *Cricket Tutor* in 1862 and a collection of '*Cricketana*' in 1865, as well as a sequence of autobiographical novels.

Men of Science

At the age of seventeen Leonard Jenyns (1800-93) was introduced to Sir Joseph Banks, the President of the Royal Society, as 'the Eton boy who lit his rooms with gas', an achievement all the more remarkable for the fact that gas-lighting was only introduced to the streets of London that very same year. Jenyns became a member of the newly-established Linnaean Society when he was just twenty-two and was

also a founder-member of the Zoological Society and the Entomo-
logical Society. Having become a conscientious village priest Jenyns
declined the post of naturalist on *HMS Beagle* in favour of his friend
Charles Darwin. In 1835 Cambridge University Press published
Jenyns' *Manual of British Vertebrate Animals*, which became a standard
work of reference. In 1850 concern for his wife's health led Jenyns to
move to South Stoke and later to Swainswick, near Bath. In 1855 he
became founder and first President of the Bath Natural History and
Antiquarian Field Club. In 1865 he was instrumental in establishing
a meteorological observatory in the gardens of Bath's Royal Literary
and Scientific Institution. In 1871, as a consequence of an inheritance
via a connection with a Norfolk family Jenyns changed his name to
Blomefield. At his death he bequeathed the 'Jenyns Library' of some
two thousand volumes to the Royal Literary and Scientific Institution.

Charles Moore (1815–81) was another founder member of the Bath
Field Club. Born in Ilminster, he worked in a bookseller's in Bath in
his twenties and settled permanently in the city in 1853, renouncing
business in favour of municipal affairs and his passion for geology.
Moore became a councillor and alderman. His extensive collection
of fossils formed the basis of the Royal Literary and Scientific Institution's Geological Museum.

A Victorian Collector

There is, at the time of writing, still no entry for Sir William Holburne
(1793-1874) in the *Dictionary of National Biography*, but by his own
generosity and foresight, he has been rescued from an obscurity to
which posterity threatened to condemn him. The story of his collection
of *objets d'art*, books and paintings is nevertheless remarkable and the
story of his early life no less so. Thanks to the patient and painstaking
researches of Lisa White of the Holburne Museum, both the story of
his collection and of his life are being substantially recovered, despite
the absence of any major cache of journals or diaries and the apparently arbitrary survival of only miscellaneous letters, bills and accounts.
Holburne appears to have been systematically discriminating in his
purchases and, as befitted a formal naval officer, orderly in his daily
routines, but seems to have regarded even his movements, much less

The Holburne Museum

his motives, as too insignificant to be worth recording, to the great frustration of generations of scholars.

Little in William Holburne's early life would appear to have prepared him for a self-chosen career as a collector. His family, though titled, was by no means rich, possessing only the usual collection of family portraits, plate and jewels and occasional items of exotica, such as Chinese porcelain, but not the galleries of Old Masters and cabinets of curiosities accumulated over centuries by the great landowning dynasties of Britain. Holburne's earliest years were passed near Swansea, far even from provincial centres of polite culture, until in 1802 the family moved to a ten-year-old house at 7 Lansdown Place West. The Holburnes did, however, have a connection by marriage with the Lascelles of Harewood in Yorkshire, whom they visited periodically. Although William as a small boy can only have been dimly aware of the lavishness of the Lascelles art collection, he did maintain contact over the years with his wealthy and well-connected cousins.

Despatched to the harsh service of the Royal Navy as a mere boy of eleven, William Holburne had not even the rough lineaments of learning imparted by the unreformed public schools of his day, much less what he might have acquired at one of the ancient universities or from a Grand Tour. Such education as he later acquired he owed to a decade of far-flung naval service and his own enquiring mind.

Before any opportunity of self-improvement could be taken up William Holburne had to face the challenge of sheer survival. Having joined the navy in July 1805, to serve as a midshipman aboard *HMS Orion*, in October he was present at the momentous battle off Cape Trafalgar which destroyed a Franco-Spanish fleet and consigned Nelson to the pantheon of heroes. This brutal apprenticeship to combat was followed by months of mind-numbing tedium blockading the French naval base at Toulon and then lengthy tours of duty in the West Indies and off Brazil, both routinely lethal, fever-ridden postings. After further service in the Mediterranean, the Western Approaches and the Channel, Lieutenant William Holburne returned to England on half-pay in 1815. In the meantime William's elder brother, Francis, heir presumptive to the baronetcy, had died of wounds at Bayonne, after serving under Wellington for five years in the 3rd Foot Guards.

THE WELL-HEELED BARONET

William Holburne inherited the baronetcy, of Menstrie, near Stirling in Scotland, in 1820 and in 1821 the Lascelles connection secured him a place at the coronation of George IV. In 1822 the eccentric collector William Beckford acquired two houses a few doors away from the Holburne family residence, where William lived with his widowed mother and three spinster sisters. If collecting is at all contagious Beckford was a prime source of infection.

Although he had the responsibility of his mother and sisters, none of whom ever married, Sir William, now titled and adequately funded, was unencumbered with a wife or children and free to indulge a taste for travel. In 1824 he undertook the Grand Tour which political and personal circumstances had to date denied him. Aged thirty-one, he could dispense with the tutor or cicerone whom custom and parental caution had traditionally assigned to English milords, usually a decade younger than himself, setting out to view the riches of Europe's heritage.

He did, however, equip himself with extensive reading-matter, including the most recent art-historical guides. Reaching Milan, where he was sketched, Sir William visited Florence, Siena, Naples, possibly Sicily, and Venice and spent two periods of residence in Rome, where he called on sculptors, founders, mosaicists and dealers in books and pictures. After making a swift excursion into Istria (modern Slovenia), he crossed the Swiss Alps to return, much more rapidly, via Salzburg, Munich, Stuttgart and Frankfurt to Mainz where he embarked on the Rhine for Antwerp and thence to Amsterdam, Den Haag and Brussels. All told the expedition lasted eighteen months.

Sir William Holburne's exposure to the arts of Italy is reflected in his subsequent passions for Italian specialisms, such as intaglio and maiolica. The return leg of his itinerary is reflected in his collections of raw and polished mineral specimens and his taste for German silver and Dutch paintings. Sir William's later travels are less fully or firmly documented – to France certainly in 1827 and 1855, to Scotland almost certainly in 1828, to Europe again quite possibly in 1829. In 1837 he hired a coach for twelve weeks; where he went is as yet, and may remain, unknown.

In 1830, following the death of his mother, Lady Alicia, Holburne and his sisters bought a new house at 10 Cavendish Crescent, commissioning Bath's leading interior decorator, John Stafford, to supply them with fittings and furnishings of damask and gold. A handsome house with generous grounds and open views, the Holburne home still had only four major rooms and a single, if striking, staircase to display a collection which Sir William continued to augment with auction purchases following the demise of HRH the Duke of Sussex in 1843 and of his neighbour, Beckford, in 1844. It seems evident then that the emphasis of the Holburne collection was governed – it is not unreasonable to surmise, pre-emptively – by the precautionary principle 'but where shall it be put?' Hence the absence of imposing items of furniture, carpets or wall-hangings and the concentration on the finely-wrought and the exquisite – portrait miniatures, rather than portraits, cameos rather than canvases, spoons rather than statuary. In Sir William's chosen fields the emphasis was on scale rather than size – eighty-five bronzes, one hundred and twenty-five decorative gems, eight hundred pieces of silverware, thirteen hundred items of ceramic.

Sir William Holburne's status as a collector of more than purely provincial significance was confirmed in the 1860s when he was approached to loan numerous items for exhibitions in London, Leeds and Paris. In 1867 he was elected to that inner élite of connoisseurship, the Burlington Fine Arts Club, whose members included such eminenti as the society artist Frederick, later Lord, Leighton, future President of the Royal Academy, and John Ruskin, pre-eminent art critic of the age. In the same year Sir William collaborated with the dealer and antiquarian, William Chaffers, to catalogue his silver and then, in a separate volume, his paintings, his engravings and his books.

Despite their collective childlessness and the fact that all four members of the Holburne family died between 1871 and 1882, the Holburne Collection was not, as might have been expected, dispersed at auction. In 1881, acting on what she believed to be her brother's wishes, Sir William's youngest and last surviving sister, Mary-Ann Barbara, sole inheritor of his entire estate, established a trust to administer the collection and an endowment for its maintenance, to be funded from the sale of the property in Cavendish Crescent and its domestic contents on her death, which occurred the following year. Not until 1891, however, was the Collection opened to the public, housed in the former premises of the National Savings Bank. The Collection was, in accordance with Miss Holburne's dying wish, subsequently transferred to the former premises of the Sydney Hotel, following its refurbishment and adaptation by Sir Reginald Blomfield (1856-1942) in 1916, where it remains today.

City Fathers

If William Beckford (see page 183) was the archetype of self-indulgent self-regard, Jerom Murch (1807-95) was the incarnation of selfless civic service. Born into a Devon family of twelve, he studied briefly at newly-founded University College, London, a radically progressive institution, before becoming a Unitarian minister. This set him outside the mainstream of Victorian religion but did nothing to hinder him. From 1833 to 1846 Murch served as pastor of Trim Street chapel, founding a day school and a Sunday school in nearby Saw Close. Murch joined Bath's council in his mid-fifties, embarking on a second career which would last over thirty years and see him serve as Mayor seven times, latterly in his mid-eighties. Murch's energetic commitment to the Victorian cult of self-improvement saw him serve as President of the local Mechanics' Institute, of the Bath Literary Club, the Bath Royal Literary and Scientific Institution and the Somerset Archaeological and Natural History Society and as Vice-President of the Bath and West of England Society. In addition to this Murch served as a governor of Bath High School, King Edward's School and the Mineral Water Hospital, as a magistrate and, despite his Unitarian background, as Deputy Lieutenant of Somerset.

Far from content to serve the status quo, Murch preached a political gospel of civic renaissance, promoting a visionary scheme to establish a modern municipal hotel with its own hot-water treatment baths, an extension of the city's water supply, an assault on local environmental problems of drainage and river pollution and, in line with his convictions as a Gladstonian Liberal, the extinction of the archaic privileges still attached to the status of local freeman. Thanks to Murch the Bath Act of 1870 improved the water supply while another Act of 1879 finally extinguished freemen's rights. The Grand Pump Room Hotel was successfully established, though dogged by management problems. Murch also gave strong support to the excavations of the Roman baths. There were setbacks. He failed to become Bath's MP and the West of England and South Wales Bank crashed under his chairmanship. Bath's flooding and pollution problems persisted. But Murch's last years ended on a triumphant note. During his last mayoralty he laid the foundation stone to an extension to the Guildhall. In 1893 he published the fruit of many years diligent labour *Biographical Sketches of Bath Celebrities Ancient and Modern, with Some Fragments of Local History*. In 1894 he was knighted.

A CHRONICLE OF CELEBRITY

If Jerom Murch was preoccupied with Bath's physical and institutional development, Thomas Sturge Cotterell (1865-1950) became the self-appointed booster of its heritage as a key civic asset. A local businessman and councillor, Cotterell devoted himself to a forty year project of biographical cartography. In 1899 the *Bath Chronicle* published the first edition of Cotterell's *Historic map of Bath* indicating the sites of public buildings and residences of famous personages connected with the history of the city. Some one hundred celebrities were identified. By the time the map reached its fifth edition on the eve of World War Two Cotterell had increased the number of identified celebrity locations to 271. Cotterell's researches provided him with the resources needed to back his pet project, to place commemorative plaques on the former residences of Bath's historic celebrities. As chairman of Bath Council's Mural Tablets Committee, Cotterell positioned himself to dominate the business. The scheme was inaugurated in 1899 and its impact amplified by inviting current celebrities to perform the unveiling. Over three decades these were to include Lord Rosebery, Ellen Terry, Admiral Earl Jellicoe, G.K. Chesterton and George Bernard Shaw. Although Cotterell's preference was for literary figures, like Samuel Johnson and Charles Dickens, he shrewdly honoured Admiral Philip to encourage Australian visitor interest and invited the US Ambassador to unveil the plaque for Edmund Burke, who had once spoken so eloquently for the cause of the rebellious American colonists.

Unsurprisingly, Cotterell was one of the few council members to involve himself in the 1909 Pageant, serving as chairman of the key Executive and Finance Committees. Cotterell went on to serve as Chairman of the Bath Preservation Trust from its inauguration in 1934 until his death. Typically its first target was to acquire the former Trim Street residence of General James Wolfe – with a view to the Canadian market. Cotterell continued to research and write throughout his long life producing publications on *Two Great Postal Reformers, John Wood, Governor Phillip* and a full-length study of Admiral Howe but his most enduring legacy is the Mayor's Corps of Honorary Guides, established in the year of his Mayoralty (1930-1) to conduct walking tours through the city he had served as he had loved it.

Architect, Archaeologist

Charles Edward Davis (1827-1902) was Bath's City Architect and Surveyor for almost forty years. An enthusiastic member of the rifle volunteer movement he was usually known as 'Major Davis' by virtue of his militia commission. Davis's father, Edward Davis, was also Bath's

City Architect, responsible for laying out Victoria Park in 1830 and for restoring Prior Bird's chantry chapel in the Abbey in 1833. Charles Davis trained in his father's office and showed an early interest in the historical aspects of his profession, becoming a Fellow of the Society of Antiquaries at twenty-three. In 1860 Davis designed the Ladymead Fountain which can still be seen on Walcot Street. In 1861 he restored the church of St Thomas a Becket at Widcombe. In 1863 he was appointed City Architect and Surveyor in succession to his father. Among his other early projects were the Shakespeare Monument erected in the Royal Victoria Park in 1864 to mark the tercentenary of the Bard's birth and the Police Station and Lock Up in Orange Grove. Built in the style of an Italian palazzo this building remained in use until 1966 and was converted into a restaurant in 1998. The former cells are now the lavatories.

Davis was also able to build up a successful private practice and was responsible for the church of St Peter and schools at Twerton, the exuberant centrepiece entrance to Jolly's (see page 174) at Nos. 11-13 Milsom St., the shops at 9-10 and 20-22 Cheap Street and the pub on the corner at No. 21. His other official projects included the bandstand in the Royal Victoria Park and the adaptation of a former dissenting chapel in York Street to become the Bath City Laundry.

RECOVERING ROMAN REMAINS

From 1869 onwards Davis began to pursue the recovery of Bath's Roman archaeological heritage, most notably exposing the Great Bath in 1880-81. Although Davis's efforts were bitterly attacked by members of the emerging archaeological profession in his own day, posterity has been more appreciative of his efforts. In *Roman Bath Discovered* (1971) Professor Barry Cunliffe observed that 'Davis may have been slack in recording his discoveries and he may have obscured much by covering the remains with cumbersome and inelegant structures, but a wealth of information remains unscathed beneath his floors and will in time be available for further examination.'

Davis's archaeological concerns had to be combined with the need to support the revival of Bath as a leading therapeutic centre. In 1885 he was sent on an extensive tour of continental spas and returned an acknowledged expert, gratefully and respectfully consulted by other spa towns like Harrogate and Droitwich. In his efforts to upgrade Bath's spa facilities Davis added a Douche and Massage Baths block to the south-west of the Pump Room. The Cross Bath was roofed over and converted into a rectangular swimming pool, an initiative subsequently denounced by Ison as 'vandalism'. The same authority condemned Davis's 'modernization' of the interior of the Pump Room as 'disastrous'. The Douche and Massage Baths block was demolished in the early 1970s 'without regrets', the other 'improvements' reversed or removed.

A MATTER OF SOME CONTROVERSY

The same cannot be said of Davis's last major project, the Empire Hotel (1899-1901) which still provokes near apoplexy among architectural critics. Bryan Little (1947) called it 'a fearful mock-Jacobean skyscraper with a touch of Lacock Abbey at the top corner' which 'insulted' all the surrounding buildings with its 'looming and far-seeing bulk'. Pevsner in 1958 dismissed it as 'an unbelievable piece of pompier architecture' without further explanation of quite what he meant by that. Charles Robertson, writing in 1975, when it was still an Admiralty office-building thirty years after the end of the war, made the uncontrovertible observation that it was 'easily the most conspicuous secular building in central Bath', then hastened to add that 'no approval of its architectural merits is implied' and conceded that 'the way its bulk obtrudes on its neighbours, especially the Abbey, is impossible to defend.' Barry Cunliffe (1986), by contrast, was almost positive, describing it as 'a mountain of eclectic styles', an expression of 'bombastic energy'. Most recently Michael Forsyth, revising Pevsner, appeared to be in several minds at once, characterizing the Empire in the space of a single paragraph as 'unbelievably pompous', 'frolicsome', 'a worthy survival' and 'a building of its time'. The 'worthy' verdict at least commands assent because the Empire was saved from demolition in 1995-6 and the upper part converted to apartments, the lower to commercial use.

Discovery and Enterprise

The very diverse lives of the men briefly described in this 'Interlude' share crucial common features. All were personifications of perseverance against the odds. None was professionally prepared for the achievement which made him famous. Each, once they had found their métier, remained devoted to it for the rest of his life.

Stargazer

The first person in history actually to discover, rather than merely to observe, a new planet was Frederick William Herschel (1738-1822). Born in Hanover, the son of the bandmaster of the Hanoverian Guards regiment, Herschel followed his father into the band as a player of the hautboy (oboe) and violin. A brief youthful visit to England in 1755 gave him a first acquaintance with the English language. A French victory over Hanover in the opening phase of the Seven Years War of 1756-63 led Herschel, on the advice of his father, to quit the army and take refuge in England. Arriving with a single (French!) coin in his pocket, Herschel initially survived as a music copyist before finding a more profitable outlet for his talents as a teacher and organist in the north of England. The reputation he established there led in 1766 to his appointment to the 'agreeable and lucrative' position of organist at the Octagon chapel in Bath (see page 120). Co-opted into the Pump Room orchestra and greatly in demand as a teacher, Herschel was soon able to earn some £300 a year. A tireless organiser of musical events and a prolific, if not gifted, composer, Herschel was also a ferocious autodidact. Studying English led him on to Latin, then to Greek, French and Italian. Studying musical harmonics led to mathematics, optics and astronomy. Astronomy became more than a passion, it became an obsession. Finding himself unable to hire a telescope powerful enough for the observations he wanted to make, Herschel set about making one. Aided by his brother Alexander and his sister Caroline, who had joined him from Hanover, he turned his house out by the Walcot turnpike into a small-scale foundry. Overcoming dozens of failures and at least one near-fatal accident, Herschel developed such expertise as a constructor of telescopes that in 1777 he attracted a visit from the Astronomer Royal and the Professor of Astronomy at Oxford. Intrigued by rumours about the frantic activities of this untrained amateur, they were nonetheless deeply impressed by the quality and power of the instruments he had been able to construct.

In 1780 Herschel moved his household to King Street in Bath and in the same year was invited by Dr William Watson FRS to become a founder member of the Philosophical Society of Bath. A few months later on 13 March 1781 Herschel observed what he at first took to be a comet but was subsequently confirmed by the Astronomer Royal to be a previously unknown planet. It was eventually called Uranus, though Herschel had patriotically wanted to name it after King George III. Herschel's discovery brought him instant celebrity, the Royal Society's Copley Medal and election to its Fellowship. In May 1782 came a summons to the royal presence for Herschel – and his telescope. When the king awarded him a pension of £200 a year to serve as court astronomer, he was at last released from the 'intolerable waste of time' represented by performing and teaching music, although it remained a favourite pastime.

Required to live within easy reach of Windsor Castle, Herschel left Bath to settle in Slough and, aided by his devoted sister, undertook what has been called 'an observational campaign second to none in the history of astronomy'. Over the course of twenty years Herschel increased the number of known nebulae from about a hundred to over 2,500. With the aid of his ultra-powerful telescopes he was also able to identify 848 double stars. Having started his professional career as an astronomer in middle-age and quite untrained, Herschel eventually contributed some seventy papers to the *Philosophical Transactions* of the Royal Society, discovered the existence of infra-red light rays and coined the word 'asteroid'. Honours were showered on him from

France, Germany, Sweden, the Netherlands, Russia and America and, unlikely though it may sound to the modern ear, while Herschel remained in residence Slough became a place of pilgrimage not just for scientists but for the crowned heads of Europe.

'The Father of British Geology'

William Smith (1769-1839) was born in Churchill, Oxfordshire, attended the village school and displayed a childhood obsession with collecting fossils. Self-trained as a surveyor, he so impressed his employers working on the Somerset Coal Canal that in 1794 they took him with them on an extended study-tour of canals and collieries which went as far as Newcastle Upon Tyne. This greatly enlarged Smith's first-hand knowledge of the geology of England and confirmed to him his hypothesis that the earth's various strata could be defined by their distinctive fossil deposits. Settling near Bath in 1795, Smith was greatly encouraged in his speculations by two clergymen, the Reverend Benjamin Richardson of Farleigh and the Reverend Joseph Townsend of Pewsey. It was in 1799 at Townsend's house at 29 Great Pulteney Street that Smith dictated his initial sketch of the stratification of Britain to Richardson, himself an amateur geologist. Abruptly dismissed from the Somerset canal scheme that same year, Smith had established a sufficiently good reputation to build up a nationwide practice as an engineer specialising in canal, reclamation, drainage and hydraulic projects, including in 1810 a rescue job on Bath's own hot springs.

Working a great deal in Yorkshire and East Anglia, Smith travelled as much as ten thousand miles a year, an incredibly punishing burden before the advent of railways and only made possible by the introduction of John Palmer's new system of mailcoaches (see page 142).

Despite the distractions of a demanding schedule of professional engagements, Smith persevered in collecting geological data and in 1815, under the patronage of the Society of Arts, finally published a cartographic summary of his findings as *A Delineation of the Strata of England and Wales, with Part of Scotland*. The reward for Smith's diligence was professional and personal disaster as Britain's post-war agricultural depression choked off interest in canal-building or land-reclamation schemes and destroyed a speculative quarry scheme in Somerset, which wiped Smith out financially. In 1819 William Smith was forced out of his London office in Buckingham Street, had to sell his fossil collection to the British Museum and spent ten weeks in debtors' prison. In 1820 his wife went mad. With no permanent home, living near whatever project he was engaged on, Smith nevertheless between 1819 and 1824, at the nadir of his fortunes, managed to publish a six part geological atlas of England and Wales on a county-by-county basis. Belated recognition came at last in 1831 when Smith became the first recipient of the Geological Society's Wollaston Medal. In 1832 he was grateful to be awarded a government pension of £100 a year.

Phonographer

The inventor of the English-speaking world's most widely used shorthand writing system was born in Devizes, Wiltshire. At sixteen Isaac Pitman (1813-97) taught himself the system of shorthand notation invented half a century previously by Samuel Taylor (1749-1811). He later went to London for five months to train as a schoolteacher, eventually settling in Wootton-under-Edge where, in 1837, his attachment to the idiosyncratic religious teachings of the Swedish mystic Emmanuel Swedenborg (1688-1772) got him the sack from his school, which was dominated by Methodists. Pitman had become convinced that Taylor's shorthand system could be used to promote greater literacy and devised a simple primer which he tried to interest a London publisher in promoting. From London came a challenge to devise a better system which, in a few months, he did, dubbing it 'phonography', from the Greek for 'sound' and 'writing'. Unlike previous shorthand systems, which had aimed to abbreviate the spelling of words, Pitman's system replicated their sound. In 1839 Pitman moved to Bath, opening his own school at 5 Nelson Place. The same year saw the publication of *Phonography, or Writing by Sound, being also a New and Natural System of Short Hand*. A second edition was produced the following year to take advantage of the newly-established penny post. Pitman, meanwhile, aided by four of his five brothers, undertook a gruelling nationwide lecturing campaign to market his new writing system to teachers. Giving up the school in 1843 to devote himself full-time to what had become virtually a crusade, Pitman produced eight editions of his course in as many years. In 1845 he set up his first printing press and in 1847 founded the Phonetic Institute at Albion Place. Turning out an ever-increasing range of teaching materials, by 1874 Pitman had become a publisher on an industrial scale. He then brought his offspring into the business and established the firm of Isaac Pitman and Sons in 1886. The main business removed from Bath to Twerton in 1888. Pitman was knighted in 1894. A memorial plaque marks his former home at 17 Royal Crescent.

Model of Enterprise

Born in North Shields, William Harbutt (1844-1921) was a product of the National Art Training School at South Kensington and only thirty years old when he was appointed head of Bath School of Art. Three years later, however, he fell out with his employers to such an extent that he set up his own, rival establishment, the Paragon Art Studio at 15 Bladud Buildings, where his wife, and eventually six of his children, joined him in what became the family business. The school later relocated to Hartley House, Belvedere, Lansdown.

Harbutt became dissatisfied with the modelling clay he used to teach sculpture as too messy and too quick to dry out. Despite the absence of any formal scientific training, persistent experimentation enabled him to develop his own formula, initially producing a malleable grey material, which he later made available in four colours. Manufactured at 15 Alfred Street and packed and distributed from his studio and annex at 22 Milsom Street, Harbutt's invention was promoted by a complementary publication on the art of modelling *Harbutt's Plastic Method and the Use of Plasticine*. Plasticine was registered as a trademark in 1899 and large-scale production begun at Bathampton in 1900. In 1912 the business became a limited company. By then plasticine had found favour beyond schools and art colleges in the offices of architects and engineers. During the Great War occupational therapists found modelling in plasticine an engrossing diversion for convalescing soldiers.

A non-smoker, teetotaller and ardent churchgoer, Harbutt proved to be a popular and benevolent employer and served Bath diligently as a councillor and Poor Law Guardian. He died on a promotional trip to the USA, leaving a not inconsiderable fortune of over £30,000. The Victoria Art Gallery has both a bust and a miniature of him. His product lives on most famously in the film *personae* of Wallace and Gromit, whose adventures are produced in Nick Park's studio in Bristol.

CHAPTER NINE

The Twentieth Century

Edwardian Expansion

After half a century of virtual stagnation the population of Bath began to increase again in the first decade of the twentieth century. This was accompanied by the substantial growth of the working-class suburbs of Larkhall and Oldfield Park. An electric tram service was inaugurated in 1904. In 1907 a new School of Pharmacy was opened. In 1909 the city celebrated its illustrious past with a massive Historical Pageant. Bath's social conservatism was manifested in the fact that religious observance remained strong in a Britain which was increasingly secular. Pro rata to the size of its population Bath on the eve of the Great War probably had the greatest number of places of worship in the country; and average Sunday attendance still represented half the population.

The advent of the private motor car, legalised in 1896, brought a new dimension to tourism. In 1901 J.F. Meehan published a guide to the *Famous Houses of Bath and District* – note that '*and District*'. This was followed in 1902 by J.M. Baddeley's *Bath and Bristol and Forty Miles Around*. Meehan's volume was sufficiently successful to justify the publication in 1906 of *More Famous Houses of Bath and District*. The glories of Bath's golden age were rehearsed anew and at length in a series of substantial new studies – William Tyte's *Bath in the Eighteenth Century* (1903), A. Barbeau's *Life and Letters at Bath in the Eighteenth Century* (1904), Mowbray Green's *The Eighteenth Century Architecture of Bath* (1904) and Louis Melville's *Bath Under Beau Nash* (1907). In 1909 the leading London publishers Ward Lock, produced a major new *Pictorial and Descriptive Guide to Bath*, which, with revisions, would be reissued in 1922-3 and 1936-7. The conference trade continued buoyant. The Society of Architects held its annual meeting in the city every year from 1906 to 1910. In 1910 Bath hosted the British Medical Association and in 1913 the National Federation of Grocers' Associations.

UNDERBELLY OF POVERTY

There was, as ever, a darker side. Although there were school places for every Bath child, the provision was so limited that even the chairman of the school board, a local solicitor, was moved to observe that 'a lot of clerks' places were taken by boys from a distance who had the advantage of a longer education than ... was given in the city.' The vast majority of Bath schoolchildren submitted for medical inspection in 1907 were, moreover, officially classified as 'dirty'. Although only 22 of the city's houses were rated as absolutely unfit for human habitation in 1912-13, a further 162 were found to be 'seriously defective from the point of view of danger to health or structural faults' and an even larger, though unspecified, number were condemned by the Medical Officer of Health as 'unsuited for family life'. Seebohm Rowntree's pioneering investigation of living conditions in the picturesque cathedral city of York had revealed that some 30 per cent of its population were living in poverty. There is little reason to believe that things were much better in Bath.

Great War, Great Loss

Of Bath's population of *ca.* 70,000 in 1914, over 11,000 served in the armed forces during the First World War. Considering that the city's population had always contained a disproportionate percentage of females, this was a high ratio of military participation. Bath also became a staging post for Imperial contingents from Australia and Canada. The Royal Flying Corps took over the Assembly Rooms. In 1917 Harry Patch, an eighteen-year-old apprentice Bath plumber, was called to the colours. Within weeks of joining the Duke of Cornwall's Light Infantry Harry Patch was pitched into the horrendous Battle of Passchendaele, where he was so badly injured that he was subsequently discharged from further service. He recovered sufficiently to resume his trade and serve with the Auxiliary Fire Service in Bath in World War Two. At the time of writing Harry Patch was, at 110, one of only four surviving veterans of the Great War.

A PLACE FOR CONVALESCENCE

When it became all too hideously apparent that the fighting would not be 'over by Christmas' Bath's long history as a centre of medical excellence made it a key reception point for an ever-mounting number of casualties. Initially accommodated in requisitioned buildings and hastily-converted church halls, convalescent soldiers were also nursed at Newton Park House, three miles from the city centre, which had been patriotically vacated by its owners, Lord and Lady Temple. Bath War Hospital, at first consisting of ten fifty-bed huts erected over a cricket pitch in Combe Park, opened in May 1915. By the end of the war it had expanded to accommodate up to 1,300 patients. There were to be still more than a thousand convalescents in Bath over a year after the war ended.

Bath's industrial capacity was likewise mobilised to support the war effort. Crane-makers Stothert & Pitt turned out some 200,000 high-explosive shells. Other engineering works manufactured torpedoes and even experimental tanks. Skilled cabinet-makers used their woodworking skills to produce military equipment ranging from fighter aircraft to humble ammunition boxes. In all over two thousand men and a thousand women were employed in fabricating munitions and materiel of varying sorts. Women also found new employment opportunities in occupations vacated by the men at the front, working as clerks, drivers and tram conductors. Many others volunteered to help out in the hospitals and convalescent homes.

WAR MEMORIALS

On Bath's main war memorial at the Rivers Gate entrance to the Royal Victoria Park of those who served in the armed services 1,172 are listed as killed. The memorial features the Cross of Sacrifice, which was devised by its designer Sir Reginald Blomfield (1856-1942) and became a standard component of war memorials thoughout Britain. Blomfield, with Sir Edwin Lutyens and Sir Herbert Baker, was one of the three official architectural advisers to the Imperial War Graves Commission. As Blomfield had been working on the conversion of the Holburne Museum (see page 196) until 1916 he knew Bath well and was present in person at the unveiling, which was performed by Field Marshal Allenby (1861-1936), the former commander of Britain's forces in the Middle East.

In Bath Abbey a memorial records the names of 241 men who fell while serving with the 4th Battalion of the Somerset Light Infantry. The colours of the 8th Battalion were also laid up there. An eagle lectern in the Abbey is for Lord Alexander Thynne DSO who had served as one of the city's Members of Parliament. The War Memorial Chapel has subsequently been redesignated the Gethsemane Chapel in recognition of the Abbey's involvement with the work of Amnesty International. Other Abbey monuments commemorate sixty former bell-ringers of Bath and Wells, three members of the St John's Ambulance brigade and a middle-aged Bath physician, Dr Almond, killed serving with the RAMC.

In the Guildhall is a monument erected by Alderman Hatt who, while himself serving as Bath's mayor, lost two sons at the Battle of the Somme, both Captains in the Somerset Light Infantry. Another Guildhall memorial records the gratitude of the Belgian refugees who had been taken into their homes by the citizens of Bath.

The enormity of Bath's loss and grief is, perhaps, better understood from the dozens of other memorials which can be found scattered throughout the city. Many recorded those who would never return to their accustomed pew – from St John's 38, St Stephen's 27, St Michael's 16, St Philip's 34, from Christ Church 44, from St Luke's 33 – and its pre-war vicar, who had died of wounds in Belgium while serving as an army chaplain. Figures for the outlying but densely populated working-class areas were even higher – Oldfield Park 63, Larkhall 81 and Twerton 147. As well as the Anglican parish churches there were memorials recording the losses of the Methodists of Claremont (9), Oldfield (11) and Walcot (8), the Baptists of Oldfield (13) and Manvers Street (26), the Catholics of St Mary's (13) and St John's (18), the Percy Congregational Church (10) and the Moravians (13). Schools also reckoned the number of their old boys who would never return to an earthly reunion – 34 from Bath City Secondary, 76 from Bath College. Others of the fallen were remembered on plaques erected by former colleagues. Nineteen men from Pitman's died, six from the Bath Gas Company and four each from Bath Tramways, the Post Office and the city's police force. Yet further memorials recall the members of the rugby clubs of the city and district, the eight lads of the YMCA scout troop and the twenty-five-year-old who was 'a scholar in Argyll Sunday School for twenty-one years.'

The impact of World War One on Bath and its surrounding district is detailed in Andrew Swift's definitive, densely-researched and profusely-illustrated study *All Roads Lead to France : Bath and the Great War* (Akeman Press 2005).

Marking Time

For Britain as a whole the inter-war years were scarred by protracted depression. After a brief post-war re-stocking boom unemployment rose past the 10 per cent mark in 1920 and never fell below it until 1940, a year into the Second World War. The impact of this curse was, however, very unevenly distributed, the main brunt falling on the traditional heavy industry and mining areas of the north of England, south Wales and central Scotland. The Midlands and the south remained relatively prosperous, thanks to the emergence of new technologically-based industries, a house-building boom and the growth of the service sector in such fields as retailing and entertainment.

Bath shared in these positive trends. Although its population increased scarcely at all between 1921 and 1931, some four thousand new houses were built in the inter-war years. Most were the product of private enterprise, many projects stringing lines of semi-detached houses along the approach roads to the city in a process of 'ribbon development'. But a thousand homes were also built by the council in five new estates. These developments required the establishment of new schools in Bath's suburbs to service them. In the city centre Georgian houses were split up, some to provide offices for doctors, solicitors and other professionals, but many to become flats, thus adding further to the city's housing stock. Other indicators of relative affluence included the opening of three cinemas, a large 'Co-op' and Woolworth's, a handsome new neo-Georgian Post Office and new offices for the electricity board. Outside the city centre the War Hospital was rebuilt as a new Royal United Hospital. Women benefited from the growing number of jobs for shop assistants, clerks and typists. Building providing male employment but this was seasonal.

VISITOR FIGURES

The census of 1921, taken in June, revealed, however, that there were 148 places in Britain where the presence of visitors increased the population by more than 3 per cent. Bath was not among them. Nor were Cheltenham or Leamington Spa. In terms of sheer numbers the most significant were the brash new resorts of Blackpool and Southend. But in terms of the sort of people who perhaps might otherwise have been in Bath the new rivals were small, seaside settlements like Broadstairs and Walton-on-the-Naze. Between 1921 and 1931 Bath experienced a substantial drop in the number of its female boarding-house keepers, from 536 to 371. The corporation continued to promote the city as a health resort with a view to boosting winter visitor numbers to the city's hotels and scored intermittent bullseyes in attracting the annual meetings of the British Medical Association (1925) and the Chartered Surveyors' Institute (1933) and by hosting two international conferences on rheumatic diseases (1928, 1938). It also promoted a John Wood Bicentennial Celebration in 1927.

DEATH BY WATER

In 1928 the corporation was involved in a major damage-limitation exercise when an outbreak of typhoid occurred at Bathwick Hill, afflicting thirty-two persons, of whom five died. The cause was a (foreseeable) pollution of the local water-supply, aggravated by the failure of council officials to act promptly in tackling it. Desperate to avoid the publicity inevitably attendant on any litigation, the corporation forked out more than £12,000 in compensation payments, almost £8,000 going to the widow of a deceased bank manager. The Waterworks Engineer resigned on health grounds, explicitly denying responsibility, and was immediately reappointed as a Consulting

Engineer. Implicitly conceding years of understaffing the Council approved the employment of three additional technical staff. Despite some limited coverage of the outbreak in the national press the full facts of the matter were successfully concealed, partly with the collusion of local newspapers in Bath. No public enquiry was ever held and the results of an internal enquiry were never published. But from 1932 onwards Bath joined the small number of towns which enjoyed the belated safeguard of a chlorinated water supply.

A CONSERVATIVE CITY

Despite the council's house-building programme and promotional efforts, at the depth of the depression, in 1932, Bath had some 3,000 unemployed. Had not improved transport links made it increasingly possible to commute to Bristol for work the figure might well have been higher. Although Bath was perceived as a city of old people the death-rate remained below the national average but there was a distinct rise in the incidence of pulmonary tuberculosis among children in the early 1930s. The infant mortality rate (deaths per 1,000 within a year of birth), perhaps the most sensitive indicator of general welfare, having plunged from 126 in 1900 to 51 by 1925, reversed to reach 57 in 1939.

Unemployment, and the wider fear of it, doubtless created social tensions but Bath remained solidly Conservative in its politics, with the Liberals, a spent force nationally, still providing the main opposition. The first local Labour candidate stood in 1918 but the General Strike of 1926, which paralysed major cities in the North, caused scarcely a ripple. In Bath members of nineteen unions came out to show their solidarity with the miners' resistance to pay-cuts and there were collections for Somerset's own local mining community; but there was no interruption to local supplies of gas and electricity and a thousand volunteers stepped forward to fill possible gaps in the provision of public services or transport. Visitor numbers dipped just 10 per cent below normal. No one was arrested.

PIONEERING CONSERVATION

The fabric of the city itself became a matter of increasing concern. The Assembly Rooms, now considered obsolete, in 1921 underwent the humiliation of conversion, the ballroom becoming a cinema, the tearoom a sales room. New Abbey cloisters were completed in 1923. An Act of Parliament of 1925 gave the council new powers over the design and materials of new buildings, which could be required to use 'Bath stone'. In 1929 Bath, Bristol and adjacent local authorities, in an early essay in 'planning', commissioned an outline regional scheme whose authors recognised Bath as 'a compact city in a setting of beautiful country especially to be preserved'. As a result the 1933 Bath District Planning Scheme became one of the first to incorporate the concept of a 'Green Belt' to limit the city's outward expansion. In 1934 the former Society for the Preservation of Old Bath (i.e. Georgian Bath), founded in 1908, was reincarnated as the Bath Preservation Trust. The Royal Literary and Scientific Institute was rebuilt in Queen Square in an approved neo-Georgian style. The Bath Corporation Act of 1937

The Royal Crescent

required the listing of all buildings dating from before 1820 and also obliged their owners to seek official approval before undertaking any alterations to them. In consultation with the Bath Preservation Trust a list of 1,251 buildings was compiled. Although only the facades were as yet protected from unlicensed alteration, this was still a pioneering scheme, predating by years the principle of listing which was to be embodied on a national scale in the 1944 Town and Country Planning Act. In 1938 the Assembly Rooms, restored to a former glory, were re-opened thanks to the generosity of an anonymous donor.

Cook's Tour de Force

Upon his death Ernest E. Cook (1865-1955), grandson of Thomas Cook (1808-92), founder of the global travel service, bequeathed a collection which was subsequently described as 'the most important that has ever been left to the National Art Collections Fund'. It consisted of over a hundred paintings, plus watercolours, drawings, furniture, tapestries, silver and porcelain. Although its component elements were to be distributed through almost a hundred museums and art galleries, the story of the collection properly belongs in this book because it was accumulated in Bath and many of its treasures can be seen in the Holburne Museum and the Victoria Art Gallery. The dispersal of the collection was at Cook's direct request, made in the characteristic hope that it would deflect public and press attention away from him.

In terms of his career in the family firm Ernest Cook was a financial technician, the developer of the company's traveller's cheque and foreign exchange business. Cook's financial expertise and acumen would become obvious not only in the way that he built up his art collection with great rapidity but also in the way that he also managed to 'collect' Montacute House and sixteen other country estates totalling 37,000 acres.

Cook retired to Bath following the sale of the family business in 1928. In 1931, learning that the city's historic Assembly Rooms were in danger of demolition, he conspired with the Society for the Protection of Ancient Buildings to acquire them for the National Trust and, typically, managed to keep his involvement a secret for over a decade. Cook thus came to collecting late, in his sixties. Acquiring Nos. 8 and 9 Sion Hill Place as staff accommodation, he extended No. 1 Sion Hill Place to create a picture gallery behind the majestic ashlar façade of a demolished town house relocated from Chippenham. A lifelong involvement in the travel trade did nothing to dilute Cook's passion for 'Old England' and English furniture and British paintings of the eighteenth and early nineteenth centuries figured prominently among his acquisitions. These included works by Gainsborough, Constable, Cotman and Crome. Another strand was represented by the Dutch masters who exerted such an influence on these East Anglian painters. Further acquisitions included works by Claude Lorrain, Tiepolo, Angelica Kauffmann, Romney, Zoffany, Morland and Turner. Stipple engravings of the notorious Georgiana, Duchess of Devonshire and the actresses Elizabeth Farren and Sarah Siddons (see page 126) can now be seen in the Victoria Art Gallery. The Holburne Museum has Gainsborough's portrait of his friend and family physician, Dr Rice Charlton, George Stubbs conversation piece *The Reverend Carter Thelwall and his Family*, Zoffany's portrait of Queen Charlotte, George Morland's *Horse and Dog in a Stable*, and *The Deserter Pardoned*, typical of the genre subjects which were his staple output, Patrick Nasmyth's *Cottage among Trees*, characteristically more cloud than cottage, and Turner's *Pembroke Castle*. Other items from the Cook collection are to be seen from Ipswich and Brighton to Sheffield and Kendal but also more locally in Bristol, Cheltenham and Oxford.

Emperor in Exile

From 1936 to 1941 Fairfield House, Newbridge, a mid-Victorian Italianate villa, was the home of His Imperial Majesty Haile Selassie I of Ethiopia. Ascending the throne in 1931, Haile Selassie gave his people their first written constitution and initiated a cautious programme of modernisation but was forced into exile by the brutal invasion of Fascist Italian forces which quickly overran his country. The emperor pleaded his country's cause with eloquence before the General Assembly of the League of Nations but to little practical effect, although *Time* magazine chose him as its Man of the Year. Settling in Bath with his family, the emperor, a slight, erect and elegant figure, became a regular sight on the streets of Bath and an habitual patron of the ABC cinema. Reinstated to power following the British liberation of Ethiopia in 1941, Haile Selassie returned to Bath in 1954 during his state visit to Britain and received the Freedom of the City. In 1958 he donated Fairfield House to the city, which converted it into a retirement home for the elderly. The emperor also gave the name Fairfield to a palace he built for himself as a rural retreat in Ethiopia. Deposed by Marxist revolutionaries in 1974, he died in captivity the following year, possibly as a result of bungled prostate surgery. He is revered by Rastafarians as an incarnation of the Godhead.

Ordeal by Fire

The outbreak of war in September 1939 brought many newcomers to Bath. Even before then there was an influx of Irish labourers, employed to build underground ammunition dumps in the quarries at Corsham and Monkton Farleigh. The evacuation of children and mothers brought in over 4,000 people in the first four days of September, although almost half of these were moved on to nearby towns and villages. One of the school age evacuees was Roger Bannister who in 1954 would become the first man in the world to run a mile in less than four minutes.

The influx of children was accompanied by the relocation of staff from businesses normally headquartered in the capital, such as the Royal London Assurance Society or the accounts department of Marks and Spencer. By Christmas 1939 the resident population of Bath had increased by 10,000.

AN ADMIRAL INVASION

The largest invasion was by the Admiralty, which moved in more than half its staff and took over the Royal United Hospital, the School of Art and many of the city's larger hotels, including the Empire, the Grand Pump Room, the Spa and the Pulteney, filling them with intelligence officers and technical 'boffins' designing submarines or minesweeping equipment. One of the boffins, transferred to Bath in 1944, was a brilliant young naval architect, Alfred Sims (1907-77), already chief designer and constructor of the Royal Navy's submarines. After the war Sims would design the Navy's first nuclear submarine, *Dread-nought*. Knighted for his services to naval architecture, Sir Alfred Sims would then become prominent in the affairs of Bath's YMCA, the Bath Choral and Orchestral Society and the Council of the University of Bath.

Bath householders were paid a guinea – one pound, one shilling – a week to take in and feed Admiralty 'billetees', who thus became known as 'guinea pigs'. Many Bathonians resented these unwanted guests who, in their turn, often felt less than welcome. One evacuated civil servant vehemently denounced to the local press the living conditions endured by himself and a colleague, obliged to:

> eat, sleep and live in a dimly-lit room where dust accumulates undisturbed. We must buy our own coal and light our own fire. A fruit basket is our coal-scuttle, a stair-rod our poker … Two wafer-like slices of a sausage, hostile in nationality if not in odour, with bread and margarine and a pot of tea is our usual repast. We grow thin while our billetor and his family grow fat on our butter, tea, sugar and meat rations. What … is the mentality of these vile things who would help the enemy by starving the workers?"

ALL CHANGE FOR WAR

Like any other British city Bath was called on to make sacrifices and undertake extraordinary exertions. Whole streets of houses lost their garden railings as they were requisitioned for scrap, supposedly to be transformed into the materiel of war, though many civilians remained sceptical of their ultimate destination or destiny. The 'Dig for Victory' campaign led to the establishment of allotments even in such aesthetically sacrosanct locations as the area in front of the Royal Crescent, where they were still being cultivated well into the 1950s. Stothert and Pitt turned once more to the manufacture of weapons, including gun mountings for tanks, 'human torpedoes', minesweeping gear and the concrete mixers used for the construction of airfield runways. The Horstmann Gear Company made fire control instruments and Bath Aircraft made wooden components for assault gliders. The Octagon on Milsom Street became the central food office and the recently-restored

Assembly Rooms were commandeered to serve as a food depot.

The city likewise prepared itself for aerial onslaught and the possibility of invasion. Shelters were built in the streets, slit-trenches in the parks. When the call went out for a volunteer defence force in May 1940 six hundred came forward within days as the core of what became two Home Guard battalions, one recruited from the city, the other from the Admiralty establishment, with an eventual combined strength of 2,700. At Coleshill House, outside the city, over three hundred specially selected recruits were put through a secret and intensive course in guerrilla warfare techniques. In case of German invasion these would operate in five or six man teams as 'Auxiliary Units' to delay, harass and sabotage the operations of the invader. Official expectations were that nearly all would be dead within a fortnight.

Efforts to establish an effective 'Fire Guard' to back up the Fire Brigade were, however, hampered by bureaucratic muddles and delay. The major tasks of the Fire Guard would be to identify fires as soon as they were started and to tackle and contain them until trained assistance could arrive. But the attempt to establish a workable roster was swamped by an avalanche of paperwork and resources were concentrated on checking out who was and was not exempt from service, rather than on creating an effective organisation. Even the council's own premises were woefully short of such basic fire-fighting tools as buckets, sand mats and stirrup pumps. This deficiency in Bath's defences would eventually have disastrous consequences, but not until almost a year after the main 'Blitz' against Britain had supposedly ended.

The Baedeker *Blitz*

Between May 1940 and August 1941 Bath experienced some 875 'red alerts' as German planes flew over the city but it remained virtually unmolested as the raiders pressed on to rain down destruction on the port of Bristol or the important aircraft factory in its suburbs at Filton. Between 19 June 1940 and 5 July 1941 Bristol was attacked fifty-three times. Although enemy aerial reconnaissance had identified new hutments and other constructions at Fox Hill, Lansdown and Swainswick, German intelligence was uncertain of their purpose and designated Bath as 'a lesser town without specific aiming points.'

Bath fire crews were regularly called into the neighbouring city to support Bristol's own hard-stretched brigade. On nine occasions in the period before the spring of 1942 Bath did suffer slight attacks, as a result of apparently stray missiles ditched at random. On 16 March 1941 three men and three evacuee children were killed and twenty-six injured at Twerton. On 11/12 April 1941 the Dolemeads area of Widcombe was hit; eleven died, including two married couples and two infants, and fifty-two were injured.

Bath's ordeal came in April 1942 as part of a retaliatory campaign ordered by Hitler in response to the RAF's 28 March devastation of the cities of Lübeck and Rostock, medieval gems whose many wooden buildings provided ideal fuel for a massive fire storm. The Luftwaffe High Command was henceforth ordered to ensure that 'when targets are being selected, preference is to be given to those where attacks are likely to have the greatest possible effect on civilian life … terror attacks of a retaliatory nature are to be carried out against towns other than London.' Selecting their targets from the celebrated *Baedeker* guidebooks, the Luftwaffe determined to exact revenge by destroying the historic fabric of such top-rated ancient cities as Exeter, York, Norwich, Canterbury – and Bath.

FIRE, DEATH AND DEVASTATION

Bath was not only poorly defended but also, being near to the coast, relatively easy for even inexperienced crews to find on a moonlit night. The first wave of the Nazi onslaught on Bath began just before 11.20 p.m. on Saturday 25 April as German pathfinders dropped flares to mark the target for the main bomber force. The attack was carried out at a low level and accompanied by machine-gunning of the streets to deter fire-fighters from trying to limit the spread of fires. The raid lasted fifty minutes and inflicted ninety-one fatalities. Unfortunately several of Bath's fire appliances had been despatched to Bristol and the severance of most of the city's telephone lines disrupted the response of the emergency services severely. Most fortunately, however, none of Bath's hospitals was hit. German losses were light, amounting to three planes shot down by British night-fighters and a further two crashing on returning to the bases in France, probably damaged by coastal anti-aircraft fire.

There was but the briefest respite before the same bombers, having rearmed and refuelled, returned as a second, even more destructive, raiding-force, to fall on the city just before dawn on Sunday morning 26 April, leaving a hundred and fifty-one dead after another raid of fifty minutes. This phase cost the raiders only one bomber lost and one other damaged. A German press release was understandably exultant – 'The attack ... went entirely according to plan and repaid the British for their wanton destruction of living quarters, cultural monuments and welfare arrangements in ancient German cities.' On the same evening the RAF struck Rostock for the fourth successive time.

A third attack pounded the city between 1.25 and 2.05 a.m. on Monday 27 April, inflicting a further one hundred and sixty-two fatalities and starting ninety fires, six of which developed into major areas of devastation. The raiders lost only a single bomber, although three more were successfully intercepted and turned back before reaching their intended target.

During the course of the three raids West Twerton School, being used as a rest and feeding centre, received a direct hit. There was also great loss of life at the Regina Hotel in Russell Street. The total number of deaths amounted to just over four hundred, including thirty-four civil defence workers, police, firemen and Home Guard. The latter included two privates in the Home Guard who had distinguished themselves, rescuing and treating the shocked and injured during the first and second raids, before themselves dying as a result of a direct hit while being on duty again during the Monday onslaught. Allan Woods was nineteen. Fred Park, who had saved at least six lives, was just seventeen. They are buried side by side in St Michael's cemetery. Nine Fire Guards, ranging in age from seventeen to sixty-one, died in action, the highest total of any civil defence unit in Bath. The remains of over a hundred of the dead were beyond identification and consigned to two mass-graves at Haycombe Cemetery. A large space was left between the two interments in anticipation of further mass-casualties. The names of the dead are inscribed in a Book of Remembrance kept in the Abbey.

In proportion to the size of the city's population Bath suffered a higher percentage of fatalities than Bristol, the target for far more frequent Luftwaffe attention. Death-tolls in the other *Baedeker* cities were also significantly lower than in Bath – at Exeter 256, Norwich 171, York 83. Of the city's landmark buildings St James's church, St Andrew's and Holy Trinity were completely lost. Individual properties were damaged by fire in the Royal Crescent, the Circus, Norfolk Crescent and the Paragon. Half of the south side of Queen Square was demolished. Seymour Place, Somerset Place and All Saints', Lansdown were totally wrecked. There was extensive destruction in the area of Julian Road. Most significant of all was the gutting of the Assembly Rooms. This may well have been, in the words of contemporary outrage 'a monument to German savagery' but what was remarkable, considering that the explicit objective of the *Baedeker* raids was to batter British morale by vandalising the nation's cultural heritage, was how little of Bath's prized architecture was harmed. By far the worst-hit areas were the working-class districts to the west and south-west of the city centre – Kingsmead, Green Park, Oldfield Park, Holloway and Twerton. In all 329 buildings were destroyed outright, over a thousand rendered uninhabitable and a further eighteen thousand damaged. It was an ironic comment on Bath's lack of preparedness that another casualty of the raids was a stockpile of 15,000 'Fire Guard' armlets, which had lain unissued in a store since October 1941. After the war the *Official History* of Britain's Civil Defence (1950) noted damningly:

... Bath ... had been considered a safe town and perhaps for that reason was virtually unprepared. Training was inadequate and equipment defective; in many buildings there were no fire guards at all and a lack of leadership contributed to an exodus of fire guards on the second night.

In the immediate aftermath of the raid the city's residents were grateful to take advantage of a mobile Post Office service which enabled hundreds to send reassuring telegrams to family and friends. A volunteer force of university students came from Bristol with their bicycles to act as message-carriers. Mobile laundries proved equally welcome, as did the positive avalanche of clothes donated from all parts of the country. John Piper (1903-92), an official War Artist, came to Bath just four days after the raids and painted views of the destruction of Somerset Place and All Saints Chapel. HM King George VI and Queen Mary made a morale-boosting tour of the city in May, by which time some three thousand building tradesmen had been recruited to set about the most immediate tasks of repair.

Later that summer Bath received a novel and bracing infusion of youth, cash and confidence in the shape of thousands of American servicemen who soon discovered that Bath, for all its respectable reserve, had much more to offer at weekends than Warminster. The Lansdowne Grove Hotel was requisitioned to serve as a leave hostel for US servicemen and one of the houses in the Royal Crescent was turned into a club for American officers.

Betjeman's Bath

The future Poet Laureate John Betjeman (1906-84) came to Bath in 1944 to deploy his literary skills in 'P branch', a secret section of the Admiralty. Rejected by the RAF, Betjeman had previously worked as a film-maker with the Ministry of Information and as a press-attaché in Dublin. Before the war he had been assistant editor of the *Architectural Review*. From the 1960s he would become nationally known as one of the pioneers of conservation and an implacable, if good-humoured, enemy of planners and developers who ignored – or were simply ignorant of – the special qualities of history and topography which had shaped or defined the character of a specific location.

In the immediate post-war period, Betjeman lived first at Farnborough and then at Wantage, both within easy driving distance of Bath. He knew the city well and wrote about it with both affection and passion and was swift to denounce its post-war 'reconstruction' in *The Newest Bath Guide*, contrasting the elegance and gallantry of the Georgian city with the tide of planned mediocrity which was about to engulf it:

> In those days no doubt there was not so much taste
> But now there's so much it has all gone to waste
> In working out methods of cutting down cost –
> So that mouldings, proportion and texture are lost
> In a uniform nothingness. (This I first find

In the terrible 'Tech' with its pointed behind.)
Now houses are 'units' and people are digits
And Bath has been planned into quarters for midgets.
Official designs are aggressively neuter
The Puritan work of an eyeless computer.
Goodbye to old Bath ! We who loved you are sorry
They're carting you off by developer's lorry.

The Plan

'Planning' and its siren handmaidens, Bureaucracy and Technology, were all the go in post-war Britain. The war had given a tremendous stimulus to all three, enormously expanding the functions of the state, enhancing the self-confidence of civil servants and, perhaps under the temporary but powerful influence of the Yankee 'can do' mentality of Britain's most powerful ally, promoting a novel belief in the possibility of a technical 'fix' for every problem and the virtues of a clean slate, target-setting approach to the problems of collective life. The undoubted contribution of brainy, backstairs 'boffins' to victory provided a further rationale for the belief that if planning could win the war it could certainly organise the peace. The Beveridge Report of 1942 looked forward to the establishment of a comprehensive scheme of social security 'from the cradle to the grave'. The Education Act of 1944 committed post-war Britain to raising the school-leaving age and envisaged slotting children at secondary level into grammar, modern and technical schools according to their aptitude as determined by supposedly objective tests of intelligence. Post-war governments were likewise also to be committed to economic policies which would promote full employment.

In the brave new world of post-war planning the great guru was Professor Sir Patrick Abercrombie (1879-1957), an internationally pre-eminent figure, with projects in hand for the redevelopment of cities on four continents. Abercrombie had grown up in historic Chester and trained as an architect. Although a superb draughtsman, he had never actually built anything major himself. Instead he became the founding editor of the *Town Planning Review*, won the international competition to redesign Dublin, founded the Council for the Preservation of Rural England and became President of the Town Planning Institute. In 1933 he published *Town and Country Planning*. In 1935 he became Professor of Town Planning at University College, London and an ardent promoter of the Green Belt policy to limit the suburban sprawl of the metropolis. In the immediate aftermath of the blitz of 1940-41 he was commissioned to devise comprehensive plans for the redevelopment of London and Greater London after victory had been achieved. Knighted in 1945, Abercrombie supervised the development of a ring of satellite 'New Towns' around London and produced plans for the reconstruction of devastated Plymouth, Hull, Edinburgh, the Clyde region and the West Midlands. Given the scale of Abercrombie's other commitments Bath might well have considered itself fortunate to merit his attention.

In 1947 Bryan Little, a Cambridge classicist turned civil servant, who had been drafted to Bath as a member of the Admiralty establishment, published an affectionate outline history of his adoptive city - *The Building of Bath 47-1947: An Architectural and Social Study*. The closing chapter was devoted to 'The New Plan'. Made public in February 1945, three months before the war actually ended, it was the work of a Joint Planning Committee, led by Abercrombie, Mr Mealand, Bath's own Town Planning Officer, and Mr Owens, the City Engineer. According to Little 'it was offered, not as a hard and fast blue-print, but as a set of guiding ideas.' Or, in the words of the Plan itself, 'an evolutionary programme of orderly progressive development for the next fifty years.' It had no legal sanction and was open to modification. Moreover, according to Little, 'it caters for no wholesale demolitions nor for any large realignments and rebuildings from the earth upwards … new work would mainly be on sites little affected by earlier building or else in areas cleared by the *Luftwaffe* in 1942.'

Bearing in mind that not only had large areas of Britain's cities been devastated by enemy action but that almost no construction had been undertaken since 1939 for anything other than military or industrial purposes, Britain faced an acute post-war housing crisis, aggravated by the fact that some five million service personnel would be demobilised, the great majority young adults eager to reconstitute their families or establish new ones. One of the Bath Plan's top priorities was, therefore, building new homes and the 'conversion of existing buildings to the servantless needs of the post war age.' The latter, Little at least foresaw, would be a 'delicate operation' given the existence of a new world 'whose social life is no longer even remotely like that of the well-staffed yet insanitary eighteenth century.' This would involve 'a matter of delicate artistic adjustments and severe economic headaches, for really good conversion is often as costly as new building…'. Little conceded the unavoidable loss of quality interiors as the price of preserving historic facades – 'it may be hard not to mourn the breaking up of large and stately Georgian first and second-floor rooms which will be sad but inevitable if hundreds of terrace houses are to be turned into flats or maisonettes.' It was envisaged that most housing would be provided in thirteen new designated 'neighbourhoods', circling the central part of the city.

A second Plan priority was to improve traffic management, routing through travellers round the city via the bombed sections north of the Circus and Crescent. Little likewise noted that proposals for 'widened local roads' had already become 'one of the more controversial sections of the Plan.' Abercrombie also envisaged the construction of a broad esplanade sweeping along the curve of the Avon and the construction of no less than five new bridges across the river.

The third component would be 'ideas for the large single units, for the public and industrial buildings of Bath.' One of Abercrombie's notions was to flatten the entire area behind the Royal Crescent to create space for a 'Centre of Civic Administration', linked to the centre of the Crescent, which would be partially colonised for the same purpose. Other possibilities included 'shops and other undefined buildings for commerce or residence', a 'new and much enlarged research centre and National Hospital for rheumatic diseases', 'a badly needed omnibus station', a Concert Hall (to be built over Abbey Green!), a 'new Great Western Station'(to hell with Brunel, apparently) and 'new shopping centres, particularly in the rebuilding of central Bath's one large bomb-wasted area in Kingsmead.' The only new public building actually to go up between the publication of the Plan and the publication of Little's book was in Broad Street 'a multi-coloured slab of architectural bad manners put up in 1946 by the Ministry of Labour'. It was not an encouraging portent. On the other hand Bath was swift to take advantage of the provisions of the 1947 Town and Country Planning Act to designate over two thousand local buildings as Grade I or Grade II and another thousand as Grade III.

Little took it as axiomatic that

> it goes without saying that nearly all Georgian Bath must stay, even the second-class streets like Alfred Street… or Daniel Street… for once kill Georgian Bath and there will be fewer golden eggs even though Bladud's springs gush merrily enough. Above all, it will be in its execution and in the actual design and detail of the new buildings that the Plan will stand or fall. Probably it will be all the better if left as much as possible to local people…

Little did Little suspect what this would mean in practice…

THE SACK OF BATH

Abercrombie's scheme was never carried through but its utopian spirit metamorphosed into a malignant spectre which, while apparently respectful of the city's acknowledged architectural gems, retained an apparently insatiable urge to 'clear' whatever failed to achieve the category of unchallengeable excellence. Apparent indifference towards the value of architecture intended for the artisan rather than the aristocrat was implicitly endorsed by Walter Ison's authoritative 1948 study of *The Georgian Buildings of Bath*, which pretty much ignored the city's humbler structures, as did the first edition of Pevsner's *The Buildings of England: North Somerset and Bristol* (1958).

As Graham Davis and Penny Bonsall have cogently observed 'vision and optimism were not in short supply in the mid-1940s but money and materials were. Repairing bomb damage and increasing the housing stock took priority over plazas …'. The Moorlands Housing Estate, consisting of semi-detached and terrace houses in Bath stone, was completed by 1950, the year that the wholesale self-devastation of historic Bath began. Between then and 1973 over a thousand Georgian buildings, a third of them listed, were demolished. Entire streets were sacrificed to the wrecking-ball and the bulldozer - Charles Street, Calton Road, Lambridge Street, Philip Street … Grade II early eighteenth century houses in St James's Street South went to make way for a new Woolworth's. Ten acres of streets and courts and alleyways were flattened for the Southgate shopping centre. No. 1 Trim Street, one of the first houses to be built outside the city walls went in 1969. Other casualties included some four hundred houses in Holloway, most from before 1875, some dating back to the seventeenth century, and the house in Twerton where Henry Fielding wrote much of *Tom Jones*.

This holocaust was irately chronicled – and shockingly illustrated – in Adam Fergusson's *The Sack of Bath: A Record and an Indictment* (1973). Written on behalf of the Bath Preservation Trust, it made the city an icon of iconoclasm. Fergusson stated the core of his case on his very first page by stressing that what made Bath so very special was not just

> a beauty unusual even for its time (but the fact that) to all intents and purposes Bath was a 'New Town'; and practically all the artisan housing ... was planned and built in conjunction with the big set pieces ... Eighteenth century Bath had virtually no decay in it. The terraced cottages ... were of brand new Bath stone ... as perfect and graceful and harmonious as the Bath of the middle and upper classes. All Bath grew old together. It was unique.

The evils of destruction were compounded by the sins of construction. In Fergusson's words 'almost every original construction for twenty years in Bath has to some degree been an environmental calamity ... not one a positive embellishment' and most 'unusually obtrusive' to boot. Offending examples singled out by Fergusson included the Technical College (1957–63) 'the squat nastiness of the bus station' (1958), Rosewell Court (1960), Northwick House (1961), Kingsmead House (1964–5) and the Sports Centre (1972–3). The climactic catastrophe was the building (1969–73) of the Ballance Street Flats below Lansdown Road. Constructed, apparently with unknowing irony, out of reconstituted stone, with sham mansards, they were designed by Bath's own City Architect and Planning Officer, Dr Howard Stutchbury, and occupied a site whose clearance involved the wholesale annihilation of 137 houses dating from the period 1773–83. Fergusson described the new flats as 'ugly, intrusive and tasteless; out of character and scale and harmony ... perhaps the most detested new addition to the Bath scene.'Writing thirty years later conservation architect Michael Forsyth, author of the Bath 'Pevsner' noted that 'their construction helped stem the tide of urban destruction by planners, not just in Bath but nationally.' But not before the completion (1972) of the Beauford (now Hilton) Hotel, which Forsyth judges now to be 'the most reviled building in Bath.'

Fergusson's judgment on the 'guilty men' was that they were 'lacking the advantage of an outsider's point of view, unable to see the wood for the trees, confused by local politics ... for otherwise only bottomless philistinism appears to explain what they have done.' And, as he pointed out, 'the professionals' were well paid for what they were doing and controlled extensive human, technical and cash resources. Their opponents fought their fight in their own time, dependent on whatever meagre assets of expertise and funds they could mobilise, all too often finding out that action was 'too late, too difficult or too expensive.' Nevertheless, as Tim Mowl could underline in 1989, *The Sack of Bath* proved to be a bombshell – 'No single literary defence of an architectural heritage has ever been so immediately effective ... Demolition of old buildings came to a virtual full stop.' Proposals for the demolition or partial demolition of Beauford Square, Kingsmead Square and New Bond Street were all defeated. Marshal Wade's House, No. 1 Royal Crescent and St Ann's Place were restored. New museums were opened to tell the story of Bath at Work and The Building of Bath. Decayed Green Park station was regenerated. The quarrying of Bath's past was set on a more systematic basis by the formation of a History of Bath Research Group and the publication of a *Bath Journal*.

Making the Working City Work

In the immediate post-war period it had been assumed that Bath's population would rise from an estimated 76,000 in 1945 to reach 100,000. By 1971 it had in fact only reached 84,670 and by 1981 had fallen back slightly to 80,771. Contrary to the popular image Bath did not have a particularly aged population profile. Only 22.6 per cent of its population was over sixty, compared with a national average of 17.7 per cent. The growth of the city's institutions of higher education over succeeding decades would, moreover, give its entertainment facilities an increasing orientation towards the tastes of a 'yoof' market.

Manufacturing continued to remain an important sector of employment in the quarter century after the war. The shoemaking firm Clark's of Street opened a new factory in the city. As late as the 1970s there were still five thousand people employed in engineering and another two thousand in printing and publishing. But by then manufacturing jobs had been outnumbered by service sector jobs in a ratio of three to one. The closure of Stothert & Pitt in 1987 was a landmark in the city's industrial history. The Ministry of Defence was still then the largest single employer but was increasingly rivalled by the new university, established in 1966. Health services remained another major job provider, as did retailing. In retailing Bath bucked national trends to maintain a large number of small, independently-operated, specialist outlets. There were no large out of town shopping centres, partly at least because there were few plausibly suitable sites.

Writing in 1961 the journalist Alistair Cooke predicted that 'Bath's best future is as a tourist town; and unlike some other tourist traps that are bedecked and bedizened for the visitor, Bath has no need to add anything. All it has to do to become a beautiful but animated museum is to clean and restore and expose the lovely shell of a town which attracted everybody there in the eighteenth century …'. The visit of the Queen in 1973 to mark the thousandth anniversary of King Edgar's coronation and the organisation of a William Beckford exhibition signalled a renewed awareness of the significance of the city's cultural heritage. By 1980 tourism was estimated to employ about one in seven of the population, although it also had a significant indirect impact on employment in transport, construction and retailing. A contemporary survey revealed that 50 per cent of visitors had shopping as their top priority, as opposed to 22 per cent who rated architecture and sight-seeing their major concern.

CORPORATION POWER

Bath Corporation continued to exercise more power over the development of the city than many of its counterparts elsewhere in Britain, not least because, thanks to a policy maintained over centuries, it enjoyed a substantial income from such lucrative attractions as the Pump Room and the Roman Baths, as well as rents from shops and cash generated from leisure facilities and car parking charges. Shaping Bath's future in the visionary tradition of Abercrombie remained a civic preoccupation. In 1963 Bath commissioned Colin Buchanan and Partners to carry out a Planning and Transport Study which resulted in a proposal to relieve the flow of east-west traffic through the city by building a 500 metre tunnel under the north-central area of the city from Walcot Street to New King Street. In 1966 the Minister of Housing and Local Government intervened by ordering an investigation of 'how to reconcile our old towns with the twentieth century, without actually knocking them down.' (For twentieth century read motor car.) Four case studies were selected for examination – Chester, Chichester, York and Bath. In each instance it was recognised that successful urban management required balancing the trade-off between the preservation of cultural assets and the efficient functioning of their setting as an economic unit.

The Buchanan Study was not formally debated until 1971. A public enquiry established the following year was quashed before it got down to work. The tunnel proposal finally died the death in 1979. By then the ground rules had been decisively changed as a consequence of the 1972 Local Government Act which had created a new County of Avon. Bath could still call itself a city and keep its mayor and coat of arms but technically it was now just a district whose powers over education and highways had passed to the county and whose hospitals were henceforth under the control of an autonomous health authority. At the same time as powers were being taken away from the corporation, planning decisions were increasingly facing determined and skilful opposition from conservationist and other activist organisations including the Bath Action Group, the Bath Environmental Campaign and the Bath Amenity and Transport Association,

Writing in 1982 the author Jan Morris, a sometime resident of Bath, detected 'the old place stirring with new life and bounciness'. It has continued to stir. The Abbey underwent a massive multi-million pound clean up in time for the Millennium. The city has acquired a second university appropriately named Bath Spa. Sir Nicholas Grimshaw's uncompromising Thermae Spa building , towering over the ancient Cross Bath, fittingly restates the city's origins as – a bath.

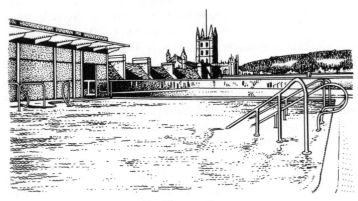

The Thermae Spa

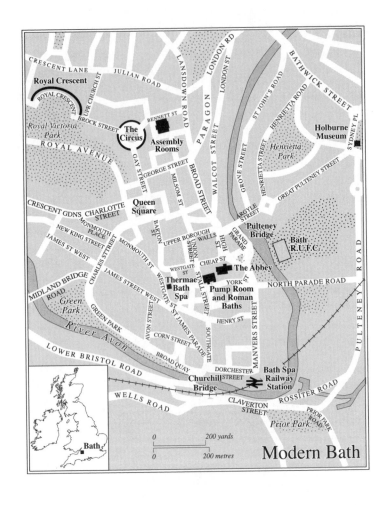

Modern Bath

Bath Walks: 1

A Quick Bath

If your time in Bath is strictly limited it should be possible to do the following walk, starting and ending at Bath Spa railway station (see page 187), in two to three hours, taking in over thirty of Bath's main sights and attractions. (The names in brackets refer to some former residents and their homes). There is a tourism centre in the station (Tel 01225 444102) and public lavatories at Seven Dials.

From the station go forward onto **Manvers Street**.

On the right is the **Book Museum**, which features the history of bookbinding, a craft for which Bath became renowned. Should you need either of them the new Southgate shopping centre will be to the left and the police station (Tel 01225 444343) further along to the right.

Turn right at the end of the parking area on the right to enter **South Parade** (No. 6 Sir Walter Scott, 7 Tobias Smollett, 14 Fanny Burney). The imposing church of **St John the Evangelist** (by Charles Francis Hansom, brother of the inventor of the Hansom cab, 1861-3) is striking evidence of both the mid-Victorian resurgence of Roman Catholicism in Britain and the disregard of Gothic Revival architects for Bath's Georgian heritage.

Turn left along **Duke Street** (note the widest pavement in Bath). No. 1 was the office of local architect John Pinch the Younger (see page 95). Exit onto North (originally Grand) Parade. **North Parade**, Duke Street and South Parade were all part of a single development (1738-48) by John Wood the Elder (see page 106) which was intended to extend further south as a 'Royal Forum'. As their name implies the Parades were intended as promenades, the North for summer, the South for autumn and winter. Here fashionably-dressed visitors to Georgian Bath would take a leisurely stroll, to see and be seen, pausing for introductions, assignations, invitations and conversation.

Look north over **Parade Gardens** (an orchard in the seventeenth century, laid out as a garden by the 1730s) for a view of Robert Adam's splendid **Pulteney Bridge** (1769-74), one of only three in the world to have shops on both sides. To its left is the bulky presence of the former **Empire Hotel** (see page 200). The area in front with the island garden (named for Alkmaar, Bath's Dutch twin town) is **Orange Grove**, with an obelisk raised by Richard 'Beau' Nash (see page 97) to commemorate the visit (1734) of the Prince of Orange to take the waters.

Go left (west) along **North Parade** (No. 5 Edmund Burke, 9 William Wilberforce, William Wordsworth, 11 Oliver Goldsmith), crossing Pierrepont Street, to pass **The Huntsman** pub. This was built (1748-50) as a shop, later became the Parade Coffee House and has been a pub since 1906. With four Ionic half-columns and three arches, it has the only surviving eighteenth-century stone shop front in Bath. Pass into **North Parade Passage**, birthplace of stagecoach pioneer John Palmer (see page 142), to reach **Sally Lunn's House** (see page 89) (Tel 01225 461634). The basement museum reveals the Roman foundations of the oldest house in Bath plus a medieval bakery and objects from recent excavations. Continue forward to enter the charming enclosure of **Abbey Green** with its massive plane tree dating from 1880. The popular Crystal Palace public house (*ca.*1780) has an attractive walled beer-garden at the rear.

Exit right (north) into **York Street** to see the south side of **Bath Abbey** in front of you. The main **Tourist Information Centre** (Tel 09067112000) is to your right and has a first-class selection of books, maps and guides.

Go left round the Abbey to admire the west front and note the entrance to the **Pump Room and Roman Baths** (see page 19)(Tel 01225 477785) and, at No. 14, the ornate upper façade of the **National Trust Shop**, (built *ca.* 1720), the former home of Field Marshal Wade (see page 104). The World Heritage symbol – a unique distinction for an English city - is set in the pavement at the entrance to the Pump Room.

Continue round the Abbey onto **Cheap Street** and then pass along the north side of Orange Grove onto **Grand Parade** for a view of the City Weir, a close-up of Pulteney Bridge and, across the other side of the River Avon, Bath Rugby Club's ground. Continue left to the **Victoria Art Gallery** at the corner for the view along Pulteney Bridge towards Bath's most imposing thoroughfare, **Great Pulteney Street**, with the **Holburne Museum** (see page 196) and **Sydney Gardens** (see page 140) at its far end.

Go left along **Bridge Street,** which has a fine shopfront of *ca*. 1830 at No. 7, and then left into the **High Street.** Pass the lively and historic covered Market (1775, rebuilt internally 1861-3) to come to the handsome Palladian **Guildhall** (by City Architect Thomas Baldwin – see page 93). Its High Street elevation (best seen when you cross to the other side of the street at the zebra crossing) is considered by local conservation expert Michael Forsyth to be 'the best in Bath and the Banqueting Hall within … the best interior.' Forsyth argues that its splendour was a deliberate architectural riposte to the aristocratic Assembly Rooms 'from which many civic dignitaries, mainly tradespeople, were socially excluded'. Look up to see the figure of Justice, supposedly modelled on the Bluestocking historian Catherine Macaulay (see page 115). The Guildhall is open (free) on Mondays 9-5 and occasionally at other times (Tel 01225 477782).

Cross on the zebra to pass through The Corridor (see page 185) shopping mall, where William Friese-Green, pioneer of cinematography, once had a photographic studio at No. 9. Glance left and right where it cuts through Union Passage to appreciate the survival of the narrow medieval street-lines in this area. Emerge onto Union Street (built up by Thomas Baldwin 1805-10), and turn right, passing Upper Borough Walls, which marks the northern boundary of the medieval walled city, then continue right as far as Burton Street to go left and immediately right into pedestrianised Old Bond Street, which is notable for pleasing shopfronts, like the double bow-fronts of *ca*.1800 at Nos. 7-8.

Enter **Milsom Street**. Built up from 1761 to connect the heart of medieval Bath with the expanding upper town, it was named for schoolmaster Daniel Milsom, a member of the City Corporation and developed by his son, Charles. It became very fashionable both commercially and residentially. General Tilney in Jane Austen's *Northanger Abbey* lived here. The street also became the focus of civic jollifications on occasions of royal or patriotic celebration.

The beautiful **Octagon Chapel** (see page 120) is down a passageway to the left of the shop at No. 46.

Nos.37-42, **Somersetshire Buildings**, were built (1781-3) speculatively as five grand houses by Thomas Baldwin. The ground floor front room of No. 39 has a fine plaster ceiling. Nos.7–14 is **Jolly's** department store (see page 174), with the most extravagant shopfront in Bath at Nos.11–13, built in 1879 by another City Architect, C.E. Davis (see page 198). At the top of the street both corner buildings were built as banks, No. 24 (east side) in 1865, No. 23 (west side, now The Litten Tree pub) in 1873–5. (The date stone of 1902 refers to later alterations).

At the top is **George Street** with the celebrated **Hole-in-the-Wall** restaurant (see page 71) on its north side. In the 1930s it was a snack bar which pioneered the local sale of 'hot dogs'. At the eastern end Selina, Countess of Huntingdon (see page 119) lived at No. 4 Edgar Buildings and the painter William Hoare (see page 163) at Nos. 5–6. Prince's Buildings are named after William's brother, the sculptor Prince Hoare (see page 164), who lived at No. 5. The Royal York Hotel was originally York Buildings (1755–9 by John Wood the Younger) but became a coaching inn by 1769 and the starting-point for one of the stage-coach services to London. The then Princess Victoria stayed here in 1830 when she came to open Victoria Park. Eminent German architect Karl Friedrich Schinkel was another guest. No. 11 George Street has a spectacular shopfront of 1909.

Turn left along George Street (note plaque on No. 13 on the north side celebrating Bath's unique contribution to philately) to reach the steep ascent of **Gay Street** (No. 8 Prince Hoare, 13 Venanzio Rauzzini, 41 John Wood the Younger). Note the differing door cases at Nos. 13, 15 and 42. Gay Street is named for landowner, Robert Gay, an eminent London surgeon.

(To divert to the **Jane Austen Centre** go left downhill to No. 40 Tel 01225 443000).

Turn right uphill and then bear right to enter **The Circus** (see page 9) – England's first circus, likened by Smollett to Rome's Colosseum turned inside out. Originally there were no trees in the centre, which was paved over with cobbles to conceal a reservoir from which servants collected water for the houses around The Circus. Note especially the frieze running between the ground and first floors which features 525 motifs and symbols, many of them occupational, nautical, military, mythical or Masonic. Imaginary lines joining the three entrances into the Circus would create a triangle within a circle, symbolising the Trinity within Eternity. There are 33 houses in all, with 11 on the west side but only ten on the north and 12 on the south-east. No. 4 houses the **Fashion Research Centre** which is attached to the Museum of Costume and has a Georgian garden open to the public in summer. No. 7 was the home of William Pitt the Elder, sometime MP for Bath (1757-66), Prime Minister, architect of victory in the Seven Years War of 1756-63 and a martyr to gout and occasional bouts of mental derangement. Missionary and Victorian icon David Livingstone, the first European to explore and map central Africa from west to east, lived briefly at No. 13. No. 14 was one of several homes of the adventurer and millionaire 'nabob' Robert Clive, inadvertent founder of Britain's 'Raj' in India. Thomas Gainsborough (see page 165) painted and prospered at No. 17. A plaque at No. 22 recalls forgotten hero Major John Andre, the British contact to whom the American traitor Benedict Arnold attempted to surrender West Point. Arnold escaped to well-pensioned exile in London, Andre was caught and, on George Washington's direct order, hanged like a common criminal, rather than being shot as a gentleman. From George III downwards, the British were outraged at the insult.

Take the first exit right, **Bennett Street** (built 1770-76) where the **Museum of East Asian Art** (Tel 01225 464640) is at Circus Lodge. Admiral Arthur Phillip (see page 157), who began the British settlement of Australia, retired to No. 19 in 1806. Turn right into **St Andrew's Terrace** to pass the **Assembly Rooms** and **Fashion Museum** (Tel 01225 477789) (see page 176) and into **Alfred Street** (built 1768-76). Sir Thomas Lawrence (see page 166), the society portraitist lived at No. 2 Alfred Street and so did historian Catherine Macaulay (see page 115). No. 14, Alfred House, sports a bust of King Alfred and has two 'link snuffers' for extinguishing torches and an unusual hoist for lowering heavy deliveries into the servants' 'area' to the left of the entrance. William Harbutt (see page 205) invented Plasticine in the basement of No.15.

At the end of Alfred Street cross busy **Lansdowne Road** with care to pass through pedestrianised **Hay Hill** and turn left into the **Paragon** to reach the **Museum of English Naïve Art** and the **Building of Bath Museum** (Tel 01225 333895), which is housed in the former Countess of Huntingdon's Chapel. Actress Sarah Siddons (see page 126) lived (1779-82) at No. 33 the Paragon. Heading north, pass the **Bath Antiques Market** and The Star pub, which has a well-preserved Victorian interior. At the junction with London Road turn left and back into Guinea Lane and on to Julian Road, to pass Christ Church (see page 154) and just past it the cul-de-sac which leads up to the **Museum of Bath at Work**.(Tel 01225 318348) housed in a former Royal (i.e. 'Real') Tennis Court of 1777, which was converted to a brewery in 1825. Opposite the entrance to the cul-de-sac is meandering **Rivers Street,** leading almost immediately into **Russell Street,** running down to Bennett Street and back to The Circus.

Leave The Circus via **Brock Street** No. 2 has an insurance company firemark. Benjamin Disraeli, wit, novelist and Prime Minister, stayed at No. 8. No. 16 has an eccentrically Gothic doorway. Note what you can, or rather can't, see dead ahead – no visual hint of the breathtaking grandeur of what you are about to encounter – **The Royal Crescent** – the first crescent built in England.

No. 1 Royal Crescent (Tel 01225 428126) is open to visitors and has extremely knowledgeable guides in each room to answer your questions, as well as helpful laminated information sheets in multiple languages. Nos. 2 and 17 were bombed out in the war but have been restored. Christopher Anstey (see page 110) lived at No. 5 Royal Crescent, Elizabeth Linley (see page 136) eloped from No. 11. No. 16 was the home of the 'Grand Old Duke of York' of the nursery rhyme and later of the Radical MP Sir Francis Burdett and his daughter, Baroness Angela Burdett-Coutts, the richest woman in England, who gave away a fortune of £4,000,000 to good causes. The prolific novelist, MP and dandy Edward ('It was a dark and stormy night') Bulwer-Lytton, author of *The Last Days of Pompeii*, lived at No. 9 and Sir Isaac Pitman (see page 204) at No. 17.

At the end of the Royal Crescent turn left and walk downhill along **Marlborough Buildings**, where the infinitely versatile travel writer, essayist and historian Jan Morris lived in the 1970s. Note the surviving lampholders on several houses.

Turn left again along leafy **Gravel Walk**, where convalescents were once carried in sedan chairs to take the air. The **Georgian Garden** along the route (on the left, north side, near the end) has been restored to its original plan of *ca.* 1760 and is open to the public (May–October 9-4.30 Tel 01225 477752). Pass the **War Memorial** (see page 209) to reach **Queen's Parade Place.** (A glance to the left reveals, on the south side, a unique pair of bijou lodges built at the rear of No. 24 Queen Square for sedan chair attendants to use while their passengers visited nearby houses).

Beyond is **Queen Square** (1729-36 by John Wood the Elder) (see page 106). The grandest façade is the symmetrical group of seven large houses (Nos. 21-27) along the north side, designed as though they were a single Palladian palace with flanking pavilions at either end. The obelisk in the central garden was another Beau Nash initiative, to commemorate the visit of the loutish Frederick, Prince of Wales in 1738 (see page 65). Note the ornamental lampholder at No. 21 and the lamplighters' snuffers over the doorways of Nos. 22-23. John Wood the Younger lived in the round-bayed house on the corner of Gay Street. Jane Austen stayed at No. 13. On the west side is the **Bath Royal Literary and Scientific Institution**.

Exit Queen Square at the north-west corner into **Queen Square Place** and go on to **Charlotte Street**, a 'new' road of 1839-40. No. 12 was originally (1841) the Bath Savings Bank. Designed by the London architect George Alexander, it was possibly the first bank building in England to be built in the style of an Italian palazzo. It later served as the first home (1893-1916) of the Holburne Museum. Next to it is a former Moravian Chapel of 1844-5, now offices. The former (1854) Congregational church opposite is now the Elim Pentecostal chapel.

Pass on to **Monmouth Place**, then left into **Little Stanhope Street** and left again into **New King Street** (built up 1764-70). Note the pretty paved cul-de-sac, St Ann's Place (*ca.*1765) on the north side. This is typical of the sort of neat artisan housing so recklessly destroyed during the 'Sack of Bath' in the 1960s and 1970s (see page 228). At No. 19 New King Street is the museum dedicated to musician and astronomer William Herschel (see page 201), discoverer of the planet Uranus. (Tel 01225 311342).

Pass the Christadelphian Hall of 1880 and turn right down **Charles Street**, which is dominated by unfortunate modern buildings which are a reminder of how much of this area was devastated by the Blitz (see page 219). At **Green Park** (formerly Queen Square) railway station (1868-9) (see page 188) cross onto the eastern section of **James Street West** and then left over the zebra crossing to Kingsmead Square (1727) (see page 93) and the remarkable Baroque confection at No. 14 that is **Rosewell House** (1735), once home to Bishop Butler (1692-1752). The son of a draper, he became a learned theologian and bishop of Bristol, then of Durham. John Wood thought the building had 'nothing save ornaments without taste.' This area has abundant provision for seating and eating if you need to pause awhile.

Exit via **Seven Dials**. Through an archway on the left, just before the **Garrick's Head** public house, is a tiny courtyard with a fountain around which can be seen the handprints and signatures, Hollywood-style, of sixteen famous British actors and actresses who have appeared at the adjacent **Theatre Royal**. The Garrick's Head was formerly one of the two homes of Beau Nash. The other, now a restaurant, is immediately on the other side of the theatre foyer. The former **Pavilion Music Hall** (see page 131), now a nightclub, is just opposite.

Turn left up **Barton Street** and right into **Trim Street**, begun in 1707 as the first street to be built up outside the ancient city walls. Glance left up enticing pedestrianised Queen Street before finding No. 5, of ca. 1720, the home of General Wolfe (1727-59), from which he left in 1759 to find death and glory at the taking of Quebec, in recognition of which the military trophies were later added to the tympanum over the door. Pass through the wide passageway called **Trim Bridge** to cross Upper Borough Walls into paved **Bridewell Lane**, which was known as Plum Tree Lane in the thirteenth century and may be Saxon in origin.

Cross **Westgate Street**, once a major east-west thoroughfare of medieval Bath, to pass into the narrow entrance to **St Michael's Place** which leads to the **Cross Bath** in **Hot Bath Street.** To the rear is the Hospital of St John the Baptist which has a delightful garden on the other side, reached down a short passageway.

Continue past Hetling Court round the spectacular **Thermae Bath Spa** (by Nicholas Grimshaw 1999-2003) left into **Beau Street** to pass the United Hospital building (John Pinch the Elder 1824-6) and **Bellots** charity (see page 78), rebuilt in 1859. Turn into **Bilbury Lane** to note the mock-Tudor St Catherine's Hospital (1829 by George Philips Manners) and come out on handsomely colonnaded **Bath Street** (1791 by Thomas Baldwin). Go right into **Stall Street** and downhill to the end past Boots the Chemist to go left into **New Orchard Street** then bear left into **Old Orchard Street** where the original **Theatre Royal** (see page 128) has been successively a Roman Catholic chapel and a Freemasons' hall. A prominent plaque here pays tribute to the great Sarah Siddons (see page 126).

Pass through **Pierrepont Place** and under a columned archway to turn right down Manvers Street and return to the station.

Bath Walks: 2

Exploring East

This is a walk full of variety with the chance to make several extended museum stops. There are public lavatories in Henrietta Park, near the beginning of the walk and on Northgate Street near the end.

The starting-point is the Victoria Art Gallery at **Grand Parade**. From here head east to cross **Pulteney Bridge** and enter **Argyle Street**.

No. 9 has a handsome eighteenth-century shop front. As commercial premises often change hands every few years and new owners are prone to refitting frontages this is a precious survival. Note the coat of arms of Queen Charlotte, devoted wife of George III.

To the left No. 22 **Grove Street** has a portico bearing the Masonic date 5792 (i.e. 1792), reflecting traditional Masonic lore that the world began in 4000 BC.

On the left at the junction with **Laura Place** is a rare hexagonal pillar box of 1866. To the right No. 15 **Johnstone Street** was once the home of William Pitt the Younger. Prime Minister at 24, he was afflicted by gout from adolescence and died at the age of 42.

No. 8 **Henrietta Street** opposite was home to coach proprietor Moses Pickwick, whose name Dickens appropriated. (The public lavatory in Henrietta Park is near the junction of Henrietta Street and Henrietta Mews).

Cross Laura Place into **Great Pulteney Street**, Bath's longest, widest and grandest thoroughfare. The Pulteney coat of arms can be seen over No. 59. Former residents on the left-hand (north) side include at No. 1 the historian Lord Macaulay ('the history of England is emphatically the history of progress'), at No.2, novelist Edward Bulwer-Lytton (see page 240), at No. 6 Thomas Baldwin, architect of Bath's Guildhall, at No. 27 William Smith ('father of English geology', see page 203) and at No. 36 William Wilberforce, anti-slavery campaigner. On the other side they include at No. 76 Christian propagandist Hannah More (see page 152), at No. 72 King Louis XVIII of France, who restored its monarchy after the fall of Napoleon and at No. 55 Louis-Napoleon Bonaparte who restored the Napoleonic regime as Napoleon III. No. 53 was the home of notorious Irish dancer Lola Montez whose affair with Ludwig I of Bavaria cost him his throne.

Edward Street, a turning to the right with another hexagonal pillar box at the corner, was briefly home to Nelson's mistress, Lady Hamilton (No.6). No. 10 features a small-paned 'Tudor' window designed to protect the occupant's privacy from the prying eyes of passers-by. It was inserted by the songwriter Frederick Weatherley, who wrote the lyrics for *The Holy City, Roses of Picardy* and *Danny Boy*.

Great Pulteney Street leads into **Sydney Place** which is overlooked by the Holburne Museum (see page 196) and **Sydney Gardens**, one of England's few remaining Regency pleasure-grounds. The Museum merits a visit not only for its superb collections but also for its controversial new rear extension. Beyond the rear extension is a reconstruction of the Roman temple to Sul Minerva, erected to commemorate the Bath Historical Pageant of 1909.

Continue left along **Sydney Place (Old)** to pass the former home of Jane Austen (see page 147) at No. 4.

At the road junction bear left along **Bathwick Street**. On the left, in **Daniel Mews**, are coach-houses of 1804, built for the carriages and grooms of the smart residents of Sydney Place.

At the end on the left note the cemetery of the former church of St Mary Bathwick with its 'Gothick' mortuary chapel, now a picturesque ruin. The locality is being lovingly restored by its 'Friends'. The graves of notable Bath residents, notably architect John Pinch and his namesake son, are marked informatively.

On the opposite side of the road (north) note the house with protruding stone 'teeth' along its right-hand side for the next (unbuilt) house to key into.

Cross the charming Doric 'Greek Revival' **Cleveland Bridge** built by H.E. Goodridge (see page 185) in 1827.

Go forward over Cleveland Place to note The Eastern Dispensary (H.E. Goodridge 1845). The interior featured an ingenious zig-zag layout of benches for waiting patients to prevent queue-jumping.

Turn left onto **London Road**. This was once a Roman road (see page 14) and later a turnpike road, with a turnpike gate further up going northwest, at the junction with Snow Hill. On the opposite side of the road **Walcot Parade** (*ca.* 1770) has the highest raised pavement in Bath.

Continue left to the junction to the junction of the road, now London Street, with the **Paragon**, which is dominated by St Swithin's Church. Built (1777-90) by John Palmer, this is Bath's only surviving parish church in a classical style. Burials and monuments include those of John Palmer, Fanny Burney (see page 134), painter William Hoare (see page 163), satirist Christopher Anstey (see page 245) and Jane Austen's father (see page 152). William Wilberforce was married here. Hedgemead Park, on the opposite side of the road, was laid out on the site of a landslip which brought down 175 houses in 1881.

Return to Walcot Street and walk down the left-hand side.

Chatham Row, a short street to the left, was built *ca.* 1767 and originally named Pitt Street, after Pitt the Elder, later Earl of Chatham. No. 12 at the bottom was the home of John Pinch the Elder in 1800. In 1967, when it was scheduled for demolition, Bath's fire brigade torched it to find out how eighteenth-century houses burn.

Further downhill at No.112 Ladymead House served as a female penitentiary for prostitutes and pickpockets.

St Michael's Church House is an Arts and Crafts composition (1904) by Wallace Gill and, as such, very unusual for Bath. Forsyth identifies the carving over the doorway as St George slaying a dragon but as the figure has wings it must be the Archangel Michael.

Notice that the backs of the houses along the Paragon, visible high up on the other side of the road, are as finished and detailed as though they were the fronts. This is untypical of many Bath houses ('Queen Anne in front, Mary

Anne behind'). In fact to take advantage of the fine view from their windows the interior of the houses has been rearranged so that the main rooms are actually at the rear.

Also on the other side of the road is an elaborate water trough of 1864. Designed by Major Davis (see page 198) this incorporated samples of all the local building stones and was much used by the cattle sold in the market which traditionally congested this street.

Beehive Yard, originally the stable yard of an inn of that name, became the site of the former tram depot and its associated power station.

A little further on, looking across the river, it should be possible to make out Atwood's City Prison on Grove Street and above it, on the skyline, the 'Sham Castle' Gothic folly put up (1762) for Ralph Allen (see page 103).

The church of St Michael with St Paul occupies a commanding but highly restricted site at the junction of Walcot Street with Broad Street. Originally St Michael's Without (Extra Muros)(see page 88), the church was established by the thirteenth century and rebuilt in classical style in 1734-42 and again in 1834-7 in exuberant Gothic by George Phillips Manners. Unusually, it is oriented north-south, rather than east-west.

At the south end of Walcot Street the Hilton Hotel (1972) is, according to Michael Forsyth, 'the most reviled building in Bath' but serves to make the neo-Georgian (1923-7) Post Office, on the corner of New Bond Street opposite, look even better.
Continue into **Northgate Street**.

The Podium Shopping Centre also houses restaurants and the main library with major collections devoted to the local history of Bath and its region.

At the end of Northgate Street turn left onto **Bridge Street** to return to the starting-point at the Victoria Art Gallery.

Bath Walks: 3

Scaling the Heights

This walk involves some fairly steep climbing to reach handsome curving Crescents which give spectacular views down over the city. It begins from the western end of the **Royal Crescent.**

Turn right along Marlborough Buildings and uphill, then right into Crescent Lane and left via Marlborough Street into **St James's Square**, the most complete surviving Georgian square in Bath, built in 1790-3 by John Palmer. (Actually it's rectangular, not a true square and its four approach roads, unusually, enter it diagonally rather than at right-angles. The irascibly self-destructive writer Walter Savage Landor (see page 190) lived (1846-52) at No. 35, where he was visited by Charles Dickens.

Exit via Park Street and Park Place onto **Cavendish Road** and continue uphill. The houses here looking over High Common, now a golf course, were built in 1808-16 by John Pinch the Elder.

Note Cavendish Villa (*ca.* 1779), refronted with a bow, and Winifred's Dale, semi-detached villas of *ca.*1810 by Pinch. Neo-Georgian Cavendish Lodge (1996) finally got the go-ahead after no less than nine previous proposals had been turned down, striking testimony to the value placed on this location.

Just before the top of the hill, to the right, is Pinch's **Cavendish Crescent**. The promoter, a speculative builder, William Broom, lived at No. 3, one of the first to be completed in 1815, but was bankrupt before the scheme was finished in 1830. The collector Sir William Holburne (see page 192) lived (1829-74) at No. 10.

At the junction with **Sion Hill**, on the left-hand corner, is the windowless,

colonnaded façade of Doric House, built (*ca.* 1805) for local artist Thomas
Barker (see page 168) by the London architect J.M. Gandy (1771-1843), a
pupil of Sir John Soane. When the artist lived there it was known as 'Barker's
Picture Gallery' and may well have served as a convenient resting-place for
Bath's more robust convalescents as they toiled up here to admire the views
back over the city.

Cross at the junction to climb the steps up to **Somerset Place**, built by
John Eveleigh from *ca.* 1790. A casualty of the French wars, the project was
abandoned only to be resumed *ca.* 1820. Note the weird 'icicle mask' keystones
above the doors of Nos. 10-11. Nos. 5-7 and 10-13 were rebuilt as student
hostels after being burned out in 1942 (see page 220).

Continue eastwards onto sinuously curving **Lansdown Place**, which is broken
into two sections by **Lansdown Crescent**. No. 8 Lansdown Place West was
bombed in the war and reconstructed, as were Nos. 5-9 Lansdown Place East.
Built (1789-93) by John Palmer for coach-builder Charles Spackman, the
Lansdown development commands spectacular views over the city, especially
at dusk and at night. Eccentric connoisseur William Beckford (see page 183)
occupied the house at the west end with the bow window and took over the
houses either side for his art collection. A brief diversion through the archway
should enable you to make out Beckford's Tower (see page 185) at the top of
the hill behind the houses.

At the end of Lansdown Place East enter **Lansdown Road**. Look uphill to
the left. The fork in the road was once the site of a turnpike gate and is now
dominated by St Stephen's church, built (1840-45) to the designs of James
Wilson. Because it was oriented north-south it remained formally uncon-
secrated until 1881. The Lady Chapel has a dramatic modern stained-glass
window depicting St Stephen's martyrdom.

Here you have the choice of turning left and then bearing left at the church
to trek out to **Beckford's Tower** and the adjacent cemetery, where Sir
William Holburne and James Wilson are buried. (You may wish to take the
bus). En route you will pass the imposing mock-Tudor Kingswood School,
built (1850-2) by James Wilson for the sons of Methodist ministers. Originally provided with a hot-air heating system but no hot baths, the school
required boys to wash their upper body twice a week and their feet once a
fortnight. During World War One the school served as a convalescent centre
for wounded Belgian soldiers.

Alternatively turn right down Lansdown Road and cross to take a diversion along **Camden Crescent**, named for Charles Pratt, Marquess of Camden (1714-94), sometime Lord Chancellor and Recorder of Bath. A lifelong friend of Pitt the Elder and brilliant lawyer, Camden was by inclination an idler who preferred reading romances to law books. Built (1787-94) to designs by John Eveleigh, the houses feature doorways surmounted by elephants' heads with a variety of expressions, a motif taken from the Camden crest. The project was originally intended to be much bigger but landslips prevented the completion of the eastern end, leaving the development asymmetrical and the 'central' pavilion notably off-centre. It also outrages architectural purists in having an uneven five columns instead of the usual four or six. As Eveleigh also installed seven columns at Grosvenor Place the oddity was presumably deliberate.

Turn back into Lansdown Road to descend to **Broad Street**. This was once the heart of a seventeenth century suburb and, despite the Georgian facades, many houses are older than they look. King Edward's School on the west side was designed (1752) in Palladian style by local builder Thomas Jelly and built over the site of the former Black Swan inn. There was once a workshop making Bath-chairs at No. 4. Between 1821 and 1854 No. 8 was the Post Office and from there the first adhesive postage stamps in the world were franked and sent in 1840. Shire's Yard, now a shopping centre, was in the eighteenth century the twice-weekly departure-point for 'Wiltshire's Flying Wagons' which made the journey to Holborn, London in two and a half days. A friend of Thomas Gainsborough (see page 165), Walter Wiltshire is said to have carried the artist's paintings up to town gratis On the east side is the gabled, rambling Saracen's Head, which dates from *ca.* 1700. Dickens stayed here in 1835 when he was still working mainly as a political journalist.

Turn right into **Green Street** which was laid out in 1717 on the site of a bowling green. The Old Green Tree at No. 12 has been a public house since the 1770s. No. 13 is believed to be where the first 'Bath Oliver' biscuits (see page 69) were sold. There are interesting shopfronts at Nos. 10, 14,15 and 19. Bear left around the block to enter **New Bond Street** which was laid out by John Palmer to replace a former narrow alley, Frog Lane, and built up between 1805 and 1825 as a classy shopping street. At the end turn right into Northgate Street which leads on to the High Street and city centre.

Day Trip from Bath

Bristol

> At Bath everything is superficial – at Bristol everything is substantial. At Bath, everything is gay – at Bristol everything is grave. At Bath they live in fine houses and are poor – at Bristol in shabby ones and are rich. At careless Bath nothing is thought of but the present moment – at Bristol no step is taken but with a view to the advantage of posterity. Charles Dibdin 1788

Bristol is famous for sherry, chocolate and tobacco, the world's first purpose-built Methodist chapel, the world's first ocean liner, the University of Bristol, Bristol Zoo, Concorde, 'Wallace and Gromit' and a very distinctive local accent.

Considering its size, however, Bristol has made little contribution to English art or letters, although it was the birthplace of Sir Thomas Lawrence (see page 166), the (preociously talented) teenage literary fraudster, Thomas Chatterton and William Friese-Greene, pioneer of cinematography. Other 'Bristol Boys' include the poet Robert Southey, E.H. Baily, who sculpted the figure of Nelson in London's Trafalgar Square, publisher Allen Lane, founder of Penguin Books, champion skater Robin Cousins and the actors Sir Michael Redgrave and Cary Grant, whose statue stands on the harbourside.

Unlike Bath, Bristol is not Roman in origin. Unlike Wells, it was not a cathedral city in origin, although Henry VIII promoted its Abbey Church of St Augustine to that status in 1542. Formerly part of Gloucestershire, Bristol was not, despite its size and wealth, a county town. Bristol originated as a Saxon settlement, part of the vast royal manor of Barton, which stretched all the way to Bath. Lying at the junction of the rivers Avon and Frome and protected by the spectacular Avon gorge from any threat of sudden seaborne assault Bristol was blessed with an enviably defensible site. Access to the Avon, Severn and Wye river systems made Bristol a natural junction of the South-West, South Wales and the West Midlands, enabling it to draw on the agricultural, mineral and later industrial resources of three hinterlands.

Even before the Norman Conquest Bristol was driving a thriving trade – exporting English slaves to Ireland. A castle was built by Geoffrey of Coutances and enlarged by Robert, Earl of Gloucester, who also founded the Benedictine Priory of St James. Robert's granddaughter was the first wife of King John, who thus acquired the castle to make Bristol a royal stronghold.

Bristol was enriched by its wine trade with Bordeaux and the export of English cloth. Its local speciality was known by the fourteenth century as 'Bristol Red'. Local manufacturing developed on the basis of leather from Wales and Ireland, lead from the Mendips and iron from the Forest of Dean. The city's medieval prosperity is attested by the fact that its Augustinian Abbey was established *ca.* 1140 by Robert Fitzhardinge, a burgess, rather than by an aristocrat. Thirteenth-century commercial expansion was accompanied by an ambitious engineering scheme to enlarge the port by diverting the course of the River Frome, thus establishing Broad Quay. Other thirteenth century urban improvements included a piped water supply, the hospitals of St Bartholomew and St Mark and the almshouses in Long Row, founded in 1292 by Simon Burton. The munificence of the Canynges family made the church of St Mary Redcliffe what Elizabeth I would praise as 'the fairest parish church in England'. The hexagonal outer porch dates from 1280, the inner porch from a century before that. Admiral William Penn, father of the founder of Pennsylvania, is buried and memorialized in the nave.

Further surviving proofs of medieval Bristol's wealth include the Lord Mayor's Chapel, St James's priory church, St Stephen, St John the Baptist and the tower and gateway of St Nicholas.

In 1373 Edward III granted Bristol a status unique for a provincial city, ranking it as a county, with its own sheriff as well as a mayor and council of forty and the right to send two representatives to Parliament. In the fifteenth century the ending of the Hundred Years War with France was accompanied by the loss of control of Gascony, a severe blow to the wine trade. Bristol merchants responded by challenging their Italian rivals in the Mediterranean and looking outwards to the Americas and the Caribbean. In 1639 Sir Ferdinando Gorges obtained a charter to colonise what would become the state of Maine.

Bristol's ancient and prestigious grammar school dates from 1532, the Cathedral School from 1542. Red Maids', a school for girls, an unusually advanced notion for the times, was founded in 1634. As a result of the dissolution of religious houses much property was acquired by the corporation, as in Bath.

As a port of crucial strategic significance Bristol suffered severely during the civil wars, being besieged by the Royalists in 1643 and the Parliamentarians in 1645. Remains of a royal fort can be seen on Brandon Hill. The castle was demolished in 1656 and its site redeveloped. Despite this major setback Bristol recovered over the latter half of the seventeenth century thanks to the strength of its maritime commerce. Daniel Defoe is supposed to have met Alexander Selkirk, the original of Robinson Crusoe, in the Llandoger Trow tavern on King Street. By the late seventeenth century Bristol, after London, was the largest and richest city in the kingdom. According to that epitome of London pride, Samuel Pepys, Bristol was 'in every respect another London'. The poet Alexander Pope was taken aback in 1739 by the sheer scale of what he saw – 'In the middle of the street, as far as you can see, hundreds of Ships, their Masts as thick as they can stand by one another, which is the oddest and most surprising sight imaginable.' Horace Walpole was less complimentary – 'the dirtiest great shop I ever saw' and Bristol's most famous Member of Parliament, Edmund Burke, confessed that 'Though I have the honour to represent Bristol, I should not like to live there…'.

A public library and new almshouses ('Merchant Venturers') were built on King Street and St Michael's Hill (Colston's). Striking survivals from this prosperous period also include Queen Square (1699), the Mayor's mansion house, the Custom House, the Music Room, Commercial Rooms and Assembly Rooms. The Royal Infirmary dates from 1737. In 1743 a fine new Exchange was completed in Corn Street by John Wood (see page 106). The Theatre Royal was opened in 1766.

The wealth on which such philanthropy and display depended was, however, increasingly generated from Bristol's involvement in the 'triangular trade'. This involved transporting the industrial products of the West Midlands hinterland (axes, knives, pans etc.) to the west coast of Africa where they were exchanged for slaves. These were taken to the American colonies and plantations of the Caribbean islands where they were sold and the proceeds used to buy tropical products, such as indigo, rice, sugar, rum, cotton, tobacco and chocolate, which were taken back to Britain for processing, some to be sold on domestically, the rest re-exported to mainland Europe.

There were few actual slaves in Bristol, except as the servants of plantation-owners. Pero Bridge records one such who declined into alcoholism and a premature death. By the third quarter of the eighteenth century Bristol had been surpassed as Britain's leading slave port by Liverpool, which had a superior natural harbour. The tobacco trade passed to Glasgow. Belatedly the city responded with the construction of the Floating Harbour and New Cut in 1804-9.

Bristol compensated for the erosion of its maritime commerce by developing its own industrial base. Coal deposits at Kingswood were used to fuel lead and gunshot works and iron-founding. At Baptist Mills Britain's first brass foundry was established. Clay-pipe manufacture was a natural off-shoot of the tobacco industry. Glass was made for windows and the bottling of sherry, wine, spirits and the spa waters of Bath, Clifton and Hotwells. Other industries included shipbuilding and distilling and the manufacture of soap and salt and an imitation Delftware pottery.

Bristol's expansion led to the formation of new parishes, in 1751 St George in the east of the city and in 1787 St Paul's, Portland Square; and also to the building of suburbs at Bedminster, Kingsdown, Clifton and Hotwells. Bristol's mercantile elite, almost uniquely among provincial cities, never decamped to London. Bath was just up the road and offered everything in the way of distractions that could be found in the capital. So Bristol's bourgeoisie stayed put and built handsome houses like 6 King Street, 66-70 Prince Street and 29 and 37 Queen Square. Beyond the city boundaries others built 'country seats', like Redland Court, Goldney House, Clifton Hill House, Royal Fort House, Blaise Castle House, Weston House and Ashton Court.

Bristol's spectacular setting is accentuated by the superb Clifton Suspension Bridge spanning the Avon Gorge. The bridge was designed by Isambard Kingdom Brunel (1806-59) when still a young man but it was not completed until after his death. Brunel's other local projects included Temple Meads station, arguably the first great example of railway architecture, and two pioneering, record-breaking steam-ships, the *Great Western* and the *Great Britain*. The *Great Britain* was the first iron-hulled, steam-powered, screw-propellered ship, and hence the prototype of every subsequent ocean liner. Abandoned as a wreck in the Falklands Islands, where its hull was used to store coal, it was rescued and gloriously restored and can now be visited in the very dock in which it was built. (www.ssgreatbritain.org)

Writing in 1937, just before the heart of Bristol was torn out by enemy bombing John Betjeman declared that Bristol was 'the most unspoiled large city left in England' and its posh suburb, Clifton, '*almost* – I say almost for it isn't quite – as lovely as Bath'.

Bristol's major museums include the British Empire and Commonwealth Museum (www.empiremuseum.co.uk), the City Museum and Art Gallery (www.bristol.gov.uk/museums) and the Georgian House, built in 1790 for John Pinney, Pero's master.

Day Trip from Bath

Salisbury

Sir Kenneth Clark, doyen of art historians, called the Cathedral Church of the Blessed Virgin Mary at Salisbury 'the most perfect building in Northern Europe'. Built in less than half a century, it displays an unusual uniformity of style. At 404 feet its spire is the tallest in England and the second highest in Europe. The Cathedral Close is the largest in England, a sublime setting for such gems as Mompesson House, a magnificent mercantile mansion of 1701, and a block of almshouses which still serve their original purpose of providing a handsome home for clergy widows. The former residence of Conservative Prime Minister Edward Heath is now open to the public. The cathedral's treasures include the best preserved of only four surviving copies of the Magna Carta and the oldest (1386) working clock in the world. A quintessential symbol of Englishness, Salisbury cathedral was painted repeatedly by that most English of artists, John Constable (1776-1837). In 1991 Salisbury became the first cathedral in England to establish a girls' choir. The embroiderers who produce its vestments and altar frontals are acknowledged as the foremost in England.

Old Sarum

Salisbury originally meant somewhere else. Old Sarum, two miles to the north, began as an Iron Age fortified town, enclosed by a large earth wall. The Romans used it as a fortress, called Sorbiodunum, where several Roman roads converged. The Anglo-Saxons expanded its fortifications and, as Seares byrig, it became a prosperous town. In 1070 William I chose it as the location for reviewing and standing down his army of conquest and built a royal castle there. In 1075 it was decreed that all bishops should have the seat (*cathedra*) of their see (diocese) in a town or city. The sees of Sherborne and Ramsbury, both held by Bishop Herman, were amalgamated and the seat of the combined see removed to Old Sarum, where a new cathedral was begun.

Herman died in 1078 and was succeeded by Bishop Osmund, who had come over with William I in 1066 and served as Chancellor of England (1074-8). Bishop Osmund completed the building of the cathedral in 1092 and died in 1099. His most important legacy was not, however, this building but the rules he laid down for its running, which, formalised as a constitution in the twelfth century, were adopted as a model by many other cathedrals. This laid down that the governance of the Chapter of Canons should be headed by four Principal Persons. The Precentor was responsible for the choir and music. The Chancellor acted as Secretary and supervised education, training and the library. The Treasurer had charge of the cathedral's treasures, ornaments and vestments. The Dean presided over all. The splendid forms of service and ceremonies carried out in the cathedral likewise became widely imitated as a model, 'The Use of Sarum'.

Five days after its consecration Osmund's cathedral was severely damaged by lightning. Around 1125 it was rebuilt by Bishop Roger on an enlarged scale - 316 feet long as opposed to the 173 feet of Osmund's. It was, however, never really satisfactory. The castle garrison nearby was often rowdy and quarrelsome. There was a recurrent shortage of water; both the Roman and Saxon names of the site mean 'dry'. The location was also exposed to wind and too cramped to provide adequate accommodation for the clergy – or the enlargement of the cathedral itself. A splendid model of Old Sarum can be seen in the north cloister of Salisbury Cathedral, showing clearly how Roger's cathedral was confined within a quadrant of the walled, cramped site.

The twelfth century was a period of economic buoyancy which sustained competitive rivalry among religious establishments. Winchester, only twenty miles away, was 500 feet long. At Wells, to the west, an entirely new cathedral was begun in the 1170s. Salisbury's leadership determined to go one better – to build not only a new cathedral but also a new city to go with it.

A Timely Gesture

In 1217 Richard Poore (died 1237), a former Dean, returned to Salisbury as its new bishop. As it happened the time was especially propitious for a major new religious initiative. King John had quarrelled so badly with the Pope that the entire kingdom had been put under interdict for five years, suspending the normal life of the church. With John dead in 1216 a new reign and a new regime was in place under his son and successor. Henry III (reigned 1216-72), a precociously pious child, would have a lifelong passion for religious ceremonies and building projects, devoting his own personal efforts to the rebuilding of Westminster Abbey. It was a time for reconciliation between church and state. A new cathedral would be an ideal symbol of a new beginning. The Pope gave the go-ahead in 1218.

The foundation stones of the new cathedral were laid in 1220. One of the leading figures involved was William Longespee the elder, Earl of Salisbury and half-brother to King John. His would be the first tomb (1226) to be erected in the cathedral; an effigy of his crusader son, another William, is in the north aisle. Another superb scale model, in the north nave aisle, depicts the various tasks and techniques involved in the building of the cathedral. Necessarily, however, it shows phases of work being undertaken simultaneously which in reality would have occurred sequentially.

The first part of the building to be completed, in 1225, was Trinity Chapel (the Chapel of the Holy Trinity and All Saints), notable for its slender Purbeck marble columns. In 1226 the bodies of Osmund and Roger were brought down from Old Sarum for re-burial. In 1228 Richard Poore moved on to become Bishop of Durham but the project proceeded unchecked. Salisbury Cathedral was consecrated in 1258 in the presence of King Henry III and his queen. The rapid speed of construction reflects an extraordinarily successful fund-raising effort, all the more remarkable considering that Salisbury had no major local saint to attract pilgrims.

The West Front, the work of Richard the Mason, was finished by 1266 and a freestanding Bell Tower built at around the same date. Salisbury's cloisters, among the earliest in England, were completed by 1270 and the octagonal Chapter House, with a single central pillar, modelled on that of Westminster Abbey, was finished by 1284. The original decorative scheme in the Chapter House was of red, gold, black and white. There is much carving worthy of careful examination, including sixty portrait heads and a frieze depicting scenes and incidents from Genesis and Exodus. The tower and spire were the work of a later generation, built sometime between 1285 and 1330. The immense weight of the spire − 6,400 tons − put a tremendous strain on the four main piers of the tower, which was strengthened by internal and external buttresses and girder-arches but still twisted out of true and had to be saved from further distortion by Sir Christopher Wren (1632-1723). The pillar at the south-east corner of the crossing shows the curvature most dramatically.

The work of construction is attributed to a master mason, Nicholas of Ely, and a canon, Elias of Dereham (died 1245), who is also associated with other major building projects, such as Becket's shrine at Canterbury and works at Winchester Castle. A man who combined outstanding administrative talent with a refined aesthetic taste, Elias enjoyed a glittering ecclesiastical career as the indispensable helpmeet to three successive Archbishops of Canterbury, as well as serving as supervisor of the Salisbury site for a quarter of a century.

The interior of Salisbury Cathedral is 449 ft (135 m) long, with a nave of

230 ft (70 m). The breadth of the nave and aisles is 78 ft (23 m) and its height 85 ft (26m) The stone, a Jurassic limestone, was quarried at Chilmark, ten miles west of Salisbury. The Cathedral close was walled in *ca*. 1333, recycling stone from the former cathedral at Old Sarum.

In comparison with the exuberance of Lincoln Cathedral Salisbury appears almost austere. Its extra long nave was intended for magnificent services which involved lengthy processions. The double transepts allowed for the provision of extra altars, so that there were fifteen in all. The choir is more richly ornamented with carving than the nave. Unlike French cathedrals, Salisbury is isolated from its city by its close. Approaching either from the east or the north via a gatehouse the visitor confronts the cathedral like an apparition suddenly risen up out of the earth, suspended for an instant in time as it soars upward to God rather than being anchored to the ground. Nor is this an entirely fanciful illusion – Salisbury's foundations are only four feet deep.

Later modifications of the cathedral include the construction of the library around 1445, the insertion of strainer arches *ca*. 1450 and the replacement of a wooden ceiling at the crossing with the present stone vaulting in 1479-80. Osmund was finally canonized in 1457, bringing a belated but doubtless welcome stimulus to the pilgrim trade.

A major reformation of the cathedral was undertaken (1789-92) by James Wyatt. He demolished the Bell Tower and the Beauchamp and Hungerford chantry chapels either side of Trinity Chapel. Major tombs, including Osmund's shrine, were removed from their original locations and lined up neatly along the nave. The choir screen was removed to the Morning Chapel. The churchyard was cleared of gravestones, drained and laid to grass. Much medieval painting was whitewashed over.

The west window, incorporating medieval and later, including French, material, was assembled (1819-24) by local glazier John Beare.

A further programme of restoration and alteration was undertaken between 1860 and 1878 by Sir George Gilbert Scott (1811-78). The noted firm of Clayton & Bell restored the painting of Christ and the apostles at the choir crossing, not entirely to Scott's satisfaction.

Post-war changes to the fabric of Salisbury cathedral include the rebuilding of the top thirty feet of the spire (1949-51), the restoration of the library (1978-83) and the insertion (1980) of Gabriel Loire's great east window dedicated to *Prisoners of Conscience*. Elisabeth Frink's *Walking Madonna* was placed outside the north porch in 1982.

New Sarum

New Sarum, modern Salisbury, was laid out to the north and east of the

Cathedral close, with streets crossing a right angles to form squares called 'Chequers'. It had a large market place and its own parish church and rapidly became a flourishing city and a major center of the trade in woollen cloth. Testimony to past prosperity survives in the shape of a fine stone market cross. A tradition of intellectual distinction among the cathedral clergy – most notably St Edmund (Rich) of Abingdon (1170?-1240), a star teacher at Oxford – attracted students and led to the foundation of the College of St. Nicholas de Vaux (1261) and the College of St Edmund (1269), whose associated church is now an arts centre. The church of St Thomas is well worth visiting for its stupendous wall-painting of the Day of Doom. Other fascinating features include wooden battlefield burial crosses from the Great War, the Lady Chapel with its medieval murals and the macabre tomb carved for himself by Humphrey Beckham who died in 1671 aged 83. The chancel reredos is by G.E. Street, William Morris' mentor. Altogether a gem of a church, well worth seeking out.

Edward Rutherford's blockbuster, best-selling novel *Sarum* uses the history of Salisbury, and especially of the cathedral, to tell the entire history of England.

The American Museum, Claverton

En route to or from Salisbury the visitor can easily make a diversion to take in the first museum of Americana outside America (www.americanmuseum.org). Opened in 1961, The American Museum uses its collection of folk and decorative arts to illustrate the varied lifestyles of American communities – Native American, Puritan, Quaker, Shaker, Amish, 'Pennsylvania Dutch' (i.e. German), African American, New Mexican and Hawaiian - from colonial times to the nineteenth century. Replicas of an austere seventeenth-century living-room, a homely eighteenth-century farmhouse-tavern and parlour, an elegant nineteenth-century New York dining-room and a flamboyant New Orleans bedroom, feature the museum's outstanding collections of authentic furniture, paintings, carvings and textiles. The museum's holdings are especially strong in quilts and maps but also include a genuine Cheyenne tepee and Conestoga wagon.

The American Museum is housed in Claverton Manor, a handsome Palladian mansion built in 1819-20 for John Vivian (1756-1828), Solicitor to the Excise. The architect was the socially ambitious Jeffrey Wyatt (1766-1840), who was later knighted by George IV for Gothicizing Windsor Castle and changed his name to Wyattville because he thought it sounded more aristo-cratic. Vivian's artistic son, George, laid out Claverton's extensive grounds in an Italianate style, complete with a grotto. The grounds now also feature a fernery, an arboretum of American trees, a colonial herb garden, gardens of dye-stuffs and vegetables and a replica of George Washington's garden at Mount Vernon – which was originally stocked with plants from the Bath area. There are also two walking trails. As you admire the fine views you might also like to pause and recall that on 26 July 1897 a political novice of twenty-three made his first ever public speech here. His name was Winston Churchill.

Day Trip from Bath

Stonehenge

'Observatory, altar, temple, tomb,
Erected none knows when by none knows whom,
To serve strange gods or watch familiar stars,
We drive to see you in our motor-cars
And carry picture-postcards back to town
While still the unsleeping stars look coldly down.'
Sir John Squire *Stonehenge*

At first sight an apparently isolated structure, Stonehenge in fact once formed part of a much larger monumental complex, itself located in a landscape crammed with more enclosures (henges), ditches, embankments, causeways and burials than any other part of prehistoric Britain. Originally there were more than 300 barrows within 2 miles (3 kms) radius of Stonehenge. Long barrows, the more ancient, were raised to hold the remains of numerous dead, often within wooden structures. The later, round barrows – variously described as bowl, bell, disc, saucer and pond, according to their shape – were for the interment of prestigious individuals. Plundered by amateur archaeologists of the eighteenth and nineteenth centuries, many barrows have yielded finds of pottery, amber, bronze and gold which can be seen in the Salisbury and South Wiltshire Museum (in Salisbury Cathedral Close). It is more than possible that the area around Stonehenge was important not just for peoples of the immediate locality but over the whole island of Britain, perhaps even attracting 'pilgrims' from mainland Europe

The building history of Stonehenge not only stretches over a millennium and a half but also includes possible periods of abandonment and rebuildings in which original materials were recycled to create quite different structures from their initial form. It is equally possible that the Stonehenge assemblage was used for different purposes at different times, later occupants utilising its location and structures in ways that earlier builders never intended or envisaged. The many suggestions advanced to explain why Stonehenge was created – as a place of worship, burial, healing or celebration or as an astronomical calculator – are not necessarily mutually exclusive.

The oldest 'monuments' of Stonehenge are three post-holes dating from just after the last Ice Age, about 8,000 BC – located under the present-day car park. This implies a history of significant construction long predating the creation of the Stonehenge we see today. A marked growth in the number of settled communities, living at least partly by farming, began around 4,000 BC and is associated with the construction of monumental architecture. Land clearances for farming may have been linked with what one might call intellectual clearances and the emergence of a new cosmology to complement the new landscape. The fact that the area around Stonehenge does not seem to have been densely forested made it especially suitable as a site for building. Another factor would be the existence of a nearby river for the transportation of heavy materials and perhaps timber and food supplies as well. It has also been suggested that some of the largest stones, like the Heel Stone and the Station Stones may already have been here and served as a nucleus for the initial construction programme.

At Stonehenge monumental construction began with the creation of a circular ditch and bank of chalk. When first constructed these would have been gleaming white and visible from far off. Deer-antler picks used to dig the ditch have been radiocarbon dated to 3000-2920 BC. The circle had two entrances. A main one, facing north-east and aligned to the midsummer sunrise and another smaller one to the south-west aligned with the midwinter sunrise. Julian Richards (see below) suggests that the midwinter, rather than the midsummer, solstice was the more crucial observance as prehistoric worshippers of the sun may have feared its disappearance and welcomed the return of lengthening days as a promise of its rebirth. Within the inner edge of the bank – and possibly dating from this first phase of construction – are 56 circular pits, spaced 13 ft (4m) to 16ft (5m) apart. These are known as Aubrey Holes, after their discoverer, the antiquarian John Aubrey (1626-97), himself a Wiltshire man. When first dug these held upright timbers but were later appropriated to bury cremated human bones. Evidence in the form of post-holes reveals the existence of numerous timber structures inside the circle, rebuilt many times over. These may not necessarily have been buildings but possibly fenced walkways to guide or channel ritual behaviour. The discovery of some 240 cremation burials, dating over a period of a thousand years, implies a location of social as well as spiritual significance, a place for the disposal of persons of exceptional importance, the Westminster Abbey of Neolithic Wiltshire, perhaps even of a much wider area. The only other known 'cemetery' from this period is at Dorchester-on-Thames in Oxfordshire.

Around 2,500 BC the area within the circle began to be built up with two sorts of stone, one almost local, the other very far from so. The massive 'Sarsen' stones, some weighing over 40 tons, are sandstone, much harder than granite. Sarsen is a corruption of Saracen, from the medieval belief that they were the work of devilish enemies of God. The nearest source of sarsens is the Marlborough Downs 19 miles (30 kms) to the north. Experiments using a wooden sledge on wooden rails show that a team of 200 could shift one to Stonehenge in 12 days.

The 'bluestones' were brought from the Preseli Hills of Wales, over 150 miles (240 kms) to the west. There were originally at least 80, some weighing up to five tons. They may once have formed a structure of such spiritual power that it was deliberately disassembled for its components to be carried away. Transporting them would have involved using several rivers, crossing the Bristol Channel and at least some overland portage. The bluestones were brought on site before the sarsens but there is no trace of their original setting before they were rearranged into their present positions.

The final (probably 2280-1930 BC) arrangement of the stones consists of four concentric settings – two circles and two horseshoes. The outermost circle was of 30 upright sarsens, capped by horizontal lintel stones. Of these only 17 still stand, with five lintels in place. The lintels were held onto the uprights by mortise and tenon joints (a bump on the upright fitting into a round hollowed out recess on the underside of the lintel).

This would have meant grinding off an entire top layer of stone on the upright to leave the two protruding tenons standing proud of the surface. This was done with a round ball of sarsen, known as a maul. Mauls have been found ranging in size from an orange to a football. The lintels are locked to each other by tongue and groove joints in which a protruding section of stone (likewise produced by removing the stone either side of it) is slotted vertically into a receiving recess cut into the end of the adjacent stone. Both systems of jointing imitate standard woodworking techniques. The lintels are not rectangular, as they seem at first glance, but were gently curved on both sides to form a continuous circle. They were raised into place either up ramps of earth or by means of platforms of stacked timbers.

Inside and concentric with the outer sarsens was a circle of some 60 bluestones. Although the majority were not shaped in any way two, later used as uprights, have mortise holes showing they were used – or at least intended – as lintels.

The next setting inwards consists of a horseshoe of five sarsen trilithons

(Greek=3 stones), each resembling a massive doorway of two uprights capped by a stupendous lintel, held in place by mortise and tenon joints. These were originally graded in height, the tallest standing at the closed end of the horseshoe. Only one of its uprights remains in position; at 24 ft (7.3m) it is the tallest standing stone in Britain. Three trilithons stand intact, although the one nearest the tarmac path is actually not a survivor but was re-erected in 1958.

The innermost setting is a horseshoe of bluestones, originally 19, a number of them elegantly shaped. At its closed end, partly buried beneath the fallen upright of the tallest trilithon, is the so-called Altar Stone, a greenish sandstone, brought from south Wales, towards the end of the final phase of construction. Both horseshoes are precisely aligned so that their open ends point directly at the main entrance.

Two of an original four Station Stones survive. They marked the corners of a perfect rectangle with its central point at the exact centre of the monument. This suggests their purpose might have been practical rather than ritual, to assist the builders in calculating positionings and alignments.

Two circles, each of 30 oblong pits about 3ft (1 m) deep, were discovered in 1923. Dubbed the Y Holes and the Z Holes, their purpose is unknown but they were dug late in the period of Stonehenge's construction.

The Heel Stone, a huge unworked sarsen, stands close to the fence at the edge of the A334, surrounded by a small, circular ditch. Originally it had a companion. On the other side of the road ran the twin banks and ditches of The Avenue, a ceremonial approach route, running 1.5 miles (2.5 kms) to the River Avon at West Amesbury and built *ca.* 2300 BC.

The Slaughter Stone lies just inside the main entrance to the circle. Originally it was flanked by other stones, now missing. Iron in the stone makes for rusty red stains – which are not residues of sacrifice, as the name misleadingly implies.

Building at Stonehenge was abandoned around 1600 BC. Having been constructed, reconstructed and used over a period of 1,400 years, the area continued in use as a preferred location for increasingly elaborate burials. By about 1000 BC its sacred character was largely ignored as the demands of farming were given priority. The medieval church regarded Stonehenge as the product of pagan barbarism and positively encouraged locals to use it as a quarry for building stone. The ever-engaging Geoffrey of Monmouth (died 1155) suggested that the stones of Stonehenge had been magically transported from Ireland by King Arthur's wizard, Merlin, an explanation which was widely accepted down to the sixteenth century. On the orders of James I his court architect Inigo Jones (1573-1652) made the first accurate drawings of the monument, attributing its construction to the Romans on the grounds

that the ancient Britons simply weren't up to the required level of sophisti-
cation of design and competence in engineering. By the seventeenth century
Stonehenge had became an established tourist attraction for travellers like
the diarists John Evelyn (1654) and Samuel Pepys (1668) and the indefatigable Celia Fiennes (*ca.* 1690). Evelyn, a highly cultured man, who thought
it 'a stupendious Monument', also found it 'so exceeding hard, that all my
strength with an hammer, could not break a fragment'. Subsequent visitors
were more persistent and left their mark in the form of carved graffiti. In 1740
the antiquarian clergyman William Stukeley (1687-1765) correctly recognised
that Stonehenge had been built for worship by the pre-Roman inhabitants of
Britain but mistakenly attributed its construction to the Druids. Bath architect
John Wood the Elder (1704-54) convinced himself that it was the remnant of
the capital of an ancient British empire (see page 12) and used it as the inspiration for the construction of Queen Square and the Circus at Bath, both of
which are based on the measured dimensions of Stonehenge. Stonehenge was
finally recognised as a treasure of national significance in 1883 but not fenced
off until 1901. In 1915 it was sold off for £6,600 and donated to the nation
by the purchaser, Cecil Chubb, a few years later. Serious archaeology began
with the excavation programme of 1919-25, under the direction of Colonel
William Hawley.

Since 2003 a projected ten year programme of archaeological research
under the direction of University of Sheffield Professor Michael Parker-
Pearson has begun to make radical revisions in our understanding of Stonehenge, the chronology and methods of its construction and its relationship
to adjacent structures, most notably the so-called 'Durrington Walls' about 2
kilometres away. Parker-Pearson's team claims to have uncovered evidence of
the existence at Durrington of the largest settled community in prehistoric
north-west Europe and of the first use of metal (copper) tools in Britain. The
settlement at Durrington, established around 2500 BC was some 500 yards in
diameter and enclosed by a circular bank, within which was a ditch 20 ft (6 m)
deep and 43 ft (13 m) wide. Inside this feature were large circular structures
of wood and houses *ca.* 16 ft (5.5 m) square, perhaps as many as a thousand
dwellings in all. Durrington is taken to be the home of the builders of Stonehenge Phase II – i.e. its first stone incarnation. It may also have been the
setting for feasting and celebrations before funerals which took the deceased
from the world of the living (who inhabited structures of wood, representing
transience) to the world of the dead (who inhabited structures of stone, representing permanence). It is speculated that the population of Durrington may
have been as large as 4,000 or even 6,000. As a labour force they may have been
split into teams of *ca.* 200, based on kinship groups attracted from different

parts of Britain, and assigned to defined collective tasks such as excavating, building or finishing off specific sections of a structure or essential subsidiary tasks, like transportation, the preparation of ropes, rollers or rails or foraging for and feeding their fellow workers.

Further light on the character of ancient peoples attracted to the Stonehenge area was the discovery in 2002 of the remains of the 'Amesbury Archer' at Solstice Business Park some 3 miles (5 kms) from Stonehenge. A man aged 35 to 45, he died *ca*. 2300 BC and was buried with an impressive hoard of grave-goods, including five pots, two stone wrist-protectors (for archery), sixteen flint arrowheads and two gold hair ornaments, the earliest gold objects to be found in Britain. The fact that he was born in the Alps, probably Switzerland, and also had three copper knives with him suggests that he may have achieved his great wealth from a mastery of the new mystery of metal-working.

Stonehenge is located in a triangle bordered to the south by the A303 to London and to the north by the A334, with the parking area on its northern side and a tunnel under the road to take visitors to the main site. The monument is in the charge of English Heritage, with adjacent areas controlled by the National Trust, the Ministry of Defence and private owners. A Virtual Tour of the area can be taken at the English Heritage Stonehenge website (www.english-heritage.org.uk). Stonehenge was designated a UNESCO World Heritage site in 1986 and now receives some 850,000 visitors a year.

The short, well-illustrated English Heritage (2005) guide to Stonehenge is written by popular TV archaeology presenter Julian Richards, who is in no doubt that it was a temple. The notion that it was a sort of astronomical computer was most fully developed by Professor Alexander Thom, a retired professor of engineering rather than an archaeologist. The history of how Stonehenge has been interpreted, misinterpreted, excavated and exploited culturally and commercially can be found in Christopher Chippindale's comprehensive and compelling *Stonehenge Complete* (2004). Rosemary Hill's *Stonehenge* (2008) attempts the same in briefer compass. The more technically minded might relish *Stonehenge Landscapes : Journeys Through Real and Imagined Worlds* (2000) by Sally Exon, Vincent Gaffney, Ann Woodward and Ron Yorston (www.iaa.bham.ac.uk) or T.C. Darvill's *Stonehenge : The Biography of a Landscape* (2006). Popular historical novelist Bernard Cornwell has attempted a recreation of the lives and mind-set of the monument's original creators in his novel *Stonehenge, a Novel of 2000 BC* (2000).

Chronology

1189	Richard I grants Bath a charter
1245	Pope Innocent IV decrees union of Bishoprics of Bath and Wells
1256	Henry III visits Bath
1279	Church of St James relocated outside the priory walls
1304	Priors granted the right to hold fairs at Lansdown and Lyncombe
1332	South Gate rebuilt
1340	106 taxpayers pay the tax of one-ninth
1348-49	Black Death
1362	St Lawrence's Bridge built
1371	Edward III's charter recognizes a twice-weekly market
1379	329 Bath residents pay poll tax
1412	Pillory erected in the market place
1435	St Catherine's Hospital founded
1502	Rebuilding of Bath Abbey begins
1536	John Leland, antiquary, visits Bath
1539	Dissolution of Bath Abbey
1552	King Edward's School founded
	Edward VI gives priory lands to the corporation of Bath
1562	William Turner appraises the medical value of Bath's waters
1572	Abbey church presented to the citizens of Bath
	West Gate rebuilt
	John Jones advocates drinking Bath waters
1574	Elizabeth I visits Bath
1576	John de Feckenham builds a leper house
1583	Elizabeth I orders the consolidation of five intramural parishes
1590	Elizabeth I grants Bath a royal charter
1597	Royal charter mandates free use of the baths by the poor
1604	Plague outbreak, 72 dead
1609	Thomas Bellott founds a hospital for poor strangers visiting the baths
1610	John Speed's map of Bath
1613	Queen Anne of Denmark visits the baths
	City scavenger appointed
1615	Queen Anne revisits Bath
1616	Bath Abbey consecrated as a cathedral
1622	Sally Lunn's house built
1625	Guild Hall and Market House built; plague outbreak
1628	Charles I visits Bath

	Tobias Venner – *The Baths of Bath*
1633	Thatched roofs banned
1634	Queen Henrietta Maria takes the waters
	Bridewell built
1635	Plague outbreak
1643	Royalist victory at the Battle of Lansdown
	Typhus outbreak
1643–45	Bath occupied by royalist garrison
1665	Charles II and Catherine of Braganza visit Bath
1673	Henry Chapman *Thermae Rediviviae: the City of Bath Described*
1675	Thomas Johnson's drawing of the King's Bath published
1687	James, Duke of York and Mary of Modena visit the baths
1688	Melfort Cross erected
1692	Visit of Princess Anne and Prince George of Denmark
1694	Joseph Gilmore's map of Bath
1702 & 1703	Queen Anne visits Bath
1705	First playhouse opened (demolished 1737)
1706	First Pump Room opened
1707	Trim Street begun
	Turnpike Trust established to surface seven access roads
1708	(Harrison's, later Simpson's and the Lower) Assembly Rooms opened
1715	Anti-Popery riots
1716	Green Street built
1722	Blue Coat School built on the site of the former Bridewell
1725	Kingston Estate map of Bath
1727	Head of Minerva found in Stall Street
	Improvement of Avon navigation begun
	Ralph Allen buys quarries at Combe Down
	Last use of public pillory
1728–36	Queen Square built
1733	Demolition of Abbey Gate
1735	Rosewell House built
	John Wood's map of Bath
1740–48	Grand Parade built
1741	John Wood – *The Origin of Building; or, the plagiarism of the heathens detected*
1742	Mineral Water Hospital opened
1742–3	John Wood *Essay Towards a Description of Bath*
1750	Theatre opened in Orchard Street

	London–Bath–Bristol turnpike route completed
1754	St Lawrence's Bridge rebuilt
1754–8	Royal Circus built
1755–62	Bladud buildings built
1761	Milsom Street begun
1762	Oliver Goldsmith *The Life of Richard Nash of Bath esq.*
	George Street begun
1765	Countess of Huntingdon's Chapel built
1766	Christopher Anstey *The New Bath Guide*
1766–67	Octagon chapel built
1767–75	Royal Crescent built
1768–75	Paragon built
1769–71	Third (Upper) Assembly Rooms built by John Wood the Younger
1769–74	Pulteney Bridge built
1771	Tobias Smollet *Humphrey Clinker*
1772–3	New Prison, Grove Street built
1775	Theatre rebuilt
1776	West Gate demolished
	Dr Samuel Johnson visits Bath
	George Ellis *Bath: Its Beauties and Amusements*
1777–90	St Swithin's church built
1781	Sir William Herschel observes the planet Uranus
1783–84	Cross Bath rebuilt
	Melfort Cross demolished
1787	Inspector of the Baths appointed
1788–93	Bathwick Estate built
1788–9	New Private Baths built
1789	Bath Improvement Act
1789–93	Lansdown Crescent built
1790–95	New Pump Room built
1790–93	St James's Square built
1791	Bath Street built
	Grosvenor Place begun
1792	Grosvenor Gardens opened
1793	Failure of Bath City Bank
	Taylor's map of Bath
	T. Pownall *Description of Antiquities dug up in Bath in 1790*
1794	Haydn visits Rauzzini at Widcombe
1795	Sydney Gardens opened

	Dissenting chapel built in Trim Street
1798	Christ Church Julian Road completed
	Thomas Rowlandson *The Comforts of Bath*
1801	First national census records Bath as the ninth most populous city in England
1801	R. Warner *The History of Bath*
1801–6	Jane Austen resident at Bath
1804–5	Theatre Royal built by George Dance the Younger
1808–16	Cavendish Place built
1810	Kennet and Avon canal completed
1815–30	Cavendish Crescent built
1817	Queen Charlotte visits Bath
1818	Jane Austen *Northanger Abbey*
1818–25	Raby Place built
1819	Gas-lighting introduced
	Pierce Egan *Walks Through Bath*
1820	Claverton Manor built by Sir Jeffrey Wyattville
1820–4	Partis College almshouses built
1824–5	The Bazaar built
1824–6	United Hospital built
1825	The Corridor opened
1826	Woodland Place built
1827	Cleveland Bridge built
1829–30	Royal Victoria Park laid out
1829–32	St Saviour, St Saviour's Road built
1830	Visit of Princess Victoria and the Duchess of Kent
1831	James Jolly's department store opened
1832	Cholera outbreak kills forty-nine
1835	Municipal Corporations Act
1836	Radicals dominate newly-elected council
	Police force established
1837	Bath Ear and Eye Infirmary opened
1838	Bath Union Workhouse opened
1840	Great Western Railway links Bath to Bristol
1841	Great Western Railway links Bath to London
1845	Eastern Dispensary opened
1848	Cholera outbreak kills ninety
	Lansdown cemetery laid out
1859	Pitman Press established on Lower Bristol Road
1860–73	Restoration of Bath Abbey by Sir George Gilbert Scott

1865	Bath Rugby Football Club founded
1866	First Medical Officer of Health appointed
	Last cholera outbreak causes one fatality
1866–70	La Sainte Union convent Pulteney Road built
1866–69	Grand Pump Room Hotel built
1867	New Royal Baths built
1869	Queen Square (Green Park) station opened
1878	Bath hosts annual meeting of the British Medical Association
1878–9	Excavation of Roman spring and reservoir
1879	Jolly's department store, Milsom Street opened
1879–81	Our Lady Help of Christians, Julian Road built
1880	Horse-drawn tram services introduced
	Abbey Green plane tree planted
1880–81	Great Bath uncovered
1881	Trustees of the Holburne Collection established
	Landslip destroys 175 houses
1883	Monk's Mill burned down
	C.E. Davis *The Mineral Baths of Bath*
1883–84	R.E.M. Peach *Historic Houses in Bath*
1887	Botanical Gardens opened
1889	J. Tunstall *Rambles about Bath*
	Douche and Massage Baths opened
1893	Guildhall extension built
1893	J. Murch *Biographical sketches of Bath celebrities, ancient and modern*
1897	William Harbutt invents plasticine
1897–1900	Victoria Art Gallery built
1899	Historic houses plaque scheme inaugurated
1899–1901	Empire Hotel built
1904	Electric tram services introduced
1909	Bath Pageant staged
1916	Holburne Museum reopened in former Sydney Hotel
1921	Assembly Rooms ballroom converted to a cinema
1923	Abbey cloisters built War Memorial unveiled
1931	Assembly Rooms bought for National Trust
1932	Edith Sitwell *Bath*
1933	Lower Assembly Rooms demolished
1934	Bath Preservation Trust established
1936–38	Restoration of Assembly Rooms
1937	Establishment of the Georgian Group

	Bath Corporation Act requires listing of historical buildings
1938	Pump Room Orchestra disbanded
1942	Baedeker raid kills 400+ Assembly Rooms gutted
1945	P. Abercrombie, J. Owens and H.A. Mealand *A Plan for Bath*
1948	Bath Festival founded as the Bath Assembly (renamed 1955)
	Walter Ison *The Georgian Buildings of Bath from 1700 to 1830*
1958	Nikolaus Pevsner *The Buildings of England : North Somerset and Bristol*
1959	Demolition of Grand Pump Room Hotel
	Ruins of St James, Southgate demolished
1963	Museum of Costume opened; Bath Excavation Committee established
1965	C. Buchanan *Bath : A Planning and Transport Study*
1966	University of Bath founded
1967	No. 1 Royal Crescent presented to Bath Preservation Trust
1969	Museum of Bath at Work opened
	Demolition of Kingsmead Square prohibited
1972	Beaufort (now Hilton) Hotel built
1973	Visit of H.M. Queen Elizabeh II to mark the thousandth anniversary of the coronation of King Edgar
	A. Fergusson *The Sack of Bath : A Record and an Indictment*
1974	The Corridor bombed by the IRA
	Avon County Council established
1976	Restoration of General Wade's House
1982	Regeneration of Green Park station
1986	History of Bath Research Group established
	B. Cunliffe *The City of Bath*
1987	Bath recognized by UNESCO as a World Heritage Site
	Closure of Stothert and Pitt
1988	Building of Bath Museum opened
1998	Bath Rugby F.C. win the European Cup
1999	Bath Abbey refurbishment completed
2003	Thermae Spa Bath opened

Reading and Reference

Christopher Anstey (ed. G. Turner) – *The New Bath Guide* (1994)

J.H. Bettey – *The Suppression of the Monasteries in the West Country* (1989)

Anne Borsay – *Medicine and charity in Georgian Bath: a social history of the General Infirmary c. 1739-1830* (1999)

Peter Borsay – *The image of Georgian Bath 1700-2000 : Towns, Heritage and History* (2000)

V.E. Bowyer - *Along the Canal in Bath* (1979)

B. Boyce – *The benevolent man: a life of Ralph Allen of Bath* (1967)

R.A. Buchanan – *The Industrial Archaeology of Bath* (1979)

Building of Bath Museum – *Obsession: John Wood and the Creation of Georgian Bath* (2004)

G. Clarke – *Prior Park: a compleat landscape* (1987)

P. Coard – *Vanishing Bath* (1970)

L. Cochrane – *Adelard of Bath* (1994)

James Crathorne – *The Royal Crescent Book of Bath* (1998)

P. Cresswell (ed.) – *Bath in Quotes: A Literary View from Saxon Times Onwards* (1985, 2006)

Barry Cunliffe – *Roman Bath Discovered* (rev. ed. 2000)

Barry Cunliffe – *The City of Bath* (1986)

Peter Davenport – *Medieval Bath Uncovered* (2002)

G.P. Davis – *Bath Beyond the Guide Book* (1988)

G. Davis and P. Bonsall – *Bath: A New History* (1996, 2006)

G. Davis (ed.) – *Bath Exposed! Essays on the Social History of Bath 1775-1945* (2007)

John Eglin – *The Imaginary Autocrat: Beau Nash and the Invention of Bath* (2005)

Kirsten Elliott – *A Window on Bath: Eight Walks in Bath* (1994)

D. Falconer – *Bath Abbey* (1999)

David and Jonathan Falconer – *A Century of Bath: Events, People and Places Over the 20th Century* (1999,2007)

Trevor Fawcett and S. Bird – *Bath: History and Guide* (1994)

Trevor Fawcett – *Voices of eighteenth-century Bath* (1995)

Trevor Fawcett *Bath entertain'd* (1998)

Trevor Fawcett – *Bath Administer'd: Corporation Affairs at the 18th Century Spa* (2001)

Trevor Fawcett – *Bath Commercialis'd: Shops, Trade and Market at the 18th-century Spa* (2002)

Adam Fergusson – *The Sack of Bath : A Record and an Indictment* (1973)

Adam Fergusson and Tim Mowl – *The Sack of Bath – And After* (1989)

Michael Forsyth – *Pevsner Architectural Guides : Bath* (2003)

R. Gilding – *Historic Public Parks: Bath* (1997)

T. Gorst – *Bath* (1997)

Kim Green – *Valley of the Sacred Spring* (2004)

M. Hamilton – *Bath Before Beau Nash: A Guide Based on Gilmore's Map of Bath 1692-4* (1978)

M.K. Hill – *Bath and the Eighteenth Century Novel* (1989)

T. Hinde – *Tales from the Pump Room. Nine Hundred Years of Bath: The Place, Its People and Its Gossip* (1988)

Holburne Museum – *A Gift to the Nation: The Fine and Decorative Art Collections of Ernest E. Cook* (1991)

Holburne Museum – *Love's Prospect: Gainsborough's* Byam Family *and the eighteenth century marriage portrait* (2001)

Holburne Museum – *Pickpocketing the Rich: Portrait Painting in Bath 1720-1800* (2002)

Holburne Museum – *Every Look Speaks: Portraits of David Garrick* (2003)

Holburne Museum – *Pictures of Innocence: Portraits of Children from Hogarth to Lawrence* (2005)

G. Hones – *Bath: Museum or City?* (1978)

J. Hudson – *Bath in Old Photographs* (1993)

Kenneth Hylson-Smith – *Bath Abbey: A History* (2003)

Kenneth Hudson – *Pleasures and People of Bath* (1977)

W. Ison – *The Georgian buildings of Bath from 1700 to 1830* (2nd ed 1980)

N. Jackson – *Nineteenth Century Bath Architects and Architecture* (1991)

Gideon Kibblewhite – *The Naked Guide to Bath* (2004)

M.Lane – *A Charming Place: Bath in the Life and Times of Jane Austen* (1988)

J. Lees-Milne and D. Ford – *Images of Bath* (1982)

Bryan Little – *The Building of Bath 47-1947: An Architectural and Social Study* (1947)

Bryan Little – *Bath Portrait: The Story of Bath, Its Life and Its Buildings* (1961)

Bryan Little – *Selina, Countess of Huntingdon* (1989)

W. Lowndes – *The Royal Crescent: A Fragment of English Life* (1981)

W. Lowndes – *They Came to Bath* (1987)

W. Lowndes – *The Theatre Royal at Bath* (n.d.)

N. Jackson – *Nineteenth Century Bath Architects and Architecture* (1991)

J. Manco – *The Spirit of Care: the eight-hundred-year story of St John's Hospital, Bath* (1998)

D. McLaughlin – *Lansdown Cemetery* (1991)

T. Mowl and B. Earnshaw – *John Wood, architect of obsession* (1988)

R.S. Neale – *Bath: a social history 1650-1850, or, A valley of pleasure, yet a sink of iniquity* (1981)

Ana O'Callaghan – *Past, Present and Future: A Recent History of the Theatre Royal*

Nikolaus Pevsner – *The Buildings of England: North Somerset and Bristol* (1958)

C. Pound – *Genius of Bath: The City and its Landscape* (1986)

N. Pounds - *The Medieval Cathedral-Priory of Bath* (1995)

Charles Robertson – *Bath: An Architectural Guide* (1975)

W. Rodwell – *Anglo-Saxon Bath and the Foundation of the Abbey* (1994)

R. Rolls – *The hospital of the nation: the story of spa medicine and the Mineral Water Hospital at Bath* (1988)

N. Rothnie – *The Bombing of Bath: The German Air Raids of 1942* (1983)

N. Rothnie – *Unknown Bath: Secrets and Scandals from the Past* (1986)

S. Sloman – *Gainsborough in Bath* (Yale University Press 2002)

A.J. Turner – *Science and Music in Eighteenth Century Bath* (1977)

M. Wainwright – *The Bath Blitz* (3rd ed. 1992)

Diana White – *Stories of Bath: A Selective History in Eleven Episodes* (2006)

Diana Winsor – *The Dream of Bath* (1980)

Cleo Witt – *Boy, 1st Class: William Holburne at Trafalgar* (2005)

John Wroughton (ed.) – *Bath in the Age of Reform* (1972)

John Wroughton – *A Community at War: The Civil War in Bath and North Somerset 1642-1650* (1992)

John Wroughton – *Stuart Bath: Life in the Forgotten City 1603-1714* (2004)

Useful Websites & Bath Calendar

The American Museum, Claverton www.americanmuseum.org
Bath Abbey and Heritage Vaults Museum www.bathabbey.org./museum.htm
Bath Aqua Theatre of Glass Workshop and Museum www.bathaquaglass.com
Bath Chronicle www.thisisbath.co.uk
Bath Fringe Festival www.bathfringe.co.uk
Bath International Music Festival www.bathmusicfest.org.uk
Bath Literature Festival www.bathlitfest.org.uk
The Bath Magazine www.thebathmagazine.co.uk
Bath Postal Museum www.bathpostalmuseum.co.uk
Bath Preservation Trust www.bath-preservation-trust.org.uk
Bath Royal Literary and Scientific Institution www.brlsi.org
Bath Rugby Football Club www.bathrugby.co.uk
Bath Spa University www.bathspa.ac.uk
Bath Tourist Information Centre www.visitbath.co.uk
Beckford Tower Museum *see* Bath Preservation Trust
Better Bath Forum www.betterbath.org.uk
Bristol City Museum and Art Gallery www.bristol.gov.uk
Bristol Tourist Information Centre www.visitbristol.co.uk
Building of Bath Museum *see* Bath Preservation Trust
City of Bath www.cityofbath.co.uk
The Fashion Museum www.fashionmuseum.co.uk
Herschel House and Museum *see* Bath Preservation Trust
Holburne Museum www.bath.ac.ukholburne
The Jane Austen Centre www.janeausten.co.uk
The Mission Theatre www.missiontheatre.co.uk
Museum of Bath at Work www.bath-at-work.org.uk
Museum of East Asian Art www.meaa.org.uk
No. 1 Royal Crescent *see* Bath Preservation Trust

Prior Park Landscape Garden www.nationaltrust.org.uk
Roman Baths Museum www.romanbaths.co.uk
The Rondo Theatre www.rondotheatre.co.uk
Royal Photographic Society www.rps.org
Salisbury Cathedral www.salisburycathedral.org.uk
Salisbury and South Wiltshire Museum www.salisburymuseum.org.uk
Salisbury Tourist Information Centre
    www.visitswiltshire.co.uk/salisbury/home
Sally Lunn's House www.sallylunns.co.uk
S.S. Great Britain www.ss-great-britain.com
Stonehenge www.english-heritage.org.uk
Theatre Royal www.theatreroyal.org.uk
Thermae Bath Spa www.thermaebathspa.com
University of Bath www.bath.ac.uk
Victoria Art Gallery www.victoriagal.org.uk

Calendar of Annual Events

Daily (except Christmas Day) free walking tours led by the Mayor of Bath's
Corps of Honorary Guides. Leave from the Abbey Church Yard
(details from www.thecityofbath.co.uk)

February / March
    Bath Literature Festival
March
    Mid-Somerset Competitive Festival of Bath
        (amateur performing arts festival)
    Bath Half-Marathon
    Bath Shakespeare Festival
    Bath International Puppet Festival
May
    Bath Spring Flower Show
    Bath Balloon Festival
May / June
    Bath Festival of Walks
    Bath Fringe Festival
    Bath International Music Festival
June
    Bath & West Show (at Shepton Mallet)
    Somerset County Cricket Festival
    Bath Banjo Festival

July/August
    The Peter Hall Company Festival
    Bath International Guitar Festival
September
    Jane Austen Festival
October
    Bath Beer Festival
    Bath Film Festival
November
    Bath Mozartfest
November / January
    Queen Square Ice Rink
December
    Christmas Market, Abbey Square

Bath and North East Somerset Council: for details of heritage events for adults and children see www.bathnes.gov.uk/heritageevents

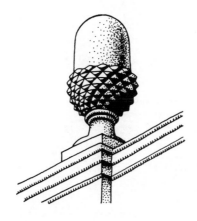

Index